FACE

Australian portraits 1880–1960

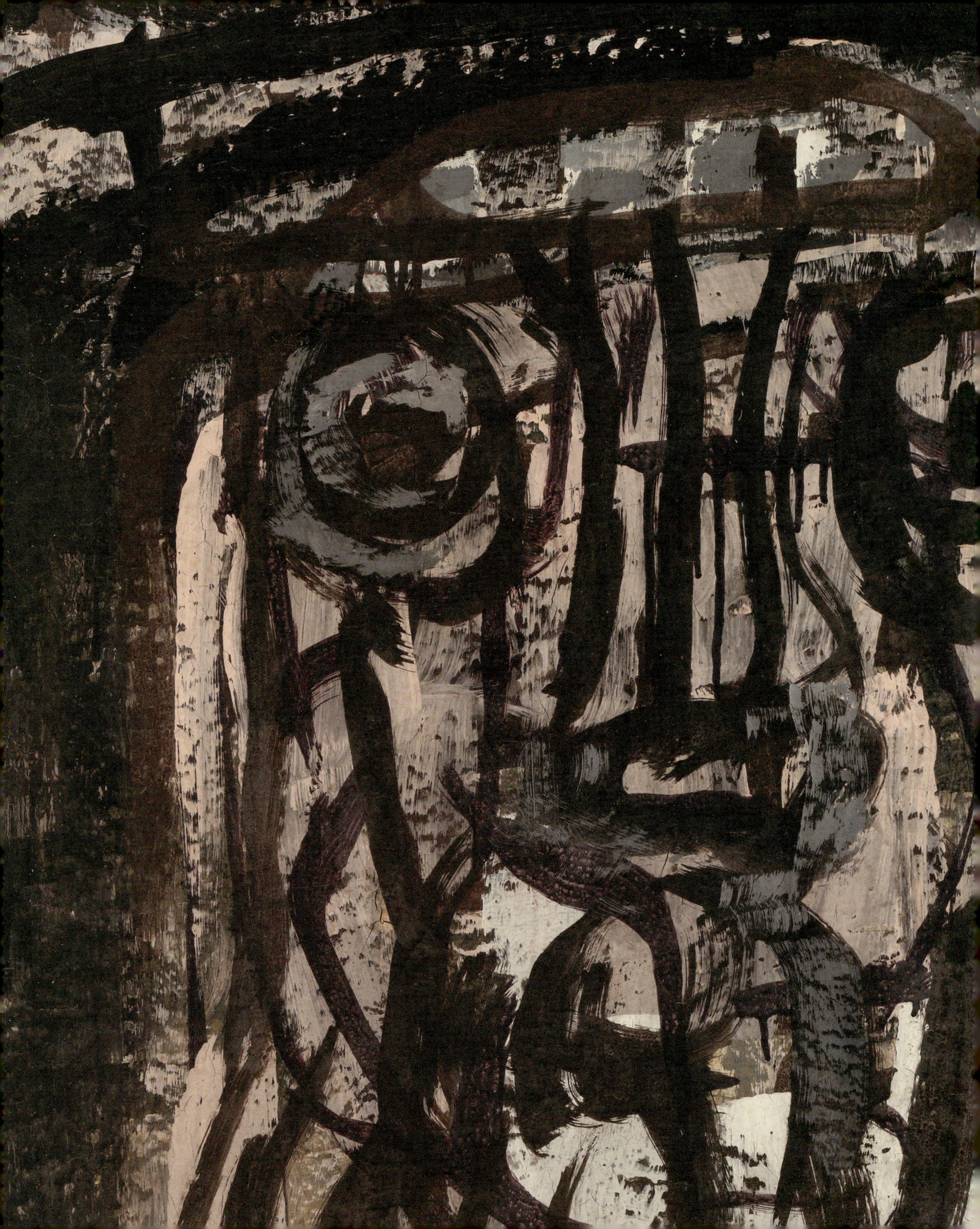

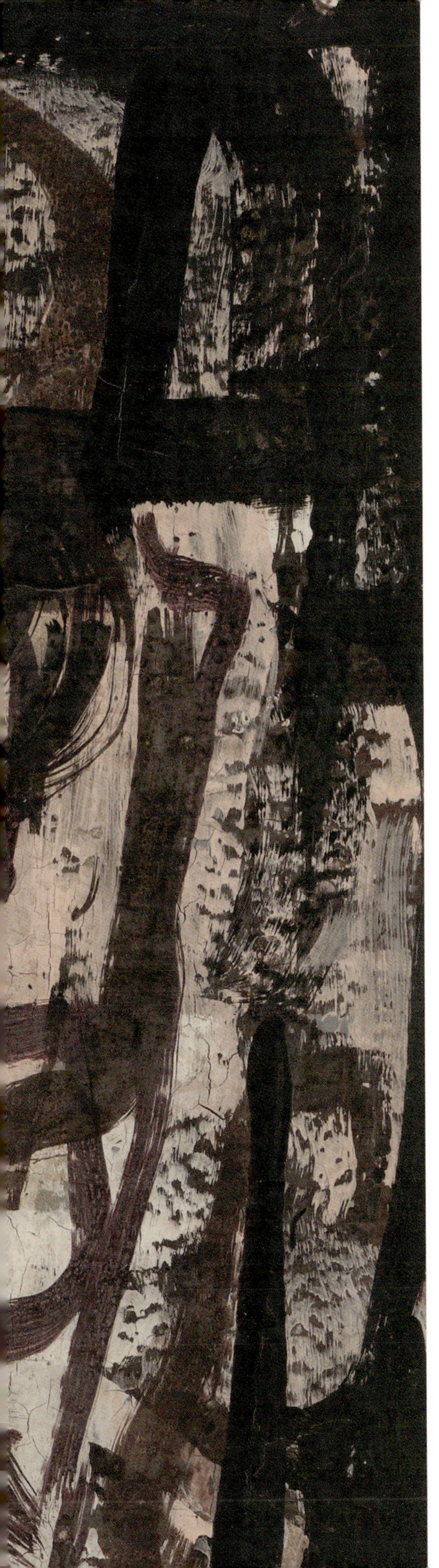

FACE

Australian portraits 1880–1960

Anne Gray

with an introduction by
Ron Radford

National Gallery of Australia

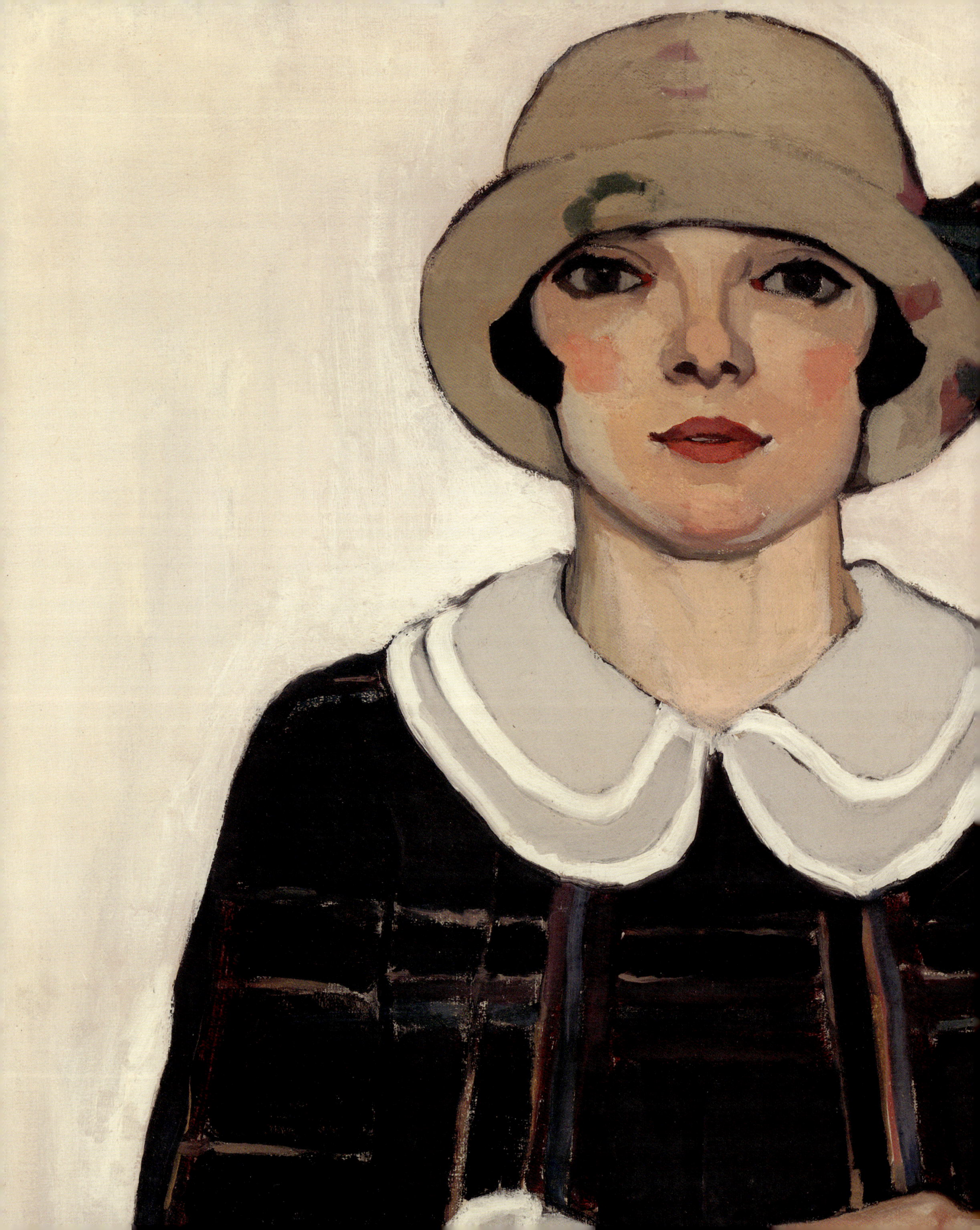

Contents

Foreword 6

An introduction to Australia's first portraits 9
Ron Radford

Face: Australian portraits 1880–1960 15
Anne Gray

The portraits 42–153

Bibliography 154

Image credits 156

Abbreviations 156

Contributors 156

Acknowledgments 157

Index 158

Foreword

This publication, and the exhibition it is published in conjuction with, are part of the National Gallery of Australia's extensive program of sharing the national collection with the whole of Australia. The theme, Australian portraiture from 1880 to 1960, was conceived as a follow-up to the highly successful *Ocean to Outback: Australian landscape painting 1850–1950* which toured regional galleries in every state and territory in Australia from August 2007 to May 2009. Like its predecessor, all the paintings in this exhibition, and main works in this book, are from the National Gallery's collection. The selection includes well-known paintings that are usually on permanent display at the Gallery as well as interesting little-known works which, because of their previous condition or poor framing, or lack of space in our galleries devoted to Australian art, have rarely been on view. All these paintings are either in oil, tempera or synthetic polymer paint; more fragile portraits in watercolour and other light-sensitive mediums have had to be excluded from this travelling exhibition. A good number of the paintings have now been specially cleaned and appropriately reframed for the tour. Several works have been acquired recently and will be seen for the first time in this exhibition. Famous images will therefore be seen along with unfamiliar and unexpected portraits.

Compared with the development of other Australian collections, the great bulk of the national art collection was acquired late—after the early 1970s. Yet even before then, major Australian portraits were among the first paintings purchased for the national collection and are seen here. These include E Phillips Fox's portrait of a figure in sunlight, *The green parasol* c 1912 (purchased 1946) as well as his portrait of a demure young girl, *Elsie, daughter of HW Brooks, Esquire* 1904 (purchased 1963); Tom Roberts's images of his friends, *Mrs Leonard Dodds* c 1893 (purchased 1959) and *Portrait study of Lena Brasch* c 1893 (purchased 1966); William Dobell's study for a commissioned portrait of the notable Australian poet and humanitarian, *Sketch portrait of Dame Mary Gilmore* c 1956 (purchased 1962); Hugh Ramsay's virtuoso portrait of Melba's niece, *Miss Nellie Patterson* c 1903 (purchased 1966); and George W Lambert's carefully posed image of the successful pastoralist Leigh Falkiner, titled *Weighing the fleece* 1921 (purchased 1966).

This national touring exhibition is truly national: it includes portraits by artists, and of sitters, from every state. In the late Victorian and Edwardian periods a revival in

Australian portraiture resulted in a number of particularly strong works by the figure painters Tom Roberts, Rupert Bunny, Hugh Ramsay and George W Lambert. The 1920s and 1930s saw the development of Modernism in Australia and with it the emergence of strong women artists such as Margaret Preston, Grace Cossington Smith, Grace Crowley and Elise Blumann, some of whose portraits are included. This was also the time when the Archibald Prize began, giving portraiture in Australia a new high-profile, if somewhat questionable and often conservative status. Then in the 1940s and 1950s artists such as William Dobell, Arthur Boyd, Albert Tucker, Sidney Nolan and Ian Fairweather developed new expressive forms of portraiture. Self-portraits have always been a strong part of the European portraiture tradition and in Australia it has been the same: this exhibition includes thirteen self-portraits, by artists as diverse as Bernard Hall, George W Lambert, Grace Cossington Smith, Albert Tucker and Ian Fairweather.

Anne Gray, the Gallery's Head of Australian Art, has curated a very absorbing exhibition and authored this book. I thank and congratulate her on an extremely interesting selection and very useful publication.

The exhibition has been sponsored by the National Gallery of Australia Council Exhibitions Fund, made up of generous personal donations by members of the National Gallery Council. It has the has generous support from the Federal Government's National Collecting Institutions Touring and Outreach Program and Visions of Australia, an Australian Government program that supports touring exhibitions. I sincerely thank these generous funding bodies.

I trust that this diverse range of portraits from the national collection by artists from all around Australia, and ranging over a period of more than eighty years, is of great interest to many, especially to audiences in regional Australia.

Ron Radford AM
Director
National Gallery of Australia

(pages 2–3) Ian Fairweather
Portrait of the artist 1962 (detail) [54]

(pages 4–5) Margaret Preston
Flapper 1925 (detail) [25]

(following pages) Robert Dowling
Mrs Adolphus Sceales with Black Jimmie on Merrang Station 1856 (detail)
oil on canvas mounted on plywood
76 x 101.5 cm
National Gallery of Australia, Canberra, purchased through the Founding Donors Fund 1984

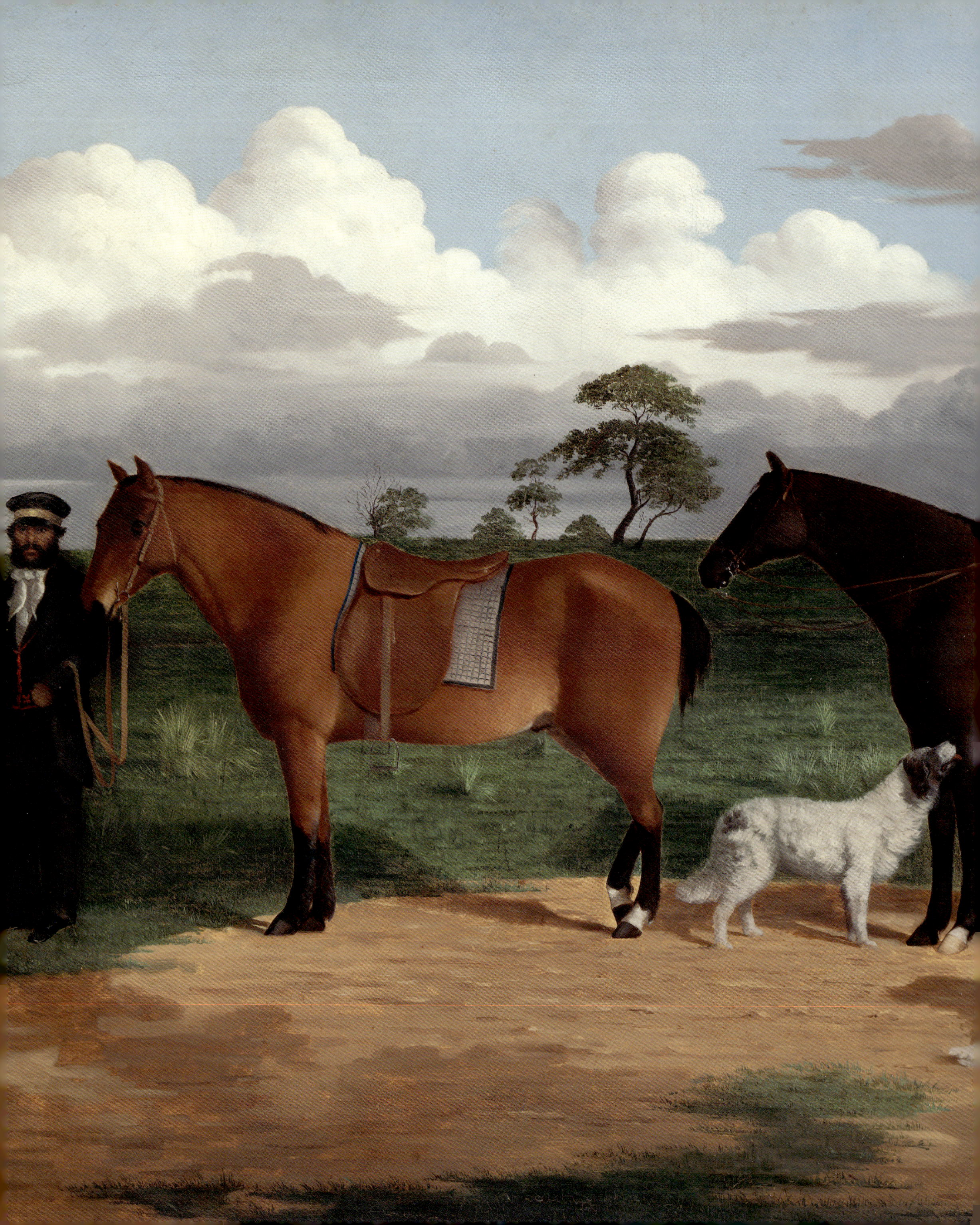

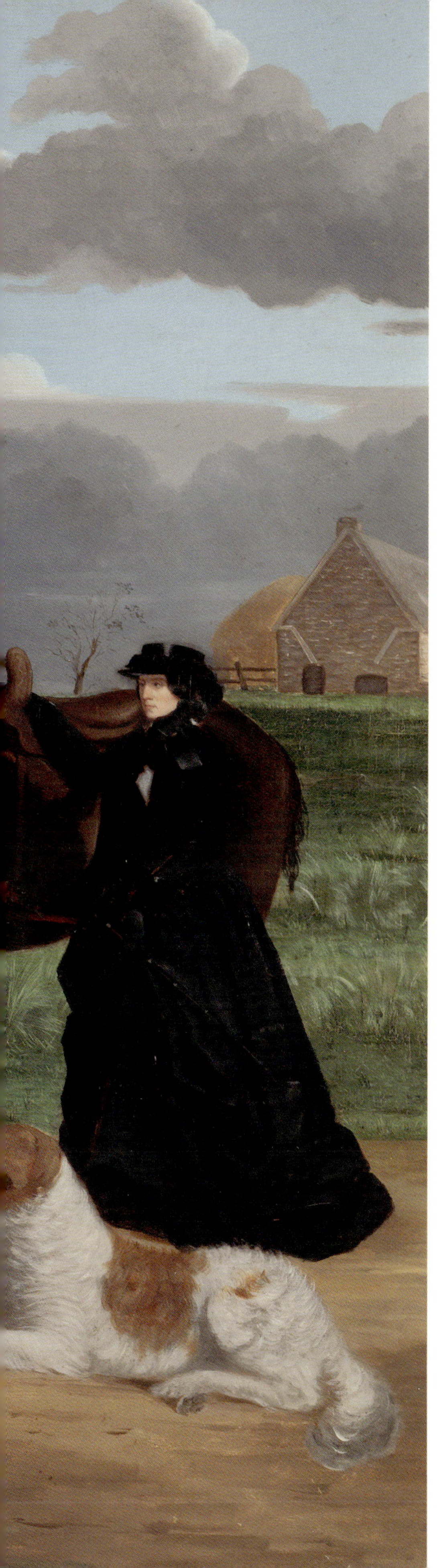

An introduction to Australia's first portraits

Ron Radford

The Australian portrait paintings included in this publication and exhibition were made between the late-colonial 1880s and the late-modernist 1960s and are among the finest from a time when portraiture was less favoured as a subject in art than Australian national life and landscape. Once a dominant aspect of painting in the early nineteenth century, portraiture had been taken over by photography. The earlier works featured nevertheless reflect a period when serious, creative portrait painting was renewed, notably within the broader practice of leading Australian artists such as Tom Roberts and George W Lambert.

From its inception in 1921 at the Art Gallery of New South Wales, the annual Archibald Prize for contemporary portraits, preferably of 'distinguished' Australians, was intended to raise the quality and status of portrait painting, and has been one of Australia's most popular and sometimes controversial art events; from the 1980s the more valuable Doug Moran National Portrait Prize, which favours intimate or critical portraits as much as the culture of celebrity, has also maintained public interest in contemporary portraiture. More significantly, in 1997 Australia established a provisional National Portrait Gallery in Old Parliament House, Canberra, and at the end of 2008 moved to a purpose-built building positioned between the National Library, the High Court and the National Gallery of Australia. Present-day Australians can be excused for thinking that portraits have always been as interesting to artists and audiences as they are now—and as they were before the 1880s and indeed especially before the 1850s.

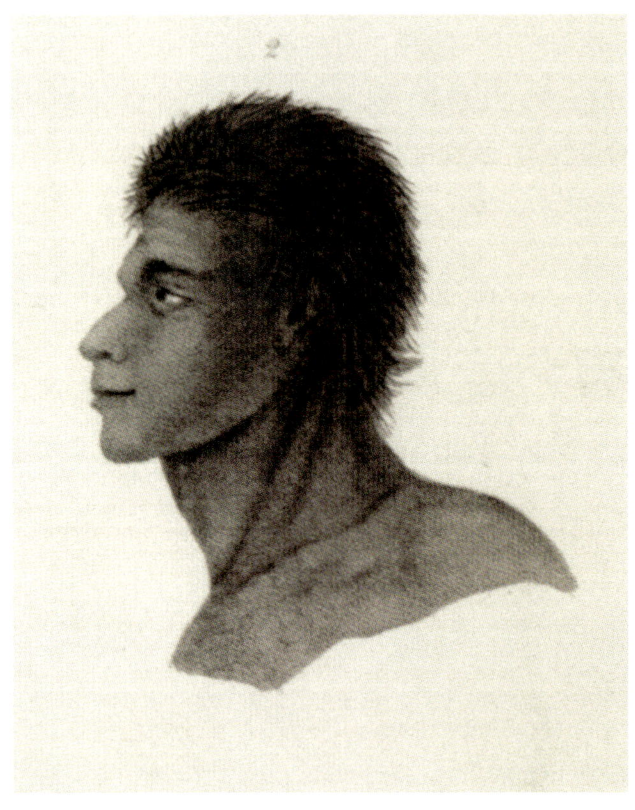

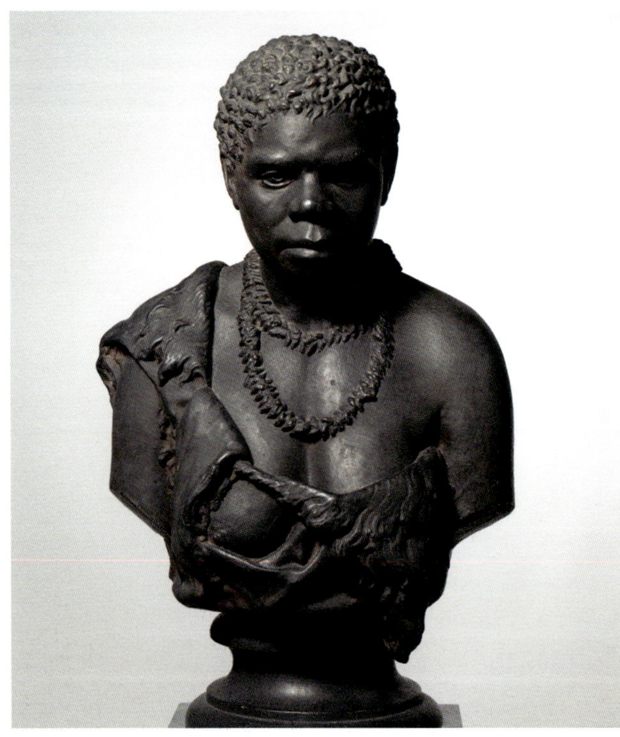

It is worth mapping here the little-appreciated profusion and excellence of Australia's first portraits. Australia was colonised by the British in the 1780s, when portraiture had already been the dominant subject of British art for three centuries; indeed, no nationality had been as obsessed with portraiture as the British. Our very earliest colonial artists from Britain produced specialised scientific records of unique flora and fauna and peoples, which included often warmly sympathetic portrait drawings of individual Aborigines; the first settler artists included military, official and convict amateurs who shared these scientific interests. Our now much-lauded national landscape tradition was a long way off. By the late 1820s portrait paintings had become the most prolific product of early colonial art; there were more professional portrait painters than painters of other subjects. Portrait photography took over in the 1850s and, although there were outstanding earlier landscape artists—John Glover (working in Tasmania) and Conrad Martens (in New South Wales)—landscape painting, too, took off in a prolific way only after the 1850s gold rushes, especially in Victoria.

Australia's first professional artist was John Lewin, trained as a specialist painter of birds, who arrived in Sydney from Britain in 1800. However, like all successful colonists, he had to be versatile. He expanded his painting repertoire to include the exotic new plants, and some landscapes, as well as birds and animals. In 1808 he advertised that he was willing to take portrait commissions for miniatures. None of the settler miniatures have been traced but earlier, on an 1802 trip from Sydney to Tahiti, he had painted a series of miniature watercolour portraits of Tahiti's island chiefs (AGSA and ML). He also painted portraits of Aborigines, known to us today only through prints. The first Australian artist to paint in oils, Lewin is probably the painter of an oil portrait, *Boy with sulphur-crested cockatoo* 1826 (AGSA).

Our first artist professionally trained as a portrait painter was Richard Read senior, who arrived in Sydney as a convict in 1813. He painted small watercolour portraits and miniatures of settlers. The second professional portrait painter was his son, Richard Read junior, who arrived in Sydney as a free settler in 1819 and, like his father, painted small portraits in watercolour.

And the first artist to produce a good number of larger portraits in the more permanent medium of oil paint was Augustus Earle, who arrived in Hobart in 1825 and a few months later moved to Sydney. His commissions included Australia's first full-length grand portraits: one of the Governor of New South Wales, Sir Thomas Brisbane (Government House, Sydney); and a pair of large portraits for the colony's then richest man, John Piper—one of Piper, the other a group portrait of his wife and children (ML). Earle painted more than a dozen smaller oil portraits of colonists during less than four years in Australia, and a notable small full-length portrait of Bungaree, a celebrity Aborigine. Charles Rodius, an architectural draftsman, arrived in Sydney as a convict in 1829 and he too did portraits of both settlers and Indigenous people, in watercolours or crayons, and also published prints.

Professional portraiture flourishes only in a self-confident and stable society; in the colonies, when the cities of Sydney and Hobart were well established and prospering. In addition to Read junior and Rodius, from the 1830s to the 1850s Sydney's portrait painters included Joseph Backler, Thomas Griffiths, William Nicholas, Maurice Felton, Richard Noble and Marshall Claxton. In Tasmania in the same period the more numerous and finer portrait painters included Thomas Bock (who had arrived as a convict as early as 1824), Benjamin Duterrau, Henry Mundy, Mary Morton Allport, W B Gould, Thomas Wainewright, Frederick Strange, Knut Bull, W P Dowling and Robert Dowling. Portraiture took hold early in Adelaide, which had been settled in 1836 without convicts, under a systematic colonisation scheme. There, during the first years of settlement, Martha Berkeley painted small portraits and miniatures and her sister Theresa Walker made wax medallion portraits of colonists and Aborigines. (Theresa

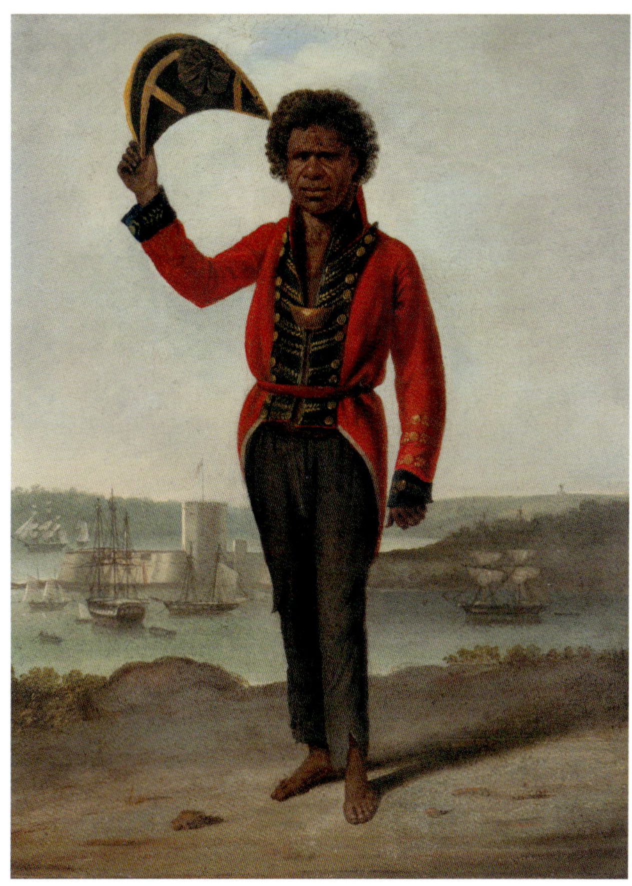

Augustus Earle
Portrait of Bungaree, a native of New South Wales c 1826
oil on canvas, 68.5 x 50.5 cm
Rex Nan Kivell Collection, National Library of Australia and the National Gallery of Australia, Canberra

(opposite above) John Lewin
Aged native of Otaheite. New Hollander 1827
engraving, printed in black ink, from one copper plate
20.2 x 12.6 cm
National Gallery of Australia, Canberra, gift of Josepf Lebovic Gallery

(opposite) Benjamin Law
Trucaninny, wife of Woureddy 1836
painted plaster, 66 x 42.5 x 25.7 cm
National Gallery of Australia, Canberra, purchased 1981

(following page) J M Crossland
Portrait of Nannultera, a young Poonindie cricketer 1854 (detail)
oil on canvas, 99 x 78.8 cm
Rex Nan Kivell Collection, National Library of Australia and the National Gallery of Australia, Canberra

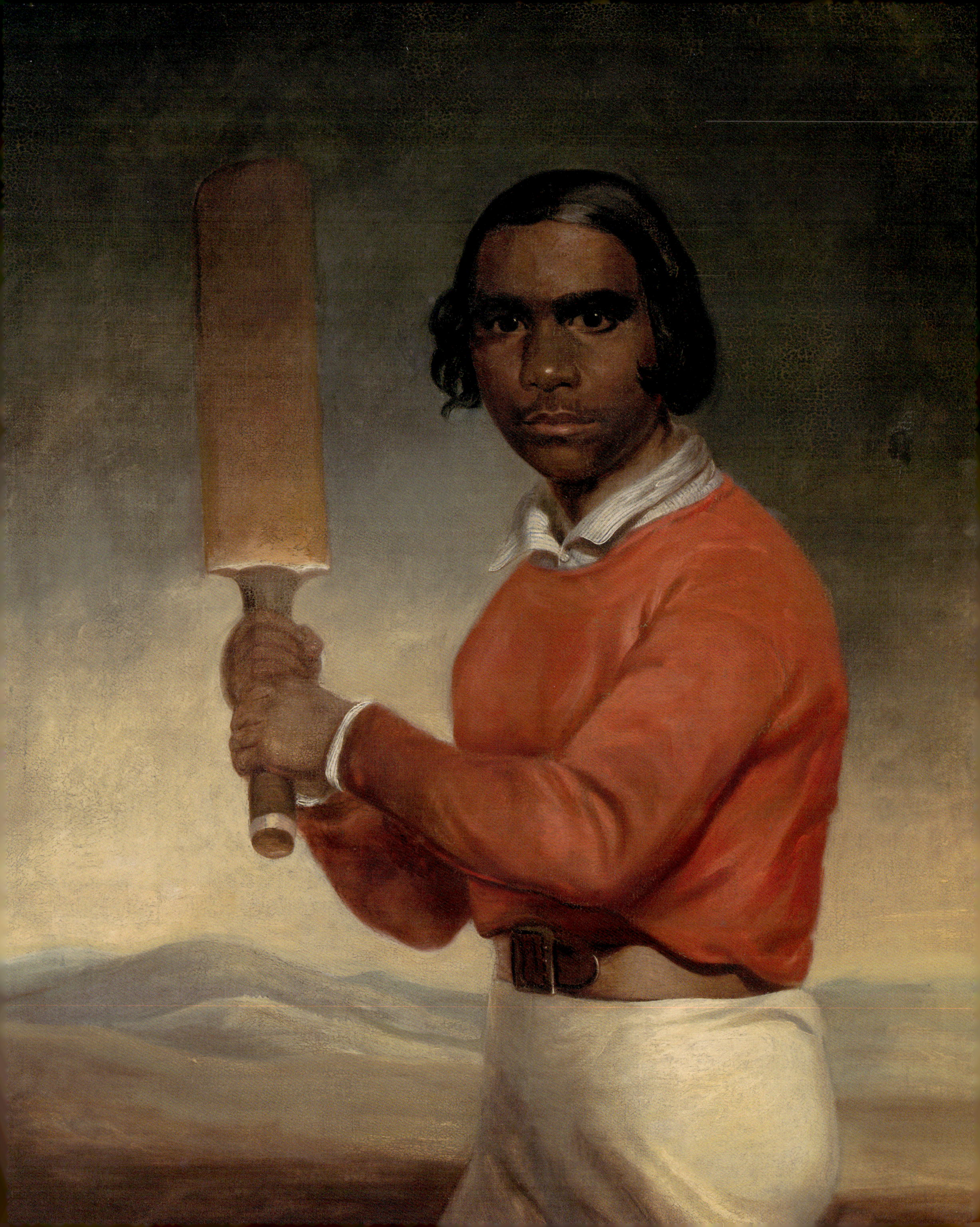

Walker was Australian's first female sculptor, and in the 1830s in Hobart another sculptor, Benjamin Law, produced a pair of wonderfully dignified portrait heads of famous Aborigines.) Melbourne attracted a small group of portrait painters, mainly after the gold rushes of 1851; they included Georgiana McCrae, Thomas Napier, William Strutt, Ludwig Becker and Conway Hart. And Robert Dowling, Australia's first locally trained portrait artist, moved from Tasmania to Geelong in 1854.

Portraiture remained a part of our colonial artists' practice throughout the second half of the nineteenth century, especially in Adelaide, where portrait and figure painting continued to dominate the art scene with such artists as Alexander Schramm, John Crossland, Charles Hill and Andrew MacCormac. However, with the growing popularity of photographic portraits large and small, the painted portrait lost the dominance it had previously enjoyed.

Early colonial portraiture followed a late-Georgian style, for which the ultimate model was provided by the extremely stylish British Regency work of Sir Thomas Lawrence (1769–1830).

The portraits in this publication and exhibition range from the beginnings of the modern portrait in the 1880s—in generally more informal and sober impressionist or realist portrait conventions—through to a huge variety of interesting modern portraits up to the 1960s—including a few painted from life in adventurous cubist and expressionist approaches.

One of the later portraits, Sidney Nolan's black-and-white 1946 painting of the long-deceased Ned Kelly, is based on a police photograph of the celebrity criminal, and thus makes a virtue of the medium that had caused portrait painting to retreat in Kelly's lifetime. It also prefigures the dominance of photo-based paintings alongside major works of photographic art in present-day portraiture.

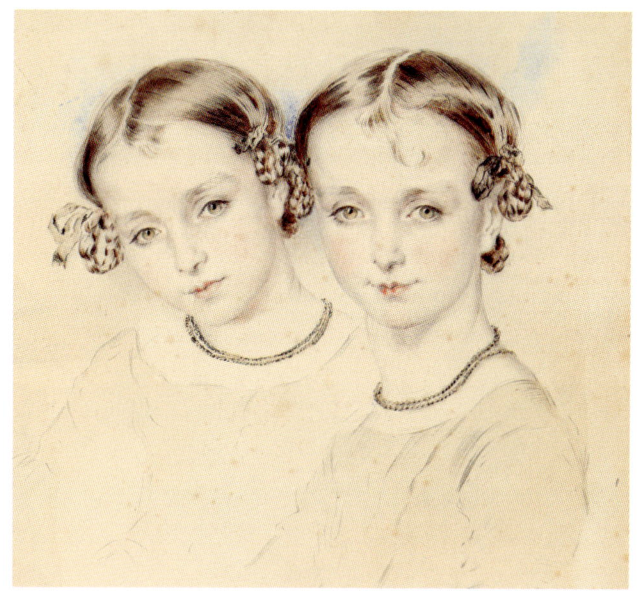

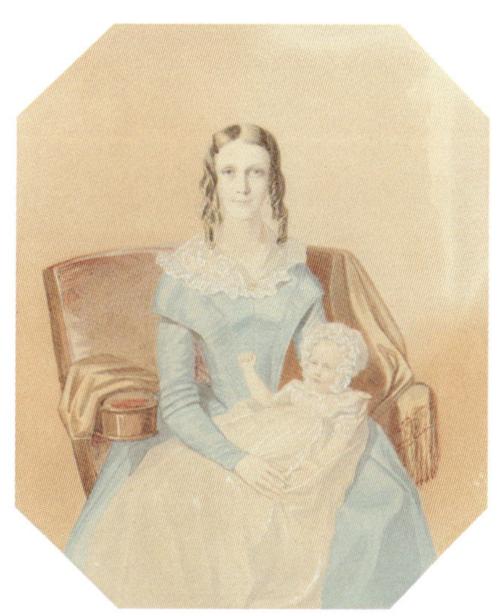

Thomas Wainewright
The Cutmear sisters, Jane and Lucy c 1842
watercolour and pencil on paper
32.4 x 30 cm
National Gallery of Australia, Canberra, purchased 1969

William Nicholas
Lady and child c 1847
watercolour and pencil, ground gold leaf and gum arabic on cardboard
24.7 x 19.8 cm
National Gallery of Australia, Canberra, purchased 2007

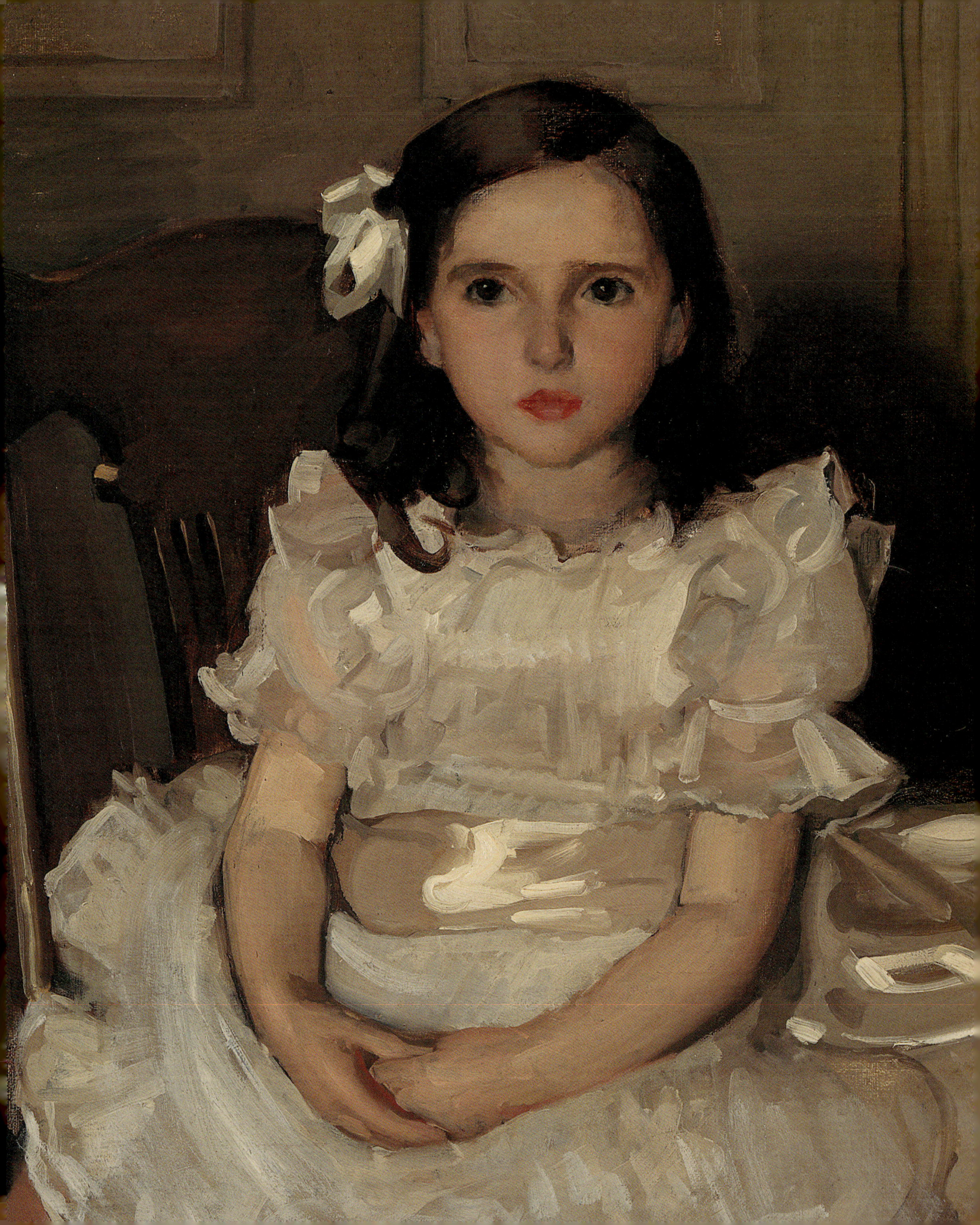

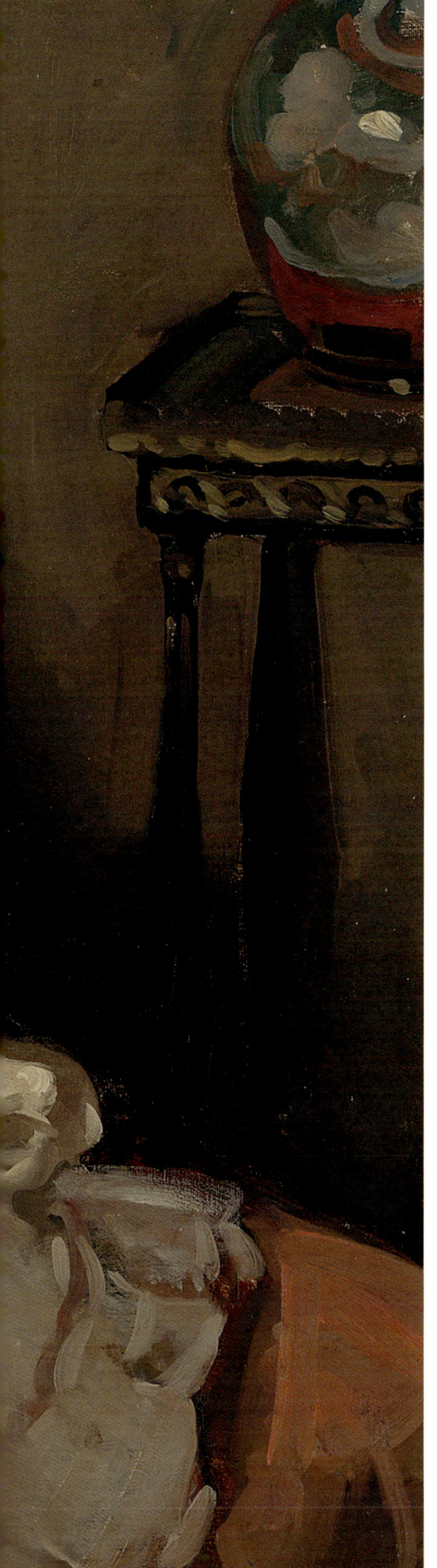

Face: Australian portraits 1880–1960

Anne Gray

There is a primacy to viewing faces and to face recognition which lies at the core of our fascination for portraits. One of the first things we do is learn to recognise the faces of our parents—and to put a name to them. We need to do so for survival: to be fed and clothed—and cuddled. American art historian Richard Brilliant observed that the child:

> gazing up at its mother, imprints her vitally important image so firmly on its mind that soon enough she can be recognised almost instantaneously without conscious thought; spontaneous face recognition remains an important instrument of survival.[1]

As we grow up, we recognise faces and facial expressions on sight and we take this for granted. Without this ability we could not recognise our friends, nor tell whether they are pleased to see us or angry with us. Curiosity about our fellow human beings is central to our very existence. In the words of French Impressionist painter Edgar Degas, 'we were created to look at one another, weren't we?'[2] This ability to recognise and respond to faces and facial expressions is crucial to the dynamics of portraiture: our ability to 'read' faces can be transferred to looking at faces in paintings.

However, as we all know, we can sometimes 'get it wrong', we can misread facial expressions and the emotional states they convey; and in these cases what helps us to 'get it right' is to rely not only on our reading of the face but also to consider the context. Furthermore, one person's reading of a facial expression—in real life or in a portrait—can differ from

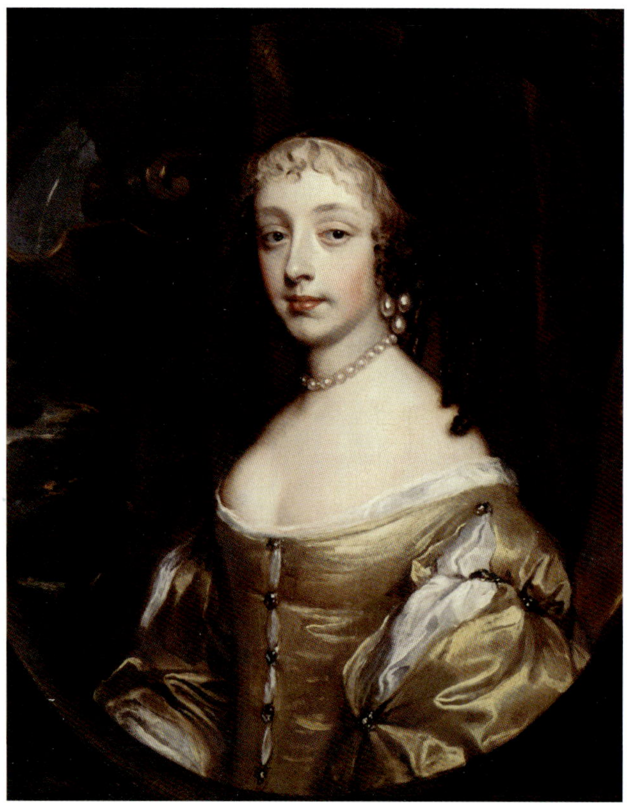

another's. Something of what we read in faces comes down to our own opinions, prejudices or expectations. Such ambiguities can, however, give portraits their strength, their fascination, and indeed the multiple possible readings may in fact capture the complexity of the subject depicted.[3]

But what *is* a portrait? Despite portraiture being one of the most accessible forms of visual art, it is in many ways among the hardest to define. The *Oxford English dictionary* tells us that it is a likeness of a person, especially of the face, made from life by drawing, painting, photography, engraving et cetera; an image, representation, type; likeness, similitude. Wikipedia goes further, to suggest that 'a portrait is a painting, photograph, sculpture or other artistic representation of a person, in which the face and its expression is predominant. The intent is to display the likeness, personality, and even the mood of the person'.[4] In a promotion for a recent Australian ABC television program about portrait painting, *Face painting*, the ABC suggested that 'with any portrait, the first thing an artist must do is find the soul of the subject'.[5] Indeed, the word portrait comes from the Latin *protrahere*, to draw forth, disclose, reveal, to capture the inner essence, to visualise the invisible.

Although likeness is central to many definitions of portraiture, it may be a likeness to visual appearance of face or body, or an evocation of the physical presence of an individual; it may be a depiction of character or personality, or the mood of a person, or their spirit or soul—or some or all of these. What portraitists have sought to achieve has differed from artist to artist, and over time, but in the twentieth century (perhaps always) most portrait painters have wanted to depict more than a mere physical likeness, more than a character study; they have wanted to create a work of art, an aesthetic object.

Artists' views of portraiture

The influential eighteenth-century British portrait painter Joshua Reynolds observed in his famous *Discourses* on art: 'Even in portraits, the grace and, we may add, the likeness, consists more in taking the general air than in observing the exact similitude of every feature.'[6] He recommended that a portrait should tend towards the idealisation of the imperfect rather than to the depiction of the particular, with all its quirks and peculiarities.

Australia's leading portrait painter at the end of the nineteenth century, Tom Roberts, remarked that when looking at art those works which held him were portraits where the 'intense feeling of humanity holds all through'.[7] In addition to a specific likeness Roberts thought it important to convey the more general 'humanity' of the subject—a sense of the living presence of a person.

In Edwardian England there were conflicting ideas about what a portrait should be; the extent to which it should be a likeness and the degree to which it should generalise or idealise. In 1908, the art critic Paul G Konody suggested that the custom of revealing a sitter's identity had been discarded in French exhibition catalogues because reference to individuals deflected from an aesthetic appreciation of the works.[8] Artists were aware that viewers were sometimes distracted from looking at portraits as works of art by their curiosity to find out what the subjects looked like, particularly if they were prominent people. Australian expatriates gave their paintings generic titles rather than the name of the sitter, as did George W Lambert in *The old dress* 1906 [14], E Phillips Fox in *The green parasol* c 1912 [20] and Max Meldrum in *Poland (Madame de Tarczynska)* 1917 [22] (painted in Australia, after working and studying abroad). These titles draw attention away from the sitters' identities and encourage the viewer to engage in the aesthetic appreciation of the paintings. These works are still portraits, and we do know who their subjects are, but the artists wanted their paintings to be regarded first and foremost as works of art.

This was not, of course, anything new. The idea of the subject of a portrait being secondary to the artist's style has a long tradition. Robin Gibson, former chief curator at the National Portrait Gallery, London, observed of the seventeenth-century British portrait painter, Sir Peter Lely: 'A "Lely" lady is always a "Lely" lady, well and before she is the countess of Nottingham or whoever.'[9] Elements of personal style have always been present in portraits. What may have been new—or been seen to be new—in the twentieth century was the conscious imposition on the sitter of Aestheticism, Formalism, Cubism and so on; it was no longer a question of producing an appropriate likeness or evoking the character of the sitter in a manner which revealed the eye and hand of the artist, it became necessary to create a 'work of art'.

Under the inspiration of British–American artist James McNeill Whistler, Edwardian artists were usually as much concerned with the careful placement of figures and the reduction of a composition to essentials as with likeness. And after about 1910 they simplified their

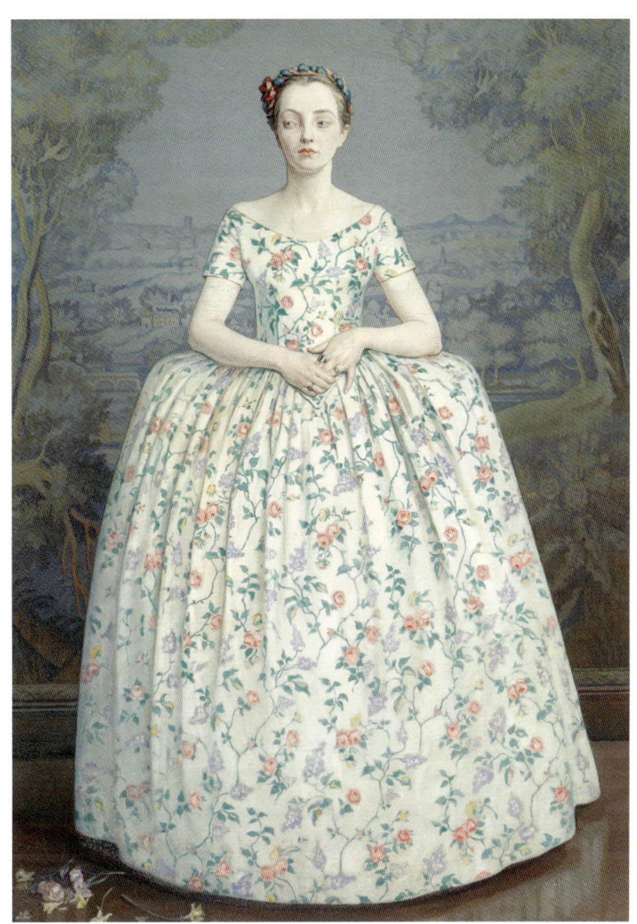

Hilda Rix Nicholas
The scorned flowers (Les fleurs dédaignées) 1925
oil on canvas
193 x 128.5 cm
National Gallery of Australia, Canberra

(opposite) Peter Lely
Henrietta Anne, Duchess of Orleans c 1662
oil on canvas
76.2 x 6.5 cm
National Portrait Gallery, London, given by Mrs ND Valpy, 1989

(previous pages) Hugh Ramsay
Miss Nellie Patterson 1903 (detail) [12]

images to elemental forms to an even greater extent, often adopting bold colours to do so. Some conservative art reviewers criticised artists who introduced an element of Formalism into their portraits and claimed (perhaps incorrectly) that the 'greatest portrait painters … did not impose a kind of abstract "art" upon the likeness',[10] while those with a more modern sensibility wrote in praise of a 'tendency to decorative realism'.[11] Whatever the attitude of critics, artists have usually been as much concerned with form as with content; indeed the two are not mutually exclusive.

Australia's pre-eminent portrait painter of the 1920s, George W Lambert, entertained his clients while he depicted them with 'a pleasant interchange of fun, fancies, and philosophy'.[12] But he claimed that once he had attained an affinity with his subject, he stood aloof and created the portrait with his emotions frozen 'to a correct working degree'.[13] He told his students that they should concern themselves with the 'outsides' of what they were painting, that they were hampered by the idea that portraits should talk with their eyes and should have 'soul' in them.[14] In this he echoed the formalist claims of British art critic and theorist Roger Fry, that 'all art depends upon cutting off the practical responses to sensations of ordinary life, thereby setting free a pure and as it were disembodied functioning of the spirit'.[15] Lambert's interest in structure was a formalist concern and his group portrait *Weighing the fleece* 1921 [24] is an example of this approach. Lambert posed the figures as if they were a tableau of modern life, and sought to render the image more durable by focusing on structure and pattern. A formalist approach is also evident in works such as Rupert Bunny's *Woman in a brown hat (Femme au chapeau brun)* c 1917 [23] and Margaret Preston's *Flapper* 1925 [25].

In the 1920s the Australian modernist painter Roy de Maistre maintained that 'the subject has to be part of the material—it isn't any more important'.[16] He depicted the facial features of his subjects but he was also concerned with the arrangement of lines, forms and colours in order to convey character. In his 1945 self-portrait [42] he did this by carefully arranging a strong pattern of interlacing forms in an almost cubist fashion.

For John Brack, likewise, structure was essential to a portrait. Helen Brack observed:

> a portrait was about identity, the disposition—not the persona—and the whole picture was a portrait. To place the figure near the frontal plain of the picture is not the same as placing it in the centre space of the picture … and to place it at the back plane implies something different again.[17]

Brack's portraits, and his likenesses such as *The baby drinking* 1955 and *The girls at school* 1959 [50, 53], are carefully constructed images in which the placement of figures in space is central to his interpretation of his subject, engaging both the eye and mind.

Other artists have suggested that their main concern in painting a portrait was with capturing the soul or the spirit of their subject. In 1982 Albert Tucker said that in his portraits he sought to create 'a social-psychological landscape'.[18] In works such as *Man's head* 1946 [45] he exaggerated distinctive features of his subjects to suggest their character and mood. And he used colour and paint texture to add to the emotional impact, to assist in conveying a sense of the physical presence of his subjects. He wanted to depict what he thought to be types or symbols, or as he described it, a 'kind of refracting prism for the human condition'.[19]

Tucker's concern was similar to that of the contemporary British portrait painter Lucian Freud: to evoke the subject, rather than create a mirror likeness. Freud commented that 'my idea of portraiture came from dissatisfaction with portraits that resembled people. I would wish my portraits to be of the people, not like them. Not having to look at the sitter, being them. As far as I am concerned, the paint is the person'.[20]

Artists have approached portraiture variously. Those included here have been less concerned with a particular visual likeness of the human body than with an idealised likeness or a generalised feeling of 'humanity'; an abstracted or structured likeness; or a psychological likeness in which the character or mood of the person is suggested, and the spirit of the subject is evoked. Andrew Sayers, former director of the National Portrait Gallery, Canberra, suggested that 'the success and interest of a portrait cannot be separated from its success in artistic terms, regardless of how otherwise interesting the subject may be'.[21]

The subjects of portraiture

This publication and exhibition intentionally push the boundaries of what might be regarded as a portrait. There is a wide range of images of people; but in every case the subject of the work, the sitter, is known or believed to be known.

Although not included here, portraits may be of men and women whose identity remains unknown. Such works are common in art galleries, and we do not question that they are portraits even though we do not know who the person was. Indeed, Jan van Eyck's *Portrait of a man* 1433 (NG, London) or Titian's *A man with a quilted sleeve* c 1512 (NG, London), for example, are two of the most remarkable portraits painted. These works can be described as being 'good likenesses', even though the subject and what they looked like is unknown. The works have a sense of 'authenticity'; we look at such portraits and imagine the existence of the individuals depicted, gathering together all the details provided by the artists: the size and scale of the work, the expressions on the sitter's face, the pose, what they are wearing, what is in the background and so forth. We do so rather as we would look at the face, stance, dress and gestures of a new acquaintance to work out their personality—or gauge the mood of someone we know.

We transfer the skills we regularly use in everyday life to help us 'read' a portrait. When looking at most portraits from earlier times, even when the subject is known, we generally do not know the person depicted and are unlikely to have anything with which to compare their portrait. In these instances, as with portraits of people whose identity is unknown, we interrogate the image to learn what we can about the person depicted.

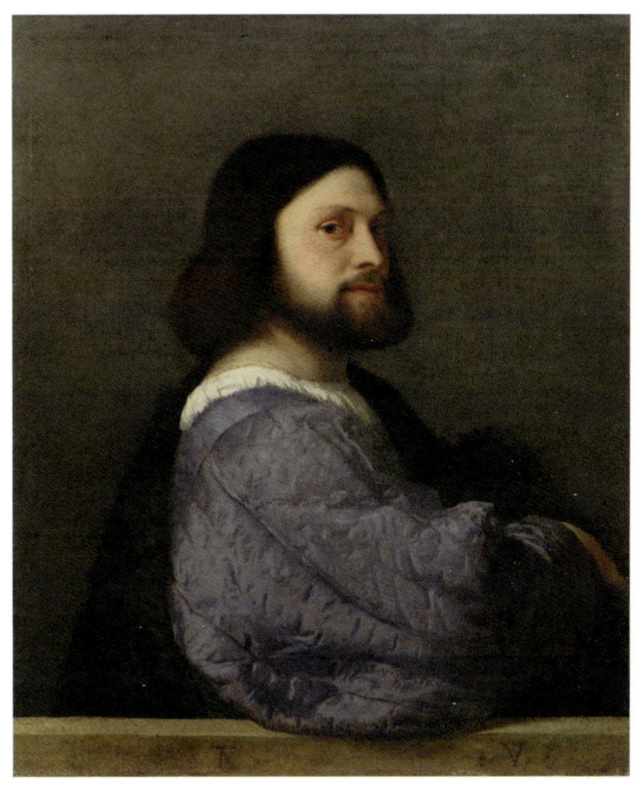

Titian
A man with a quilted sleeve c 1512
oil on canvas
81.2 x 66.3 cm
The National Gallery, London, purchased 1904

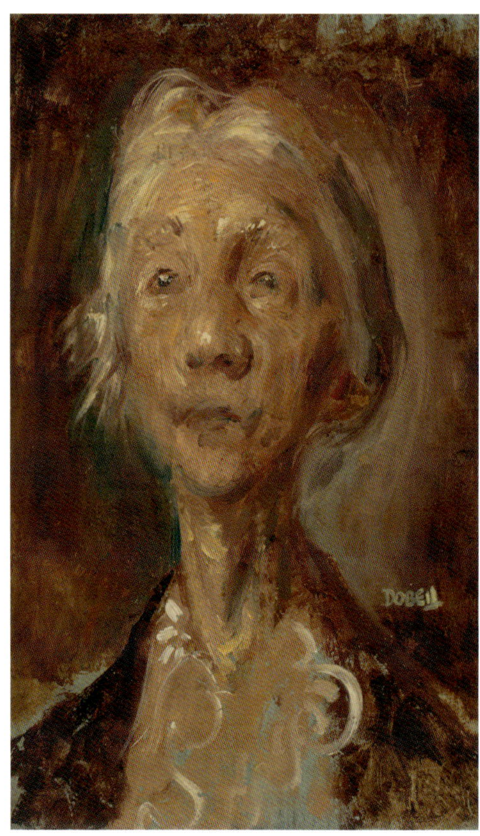

Commissioned portraits

With commissioned portraits, usually the purpose is to pass on to future generations a plausible image of an individual, conveying not only what they looked like, but also their place in society. 'State' portraits are those of eminent people such as the politician Senator J T Walker [9]; 'professional' portraits include celebrity subjects such as Myra Kemble, Dame Mary Gilmore and Helena Rubinstein [4, 51, 52], people famous for what they have done. These are the kinds of public portraits traditionally collected by portrait galleries and public institutions. In classical antiquity such official portraits were thought to be of 'noble characters' worthy of imitation—and for Joshua Reynolds remained so into the eighteenth century. Now they are more likely to be viewed as historical documents providing insight into the subjects and their society.

There are also commissioned 'family' portraits of people with wealth and status like Miss Robertson of Colac (Dolly), Abigail Pirani, Leigh Sadleir Falkiner and his wife Beatrice [3, 8, 24], as well as the more humble private commissions like those of Nellie Patterson, Elsie Brooks and Mary Widney [12, 13, 27]. These portraits are frequently kept in a family and passed down from one generation to another. And there is the 'memorial' portrait, painted after the subject's death, of which there are no examples in this exhibition. All, if they excel as works of art, may end up in an art gallery.

Official commissions have often hindered artists and limited their work because the artist generally has to meet the needs of the client. Indeed, many commissions have brought out the worst in an artist. But this does not appear to have been the case with any of the commissioned portraits here. Robert Dowling painted an even better portrait of Miss Robertson of Colac when he was asked to repaint it. And he appears to have done so with considerable goodwill. In *Miss Nellie Patterson* 1903, Hugh Ramsay created one of his best portraits, capturing the wide-eyed, alert face of young Nellie [12]. E Phillips Fox created an insightful portrait of a stately, elderly dowager in *Mrs James Pirani* 1893 [8] and a sensitive rendering of childhood in *Elsie, daughter of HW Brooks Esquire* 1904 [13]. Tom Roberts was hampered when painting his *Opening of the First Parliament of the Commonwealth of Australia by HRH The Duke of Cornwall and York (later King George V), May 9 1901* 1903 (Parliament of Australia), with its 269 miniature portraits of famous people. But his unrestrained, energetic brushstrokes in the sketch portrait of Senator Walker [9] animate the subject in a way not possible in the official 'big picture'. Likewise William Dobell may have been constrained in his full-scale commissioned portraits of Dame Mary Gilmore and Helena Rubinstein [51, 52], but the sketch portraits for these works are full of life. He conveyed the feisty spirit of the poet at the age of 90, through his depiction of Gilmore's face. The artist commented:

> She hasn't a neck like that but I wanted to get her the way she sits and spouts poetry … so I had to lengthen the neck to get it.[22]

And George W Lambert was in no way constricted by his commission to depict the Falkiners [24]. He painted the work as he chose, and if they did not like it, so be it—he would sell it to someone else, and he did.

Self-portraits

Artists have often painted themselves as subjects because they were in need of a readily available, patient model. What is more, they could depict themselves more freely than any other subject. Indeed, the self-portrait is the artist's most personal form of expression, a means of self-evaluation, promotion—and deception. Those who regularly paint self-portraits produce a kind of visual autobiography, as well as charting their development and changes in artistic approach.

Frederick McCubbin painted at least six self-portraits, recording the aging face of the artist, and presenting different aspects of his personality. McCubbin's *Self-portrait* 1908 [15] is one of his most intimate and searching portraits. Here, he pays homage to Rembrandt's *Self-portrait at the age of 34* 1640 (NG, London), a work which he would have viewed in 1907. In referencing Rembrandt—by default—he made a claim for himself as a master painter. Four years later, in his *Self-portrait* 1912 (AGSA), McCubbin depicted himself looking at the viewer with quiet satisfaction, having just been elected the first president of the Australian Art Association. This is his most 'official' and least revealing portrait; all his physical features are there but he conveyed little of his genial, fun-loving, warm-hearted personality. McCubbin's 1916 self-portrait (AGWA) is similar to that of 1908 in both composition and colouring. There is, however, an even greater frankness in his last portrait—an honest interrogation of his own face to reveal a sense of frailty, a hint at the impermanence of life.

Self-portraits not only show what an artist looked like but also how they wanted to be seen. Hugh Ramsay and George W Lambert had fun with their self-portraits. Like other Edwardians, they enjoyed dressing up and play acting and consciously explored ways of presenting

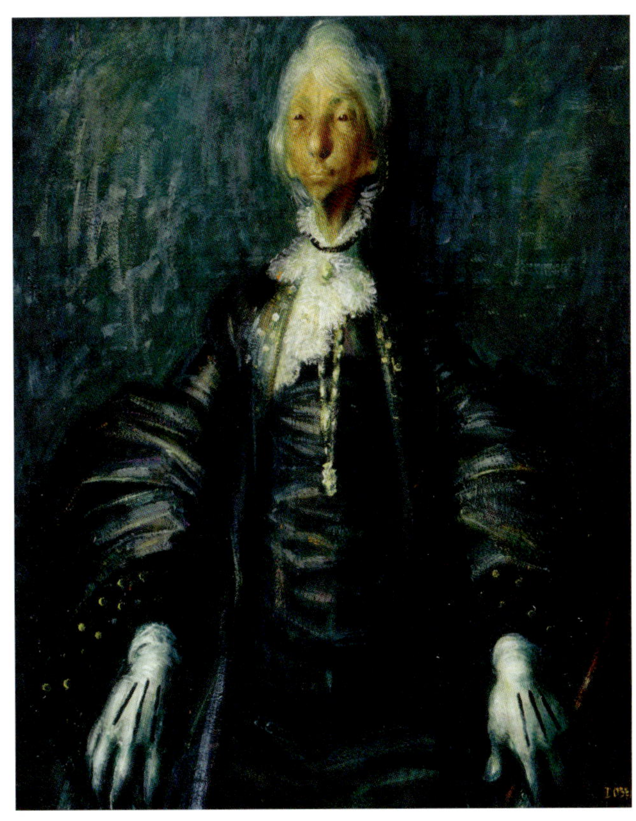

William Dobell
Dame Mary Gilmore c 1956
oil on hardboard
90.2 x 73.7 cm
Art Gallery of New South Wales, gift of Dame Mary Gilmore 1960

(opposite) William Dobell
Sketch portrait of Dame Mary Gilmore c 1956 (detail) [51]

themselves. *Self-portrait, bust showing hands* 1901–02 [10] is one of over 25 self-portraits that Ramsay produced; here, he emphasised his facial expression—a quizzical look with a half-smile and the right side of his face in darkness. This is just one of his many 'faces'. Through his many self-portraits, Ramsay constructed a composite image of himself and also, perhaps by default, showed that the face an artist presents in his portrait, of himself or of any sitter, is an artifice; merely one way of looking at this person.

There is a naive expectation, the German art historian Max Friedlander suggested, of assuming that the artist has a superior opportunity to convey both the likeness and character of their subject in a self-portrait, because the observer is identical with the observed. But even the most objective persons have difficulty in remaining objective about themselves; moreover, the artist does not depict a passive subject when they paint their self-portrait, but an intensely active subject—which may make the self-portrait theatrical, and appear artificial. We do not expect an autobiography to be more truthful than a biography and, indeed, we often expect it to be somewhat artificial.[23] The knowledge that we have of our own face and body by inhabiting them is quite different from the image that we see in the mirror.

The complicated relationship between the artist and their self-portrait is dramatically visible in Lambert's *Chesham Street* 1910 [19]. The artist's friend Hardy Wilson named 'Williams, Lambert's model' as the model for the central figure.[24] The features of this half-clad man, however, resemble those of Lambert himself and, moreover, Lambert intended this work to be a self-image. So if Hardy Wilson was correct and Lambert did indeed use another man's body for the torso, Lambert may well have been playing with, or questioning, the authenticity of 'the real'. This 'now you see me' image is a construction; it is artificial in that it might not be Lambert's actual body. It is also a pretence because the apparent honesty or truth is a mask. Lambert played a game by using nakedness to distract the viewer from penetrating his 'self'.

In real life, facial expressions are in a constant state of flux, forever mutable, whereas those in most portraits are static, caught for a moment in time. In his self-portraits, *Before the ball (Avant le bal)* and *After the ball (Après le bal)* [17], both 1910, Charles Wheeler attempted to overcome this changelessness by depicting himself with two different expressions—a smiling face before the ball and a yawning face afterwards. Certainly these images are fun, and are further examples of the way in which artists use their own face to explore the possibilities of portraiture. But rather than overcoming the problem of how to capture the constantly changing nature of facial expressions, these two portraits accentuate it, emphasising that this face has been frozen in time—twice. Indeed, the fixed features of the face seem to become, in these portraits, a little like a mask. Herbert Badham, in his 1937 *Self-portrait* [35], portrayed himself pulling a face, literally, with his hand pulling at his mouth and distorting it. In doing so he too questioned the extent to which any image of any person can truly capture the complexity of the self.

Australian artists of the 1940s and 1950s also painted self-portraits in which they explored their own identity. Albert Tucker, in particular, painted many self-portraits that mirror his ongoing self-interrogation, with over twenty, in a variety of media, held by the National Gallery of Australia. Tucker's self-portraits suggest a man in search of his self, someone constructing his persona. In *Self-portrait* 1937 [33] he presented himself neatly, dressed in muted colours of blues, greens and dark pinks. Only four years later in *Self-portrait* 1941 [38] he pulled his face apart in cubist fashion, dramatising his eyes and nose and black moustache. The softer colours of the earlier portrait are no longer there; instead there are strong yellows, darker reddish pinks and bold black outlines. Indeed, this self-portrait seems to exemplify the view of British impresario and author Jonathan Miller that it would be interesting for a self-portrait to be painted on the basis of non-visual experience; that is, an artist's representation of the 'self' according to feelings rather than appearances.[25] In *Self-portrait* 1954

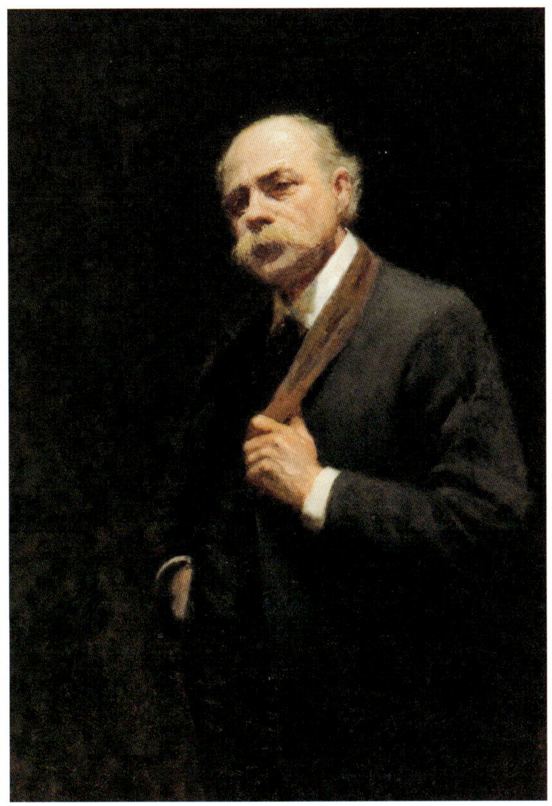

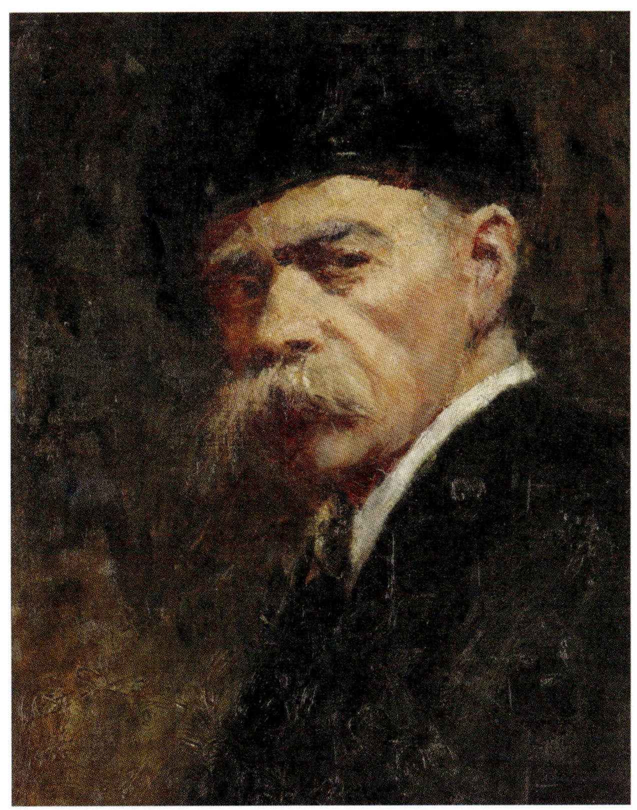

(p 132), Tucker returned to a full-frontal, intense, close-up image, his deep-set eyes looking directly at the viewer. The image is severe and the colours bold reds and browns. This is an earnest, questioning self-image, perhaps even a 'social-psychological landscape'. Painted over almost twenty years and showing different aspects of the same person, these images enhance our understanding of Tucker, the subject. They exemplify a comment made by the sixteenth-century French philosopher Michel de Montaigne: 'I give my soul now one face, now another, according to which direction I turn it. If I speak of myself in different ways, that is because I look at myself in different ways. All contradictions may be found in me.'[26]

John Brack, however, in *Self-portrait* 1955 (NGV, p148), engaged with traditional conventions of portraiture by depicting himself in a mirror, thereby enhancing the

(left) Frederick McCubbin
Self-portrait 1912
oil on canvas
106.6 x 66.6 cm
Art Gallery of South Australia, Adelaide, Elder Bequest Fund 1912

(right) Frederick McCubbin
Self-portrait 1916
oil on canvas mounted on panel
50.3 x 35 cm
Art Gallery of Western Australia, Perth, purchased with funds from the Great Australian Paintings Appeal, 1981

(page 25) John Brack
The girls at school 1959 (detail) [53]

meaning of his work. He said:

> Naturally, for the painter, the portrait of himself tends to stand a little apart from the main body of his work. It is one thing he cannot be objective about. A good many people have asked me why I chose so inauspicious an occasion as the harsh pre-breakfast hour, and the answer is that shaving is the most obvious time to look at oneself in the mirror.[27]

Brack balanced flat planes with the modelling of shapes, the low viewing point and the glowing acid yellow tone. But he did so to contribute to the emotional field—one of apprehension and defiance.[28]

Family portraits

Artists often portray their family members, and probably for the same reason that they paint their self-portrait; because the wives, lovers, mothers, husbands, fathers and children are available and willing as models. In such works the artist is able to paint their portrait with particular knowingness. Artists may feel, as did Lucian Freud, 'whom else can I hope to portray with any degree of profundity?'[29] Or they may, like the Italian sculptor Alberto Giacometti, believe that 'the great adventure is to see something unknown appear each day in the same face'.[30] But this insight into personality is also coloured by the specific nature of the relationship between artist and relative—particularly that of husband and wife. Napier Waller's portrait of his first wife [29], for instance, not only conveys much about Christian but also about their marriage. Waller suggested her absorption in theosophy and other-worldliness through her white dress and vague, distant look; he emphasised the formality of their partnership through stylised design, cool colours and the decorative leaves of the willow tree.

Although Rupert Bunny, Sali Herman and Dušan Marek were concerned with pattern and design in their paintings they still conveyed the character of their wives. Bunny and Herman [23 and 37] employed an almost identical pose in the formalist images; showing the subjects looking directly at them, and asserting their presence and strength through an intense steady gaze and crossed arms. In other ways the portraits reveal two quite different personalities; the commanding feminine presence of Jeanne and Paulette's inner strength, with just a hint of unease. Dušan Marek, in his portrait of Helena [48], used an abstracted approach, reducing the figure to a cubist structure without abandoning characterisation. Indeed, the fragmentation of the figure into bold colour forms conveys both his wife's elegance and her vitality.

Mother–son and father–daughter relationships can produce strong portraits. Eric Wilson's portrait of his mother [32] was painted at the beginning of his career and with a brutal honesty. Her ageing face and rather drab, Sunday-best, outdoor clothes reveal the frank awareness that children have of their parents. She sits upright and looks directly outwards through unfashionable spectacles with an expression of quiet resignation. We sense that she considered posing to be a duty rather than a pleasure. The way her figure dominates the canvas, however, indicates the closeness of their relationship. The same may be said of Elise Blumann's portrait of her son [36]. The model could be almost any gangling youth. But Blumann's placement of his figure in the composition, filling it from top to bottom, suggests that he enjoyed a vital place in her world. While not especially fatherly, John Brack's likeness of his three daughters in *The girls at school* 1959 [53] reveals a unique, loving knowingness of their personalities and the dynamics between them.

Arthur Boyd's *The brown room* 1943 [41] depicts an interior emotional world. He placed Merric, his silver-haired father, within the central room of the home. Merric was a noted potter, sculptor and painter but for Boyd his subject was the patriarch, a loving but dominant father, who would read the Bible to his children every night in this very room. Merric's over-large head visualises his ever-alert mind and frail body. Boyd added to the sense of family by including his brother David and his nephew Laurence playing with Peter the family dog. And yet none of the three appear to relate to each other, seeming to exist only for themselves (and Laurence for the dog).

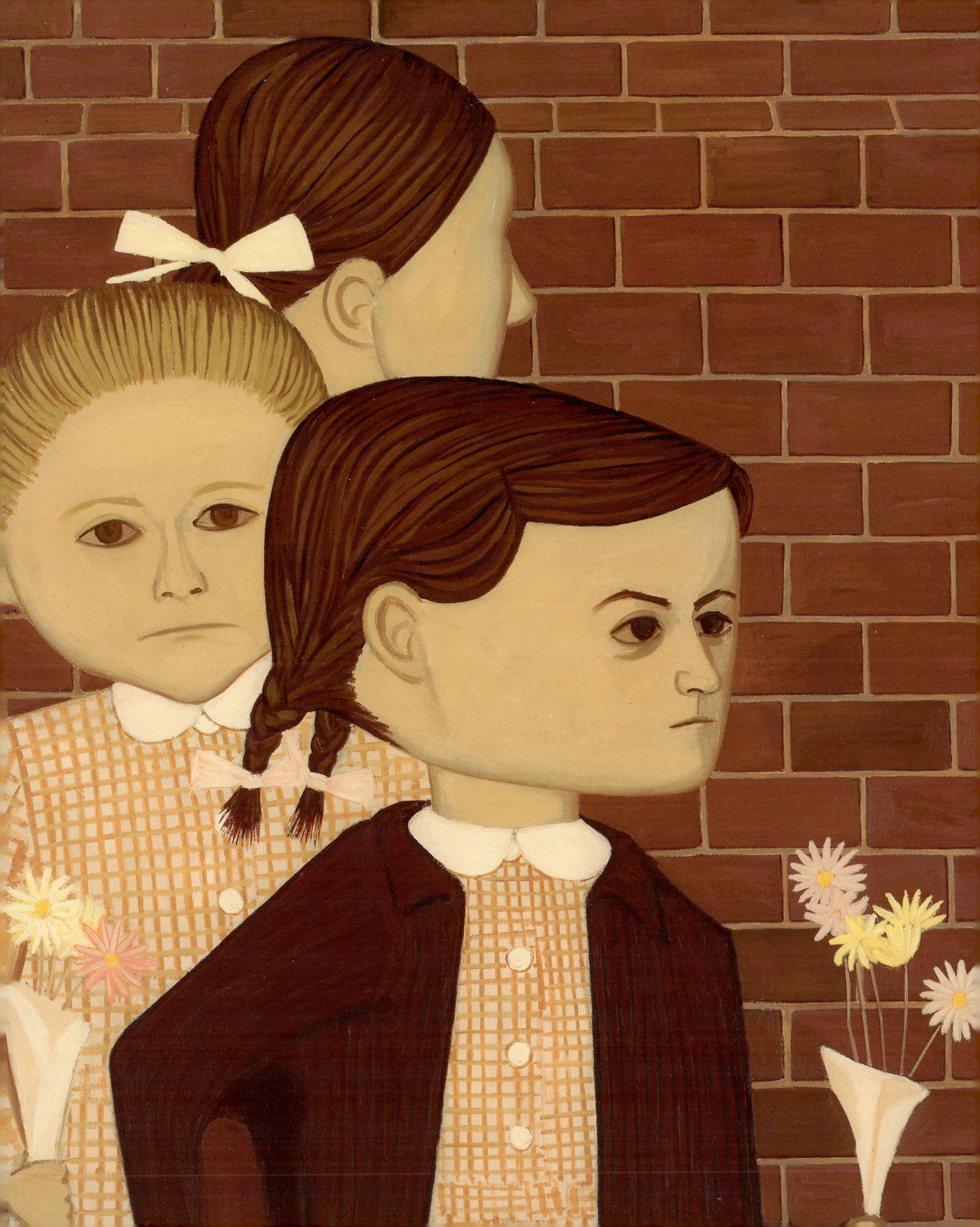

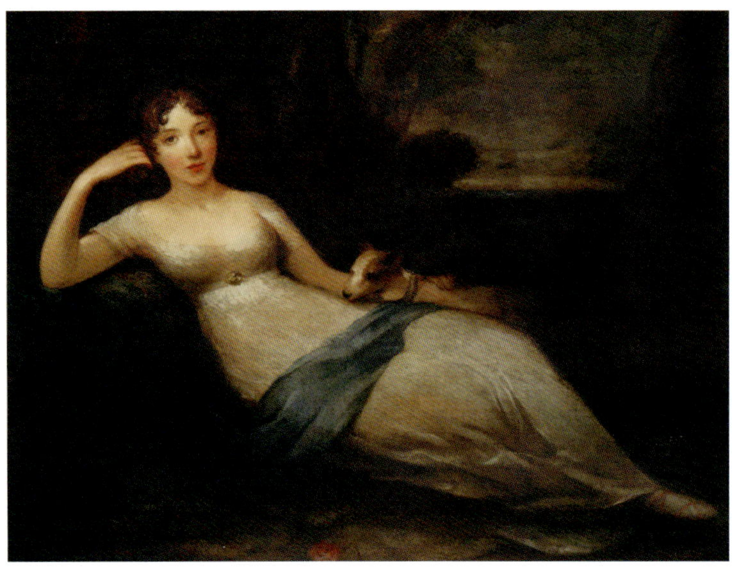

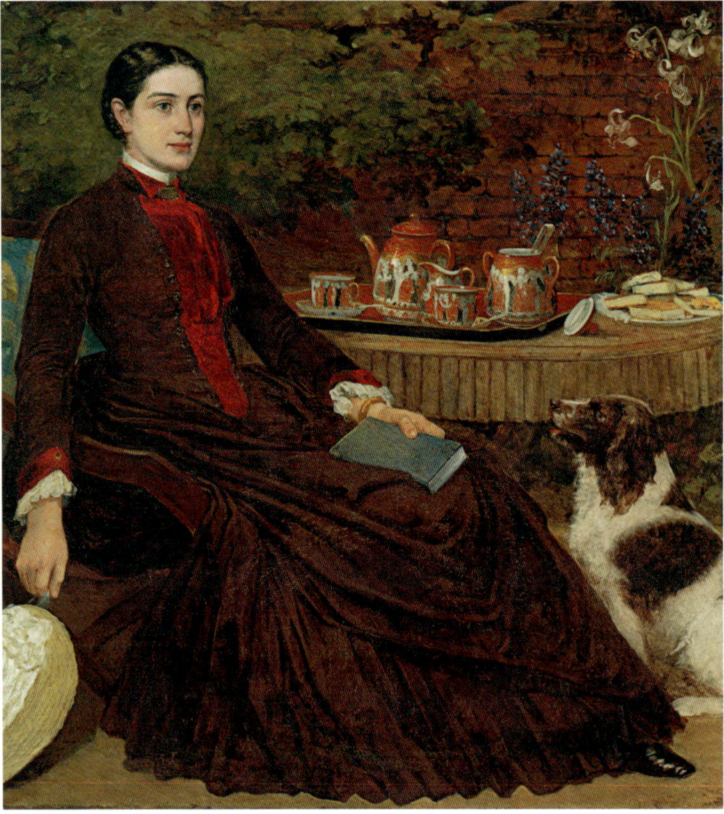

In 1937, six years earlier, and when he was still a very young artist, Boyd painted a portrait of his eleven-year-old sister Mary [34] (later to become John Perceval's wife and later still, Sidney Nolan's). In its daringly close-up viewpoint, Boyd indicated the relaxed, comfortable, companionable relationship between artist and sister. And through this viewpoint, the leaning pose and unruly mass of hair, together with the high-key palette and energetic brushstrokes, he conveyed her youthful light-heartedness and vivacity. Showing her staring distractedly out of the picture, Boyd presented Mary caught up in her own imagining—or boredom.

Portraits of artists' close friends can be extensions of the artists' families, with the artists depicting their associates again and again, and with a particular insight into their 'being'. These regular subjects include Roberts's friend Lena Brasch [7], Fox's oft-painted Edith Anderson (in *The green parasol* c 1912 [20]), Agnes Goodsir's companion and regular model, Rachel Dunn (*The Parisienne* c 1924 [26]), and Evie Stokes, Heysen's flatmate, with whom Heysen took turns in posing [30].

Situation portraits

Arthur Boyd depicted his father and brother within the environment of the family home in *The brown room* [41]. Other artists have created images in which they do not show their subjects 'posing', but rather place them in familiar surroundings, engaged in everyday activities, a mise-en-scène. In such works the distinction between genre painting and portraiture becomes less clear. Robert Dowling, for instance, depicted Miss Robertson of Colac (Dolly) [3] in the garden with her favourite Japanese tea service and vanilla slices laid on a tea table, her faithful brown-and-white spotted spaniel at her side. In so doing Dowling presented not only what Dolly looked like but conveyed aspects of her way of life.

George W Lambert located Mr and Mrs Falkiner in their brick-walled woolshed watching their prize-winning fleece being weighed [24]. He not only conveyed the appearance of the couple but also emphasised their good fortune as woolgrowers and, by implication, the importance of wool to the Australian economy. The composition recalls those of the sacred conversation in which the saints are portrayed standing in silence around the Madonna (here replaced by the fleece). And, as in these traditional images, none of the figures talk to, or appear to relate to, each other.

Edith Anderson sat at ease in E Phillips Fox's Parisian garden when he depicted her in *The green parasol* c 1912 [20]. She is shown in harmony with her surroundings as the afternoon sunlight filters through the parasol onto her face. Fox also portrayed her as a modern woman, wearing looser garments and relaxing outdoors. In *London breakfast* 1935 [30] Nora Heysen depicted her friend Evie similarly at home in their London flat. We see Evie engaged in her usual routine: reading a book, enjoying a pot of tea and a simple meal of bread and jam. The people may have been posed, the compositions may have been carefully arranged, but the subjects are portrayed doing something they might do during the course of their daily lives.

An artist's inclusion of an animal in such daily-life portraits is sure to carry a significant message about the sitter. Fidelity has traditionally been one of the principal reasons for including a dog in a portrait. Cats were originally seen as being creatures of the night, and sometimes associated with the devil or witches and, since they are inclined to sleep during the day, with sloth; but during the eighteenth century they underwent a dramatic change of fortune and began to be seen as they are today, as cuddly and playful.[31]

Although often symbolic, animals are usually included in portraits in a way that makes their presence totally natural and believable. In earlier portraits a pet sometimes indicated a missing person. Eliza Trotter included in her portrait of Lady Caroline Lamb the miniature bull terrier that Caroline's lover Sir Godfrey Webster had given her as a present. In so doing she publicly acknowledged this illicit affair.[32] The little black Scottish terrier being lovingly fondled on the lap of Edith Anderson in *The green parasol* c 1912 may perhaps

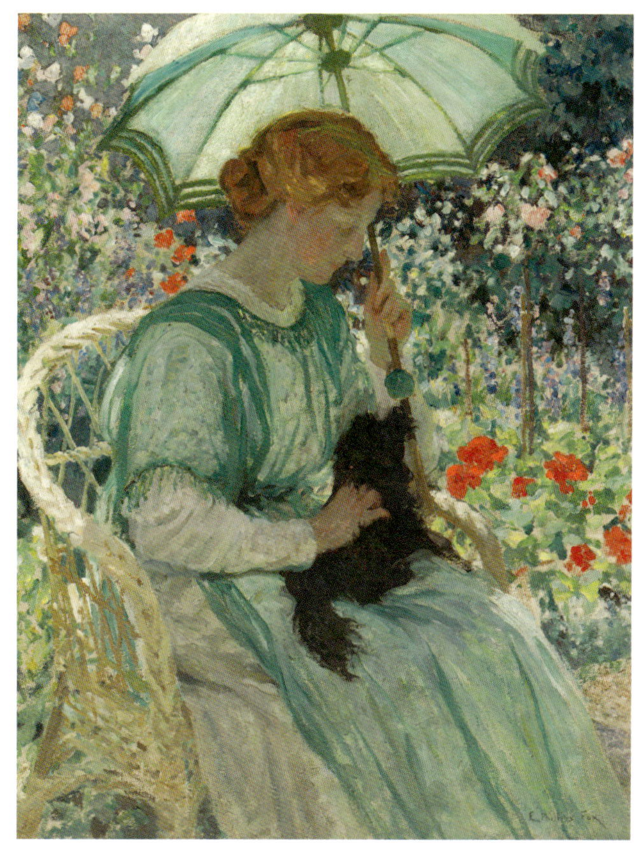

E Phillips Fox
The green parasol c 1912 (detail) [20]

(opposite above) Eliza H Trotter
Lady Caroline Lamb c 1811
oil on canvas
114.9 x 140.3 cm
National Portrait Gallery, London, given by Lady Lett, 1946

(opposite) Robert Dowling
Miss Robertson of Colac (Dolly) 1885–86 (detail) [3]

be taken to represent Edith's legitimate amour and future husband, Penleigh Boyd.

In *Domestic interior* 1935 [31], Eric Wilson portrayed his mother and a young neighbour in the living room of his home with a tabby cat. The two women recall Martha and Mary in the biblical story, one active the other more passive. It shows the mother at work, concerned with household activities, and the young girl more concerned with her mind and spirit, reading from an illustrated book. The cat may well have been included to suggest playfulness. It is alert, with its ears pricked, perhaps in empathy with the young girl. But the cat with sharp claws and red eyes in Perceval's *Boy with cat 2* 1943 [40] is another thing entirely. In this searing psychological portrait of the artist the cat is a negative force, an inner devil that the boy is struggling to fend off.

Imaginary portraits

Many artists have painted imaginary portraits, blending truth with fiction. Nineteenth-century essayist and art critic Walter Pater possibly coined the expression 'imaginary portrait' in 1887 when he published a series of *Imaginary portraits* or literary vignettes blending elements of biography, prose poem and short story. But many artists had painted imaginary portraits before then. For example, most portraits of saints are imaginary, and several if not all of the portraits of William Shakespeare are imaginary images, created after the Bard had died.

Sidney Nolan's *Daisy Bates at Ooldea* 1950 [47] may have been based on a photograph of Daisy Bates, but it is essentially an imaginary portrait in which the artist conjured the spirit of Daisy Bates and placed her within a Central Australian desert landscape. Bates is wearing clothes similar to those in a photograph—but there is no known image of her in such a landscape. (She was still alive when Nolan painted this portrait; no longer living at Ooldea, but in a nursing home in Adelaide). By depicting her as a small figure, dressed in city finery and hovering like an apparition in a vast landscape, Nolan showed how this eccentric woman was both alien to the outback and made it her own. He also created a metaphor for the way in which so many white Australians feel (rather contradictorily) both strangers to and at one with the great Australian expanse.

Nolan's *Ned Kelly* and Tucker's *Man's head* [43, 45], both painted in 1946, were based on photographs and therefore are not entirely imaginary. But the artists never met their subjects. Indeed, Nolan painted Kelly's portrait 66 years after Kelly had died. He based his portrait on a photograph of the bushranger, taken when Kelly was 18 years old, and preserved in his file at Beechworth goal. Nolan deliberately blurred and simplified the face to resemble an historic record and a criminal 'mug-shot'. Tucker exaggerated the distinctive features of the subject of his portrait rather than blurring them. When he later found the newspaper photograph on which he had based the portrait, Tucker realised it was nothing like the man's face. He had imagined the portrait by extracting 'the corrupt disintegrating element in it'.[33]

The development of Australian portraiture 1880–1960

Late Victorian and Edwardian portraits

There is considerable variety in Australian portraiture. And it has waxed and waned in popularity over the years. Ron Radford has observed:

> Although the history of Australian art has been written largely through the development of Australia's distinctive landscape painting, it was portraiture which from the 1830s to the mid 1850s dominated the art of the older colonies of New South Wales, Tasmania, and later South Australia ... As the century drew on, the portraits became larger, in adaptation to grander houses and larger public buildings but also to out-scale the rival photographic portraits which from the late 1850s were becoming an increasingly popular alternative to painted portraits.[34]

For two years, between 1884 and 1886, Robert Dowling became Melbourne's most sought after resident portrait painter, fulfilling at least 18 portrait commissions. Among these was his remarkable *Miss Robertson of Colac (Dolly)* 1885–86 [3], considered by Dowling's biographer, John Jones, to be 'a refreshing change' in Australian portraiture and consistent with Royal Academy portrait exhibits in the 1880s.[35] Through the portrayal of an individual it conveys an idea of the life of fashionable women in the Western District of Victoria towards the end of the nineteenth century.

From the mid 1880s to the 1920s a new group of Australian artists emerged who were particularly strong portrait and figure painters, and who again chose to depict people in preference to landscape. These artists included Bernard Hall, Tom Roberts, Hugh Ramsay, E Phillips Fox, George W Lambert, Rupert Bunny and Max Meldrum, as well as the women artists Violet Teague, Agnes Goodsir and H R N. Indeed, this was an age not only of opulence and elegance among the wealthy, but also a golden age of portraiture.

Tom Roberts became Australia's foremost artist and pre-eminent portrait painter during the 1880s and 1890s. He earned his living from portraiture, and over one third of his output was in this genre, in pastels as well as oils. Most were commissions. As Ron Radford observed, 'some would argue with much justification that Roberts is Australia's best portraitist of all time'.[36]

In *An Australian native* 1888 [5], Roberts depicted those Australian-born people of Anglo-Celtic descent who were asserting themselves during the Centennial celebrations of 1888 and the run-up to Federation. Humphrey McQueen suggested that portraiture manifested this phenomenon through 'the creation of a national physical type: healthy and vigorous young Australian-born men and women, capable of producing strong children'.[37] Such portraits played an important role in helping Australians construct an idea of who they were—and who they wanted to be.

In the 1890s Roberts painted a group of twenty-three sketch portraits of 'familiar faces and figures' from the arts and society, believing that this group of portraits would provide a gallery of Australian characters or types. He portrayed modern people and contemporary life, and in doing so he wanted to promote a national

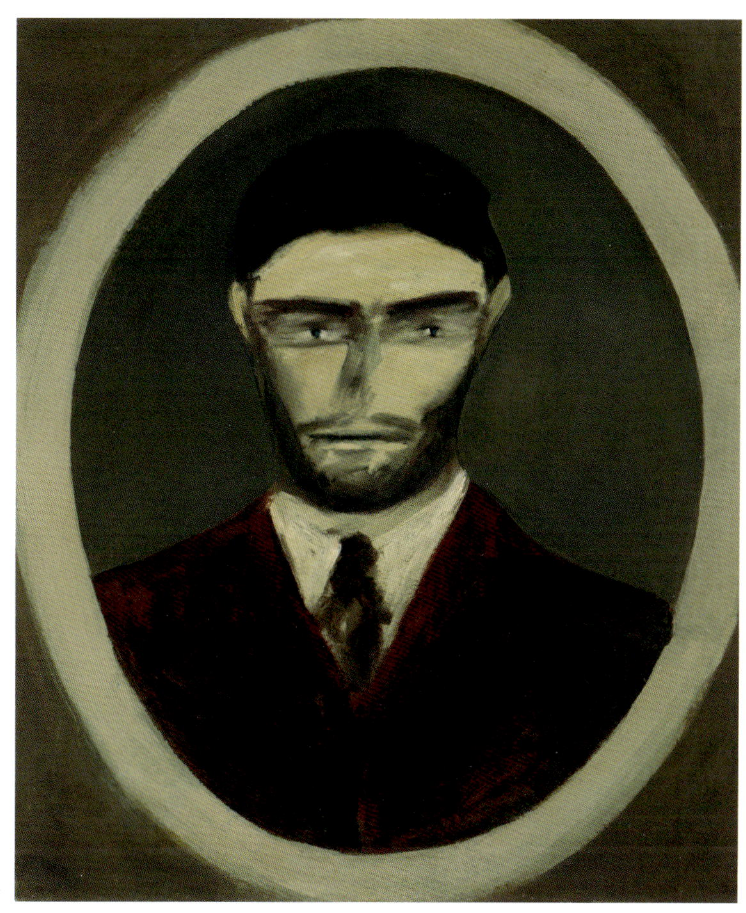

Sidney Nolan
Ned Kelly 1946 (detail) [43]

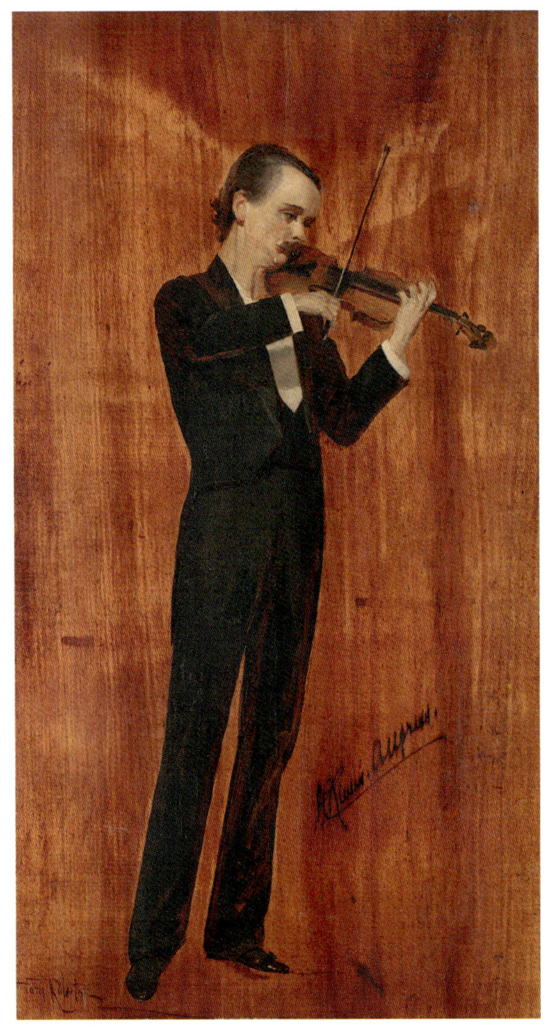

'home-grown' culture. Yet, in his use of small wooden panels, in the way he made his figures live within their space, contrasting their dark suits against the brown tones of the wood, he modelled his paintings on those of James McNeill Whistler—paintings such as *Arrangement in black: Portrait of Señor Pablo de Sarasate* 1884 (Carnegie Institute of Art, Pittsburgh).[38] It is ironic, however, that in depicting his Australian types Roberts adopted an international style—or artistic approach.

Many of the Australian artists who painted portraits during the late nineteenth and early twentieth centuries spent a substantial time living and working abroad, where they mixed with artists, musicians and writers from all over Britain, Ireland, the United States and Europe. Among the successful portraitists was George W Lambert, who, in one of his most productive years in London (1910), earned about £1000. This at a time when an upper-middle class family led a comfortable life on £2000 a year, and the average annual income for doctors and lawyers was £400, and for a labourer £50.

Portraits formed a major part of exhibitions in London and Paris at the turn of the century and portraitists such as Whistler, John Singer Sargent and Giovanni Boldini were in high demand. Australian artists admired Whistler's work, with Hugh Ramsay commenting that his work 'doesn't seem to have been painted, but just thought on by a most refined and distinguished mind'.[39] Rupert Bunny's painting *Madame Sadayakko as Kesa* c 1907 (Philip Bacon collection) was inspired by Whistler's economy of expression, subtlety of tone, and fluid application of paint, as well as by his use of Japanese themes. By depicting his subject from behind, with her face hidden, Bunny demonstrated how Sadayakko was able to convey emotion through pose and gesture, while at the same time maintaining a degree of privacy, or oriental inscrutability. Violet Teague was also influenced by Japanese printmaking as well as by Whistler, Velasquez and Manet. In *The boy with the palette* 1911 [18] she took from them the dramatic simplicity of design, restrained colour harmonies and the studied elegance of the boy's pose against the thinly painted background.

Australian artists also appreciated Sargent's opulent portraits, with Ramsay commenting that 'he gives us the beauty of life, the palpitating flesh … it isn't cleverness, it's absolute mastery'.[40] In the portrait commissioned by Dame Nellie Melba of her adored niece, *Miss Nellie Patterson* 1903 [12], Ramsay achieved a similar bravura to that of Sargent. In his luscious portrayal of the pink bow in Nellie's hair, the brilliance of her sash and the sheen of her party dress, he demonstrated his 'absolute mastery' of paint.

A number of those who commissioned portraits during the Edwardian period wanted their paintings to have the ambience of a masterpiece by earlier artists. Successful Edwardian industrialists and businessmen, as well as professionals, believed that portraits showing them and their families in a historical style conferred social credibility. E Phillips Fox painted *Elsie, daughter of HW Brooks Esquire* 1904 [13] in the tradition of eighteenth-century English portraiture. He depicted her seated patiently on a bench, with sweet expression and hands demurely clasped on her lap. In doing so, he paid homage to Sir Joshua Reynolds's portrait *Penelope Boothby* c 1788 (private collection), which had been popularised through an engraving. (Reynolds's portrait also inspired one of the most popular Victorian images, John Everett Millais's famous *Cherry Ripe* 1879, of which 500 000 chromolithographs were sold throughout the Empire.) By suggesting Elsie's British heritage and assimilating an Australian child into the broader British tradition, Fox visualised the aspirations of many wealthier Australians to be accepted within British society, in the place they still called 'home'.[41] At the same time, Fox demonstrated a characteristic Australian egalitarianism, treating his bourgeois subject as an equal to anyone.

1920s and 1930s: modernist portraits

At the beginning of the 1920s a version of Modernism flourished in Australia, following its development in Europe at the turn of the century. With Modernism came a new approach to portraiture, one in which artists experimented with an even greater degree of abstraction, a concern with composition, form and colour, and with a shallow picture plane. Artists presented their figures as objectively as still-lifes. Their subjects were not, by and large, leaders of society or the arts—not even familiar figures, but rather images of family and friends. Even Stella Bowen, who relied on portraiture for an income, mostly received commissions from people who were within her 'circle'.[42] With this trend, the distinction between the portrait sitter and the artist's model became less clear. These artists were moreover modern in their choice of subject, as well as

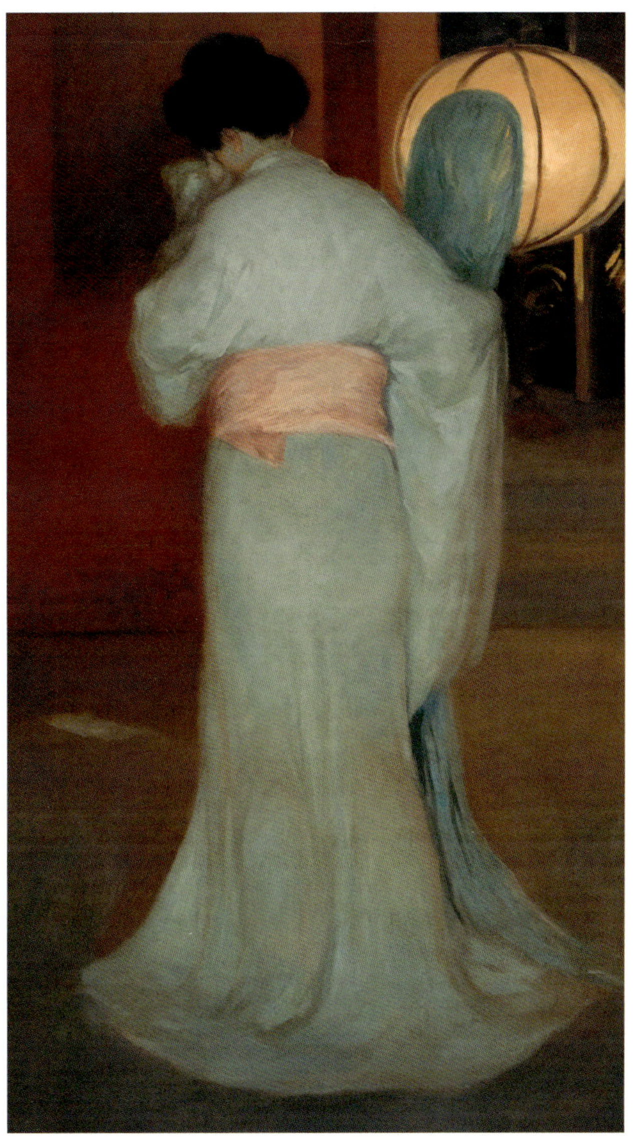

Rupert Bunny
Madame Sadayakko as Kesa c 1907
oil on canvas
175 x 95 cm
Philip Bacon collection, Brisbane

(opposite) Tom Roberts
G Rivers Alpress c 1895
oil on wood panel
61 x 33.3 cm
National Gallery of Victoria, Melbourne, purchased 1979

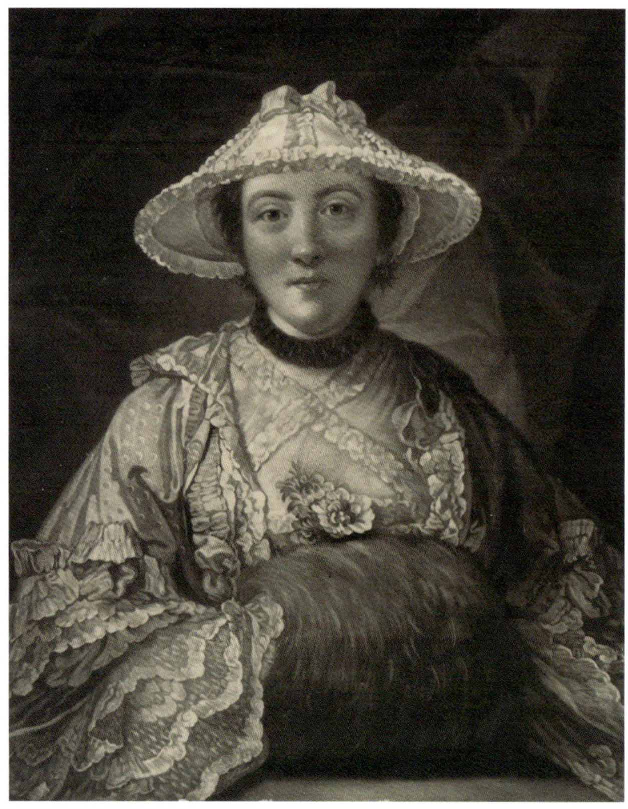

their approach—depicting 'modern women', as well as people who were not traditionally the subjects of portraits, such as members of the working class.

According to early twentieth-century Australian art critic William Moore, Rupert Bunny's return to Australia in 1911 prompted a boom in Australian portraiture.[43] His *Woman in a brown hat (Femme au chapeau brun)* c 1917 [23], painted around 1917, after he had returned to Europe, is an essay in strong forms and bold, contrasting colours. He used a series of simplified shapes, focusing on pattern to create a knowing image of his wife. He may also have looked back to earlier artists, making reference to Joshua Reynolds's *Anne (Day), Lady Fenoulhet* 1760 (private collection) portrayed in a like pose with similar large hat (an image that had been widely popularised through an engraving). Bunny may also have been aware of a half-length frontal portrait of a woman with clasped arms by the French eighteenth-century painter François-Hubert Drouais, *Elizabeth, Duchess of Argyll* 1763 (His Grace the Duke of Argyll).[44]

Margaret Preston's portrait of her maid Myra Wardell, *Flapper* 1925 [25] and her *Self-portrait* 1930 (AGNSW, p 92) are typical of a modernist approach to portraiture. Preston depicted both the flapper and herself using simple shapes and flat areas of colour. As in Bunny's portrait of his wife, in Preston's portraits the subject looks directly at the viewer. The 'flapper' was traditionally a bohemian woman with cropped hair who wore short skirts, smoked cigarettes, drank cocktails and frequented late night parties. Preston's flapper seems more staid than daring, squat rather than lithe, with her wool dress and knitted stockings too practical to be stylish. Indeed, her only adventurous feature is the quirky feather in her hat.[45] What is more, in her choice of subject, in painting a portrait of her maid, Preston was 'modern'—turning away from portraying a 'pillar of society', or a celebrity, and depicting a 'working girl'.

An image of a more modern woman—although a less Modern painting—is Agnes Goodsir's *The Parisienne* c 1924 [26], painted in Paris a year before Preston depicted her maid. The subject seems more modern because she appears to be self-assured, wearing her clothes and hat with style, holding a cigarette in her carefully manicured hand, and having the androgynous figure of the 'new woman'. We can see this in the portrait, but when we have additional information about the subject we view the Parisienne as an even more modern woman. She was Rachel (Cherry) Dunn, Goodsir's companion, whose lifestyle and attitudes were advanced. In approach, this portrait has modernist qualities: it is simple and severe, and is painted with a limited palette—but it does not have the direct frontal approach, the focus on geometrical forms of Preston's painting. Rather, by placing the framed portrait in the corner, depicting the figure half turned, and adopting a soft, tonalist approach, Goodsir referred back to Whistler and his portrait of his mother. But there is an element of concealment in this portrait: in contrast to the frontal gaze of Preston's works, Goodsir showed her subject looking to the side, with her hat pulled down (casting her eyes in shadow), and in so doing she created the atmosphere of an intimate, private world.

Another expatriate woman artist, Stella Bowen, also lived an unconventional life, sharing it in Europe with the writer Ford Maddox Ford, twenty years her senior. In her portrait of *Mary Widney* 1927 [27], as in her own *Self-portrait* c 1929 (AGSA, p 96), Bowen looked at her subject from a close vantage point, focusing on the facial features. She went beyond straightforward representation by adding a reflected image in the (invisible) mirror behind Widney. In so doing the artist added another dimension to the portrait: the decorative, patterning effect of duplication, and a modernist interest in looking at an object or a person from several viewpoints. Widney gazes out towards the viewer but her reflection—her other, alternative self—turns away towards the back of the room, apparently preoccupied with something or someone we cannot see.

After being commissioned to paint her portrait by the Art Gallery of New South Wales in 1930, Preston lectured to women artists on the importance of painting good portraits of outstanding Australian women as 'proof that women who think for themselves do not necessarily look like something out of the dust-box, which seems to be the general impression'.[46] Certainly, during the 1920s and 1930s women artists such as Preston, Grace Cossington Smith and Grace Crowley in Sydney, Nora Heysen in Adelaide, Elise Blumann in Perth, to name but a few, came to the fore in Australian art. All painted portraits. For most of them, however, portraiture was just one of many approaches to art—rather than being their principal genre—and their interest was as much with the elements of composition as with subject.

For Nora Heysen, portraiture was significant as a means of establishing herself as an artist—with a separate identity from her father, the famous landscape painter Hans Heysen—as well as a way of advancing

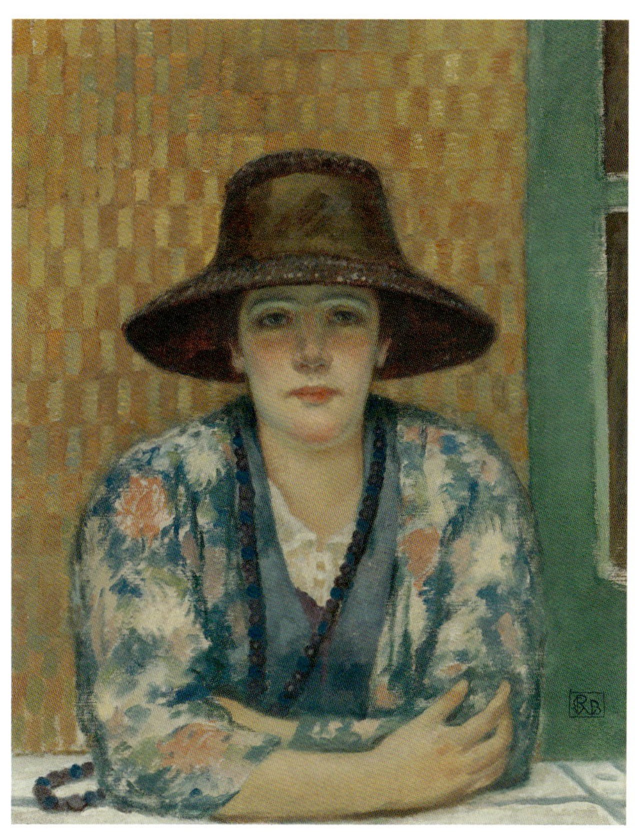

Rupert Bunny
Woman in a brown hat (Femme au chapeau brun) c 1917
(detail) [23]

(opposite) James Macardell after Sir Joshua Reynolds
Anne (Day), Lady Fenoulhet 1760
mezzotint
30.8 x 22.6 cm
National Portrait Gallery, London, purchased 1966

(following page) Stella Bowen
Mary Widney 1927 (detail) [27]

her reputation. In 1938 she became the first woman to win the Archibald Prize. Some disaffected artists met in secret to discuss the judgment.[47] Max Meldrum declared that 'to expect [women] to do some things as well as men is sheer lunacy', and that 'a great artist needs all the manly qualities, courage … [and] endurance'.[48]

1920s–1930s: the Archibald Prize

Despite such attitudes, portraiture gained a new, if somewhat questionable status in Australia in the 1920s and 1930s, through the Archibald Prize. It was the result of a bequest from J F Archibald, the former editor of *The Bulletin*, and was first awarded in 1921 to WB McInnes for his portrait *H Desbrowe Annear* c 1921 (AGNSW). Archibald stipulated that the prize should be awarded for 'the best portrait, preferentially of some man or woman distinguished in Art, Letters, Science or Politics, painted by an artist resident in Australasia during the twelve months preceding the date fixed by the Trustees for sending in the pictures'.[49] Archibald directed that the portraits should be of leaders in society, rather than of friends or family, or members of the working class—let alone images of criminals. Moreover, he protected home-grown artists, so that the returning expatriate painters, who had developed international reputations for their portraits in London and Paris, were ineligible for at least one year after their return to Australia.

From the beginning the judges—the Trustees of the Art Gallery of New South Wales—had a preference for likeness over character, and for bland over bravura, with the result that the prize did not support the most innovative of Australia's portrait painters or, indeed, the best. For instance, McInnes was awarded the prize in 1924 for his *Miss Collins* (AGSA), a tame depiction of a young woman who had been portrayed far more adventurously by George W Lambert a few years earlier in *The white glove* 1921 (AGNSW). Lambert arranged Gladys Collins's individual features to denote the artificial 'society woman' and used her luscious blue stole and elegant feathered hat to contribute to a sense of opulence. He disclosed, moreover, an audacious, uninhibited sexuality. McInnes, on the other hand, was far more serious in his approach: he portrayed Miss Collins as a polite, mild young woman with none of the sense of fun, freedom or sensuality that Lambert exposed. These two portraits reflect the Archibald Prize judges' milk-sop approach to portraiture. But more significantly, they show the extent to which various artists can perceive their subjects differently, and the way in which, as Marcel Proust declared, 'our social personality is a creation of other people's thought'.[50]

Modernist portraits were not rejected outright, but they were not favoured by the Archibald Prize judges. In 1931 Grace Crowley's portrait of her cousin, *Miss Gwen Ridley* 1930 (AGSA), one of the first cubist portraits in Australia, was hung in the competition. It was, according to Daniel Thomas, 'a startling sight in the exhibition'.[51] Inevitably, Crowley's work with its static geometry was too 'different' for the conservative judges with their aversion to anything that appeared 'advanced', and it did not receive the prize.

Over the years the prize has attracted controversy. The most famous debate was that of 1943, when Dobell's winning portrait of Joshua Smith, *Portrait of an artist*, was contested by two unsuccessful artists, Mary Edwards and Joseph Wolinski. They brought a lawsuit against Dobell and the Gallery's Board of Trustees on the grounds that the painting was 'not a portrait but a caricature'. On 19 February 1944 the *ABC Weekly* published the transcript of a radio talk by Dobell:

> To me, a sincere artist is not one who makes a faithful attempt to put on canvas what is in front of him, but who tries to create something which is a living thing in itself, regardless of its subject … I have been trying to develop a style of my own derived from the Old Masters. The leaders of the so-called 'modern' movements have done the same—although they have developed in different directions.

The suit against Dobell was dismissed, and the award was upheld, but Dobell suffered severe humiliation and

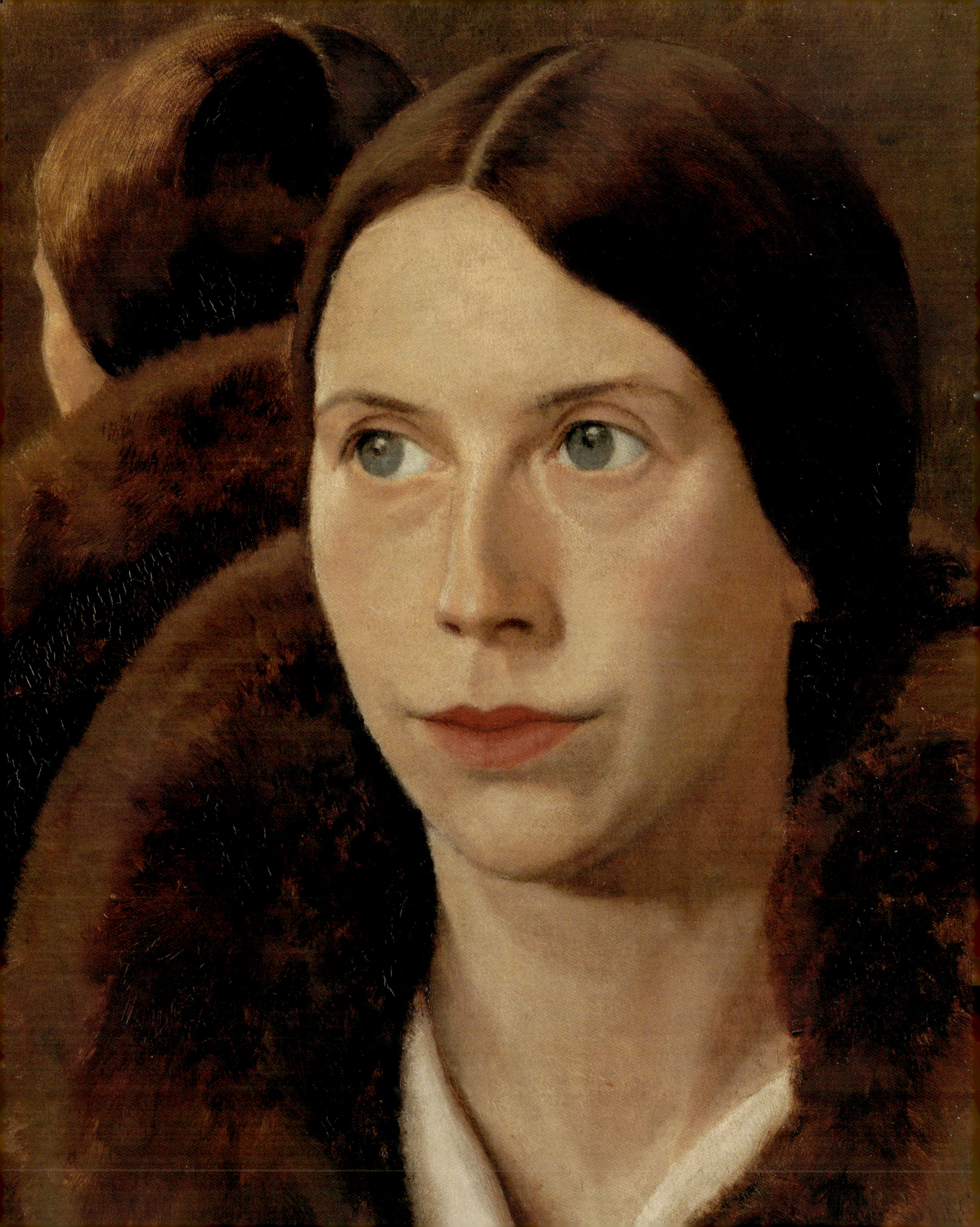

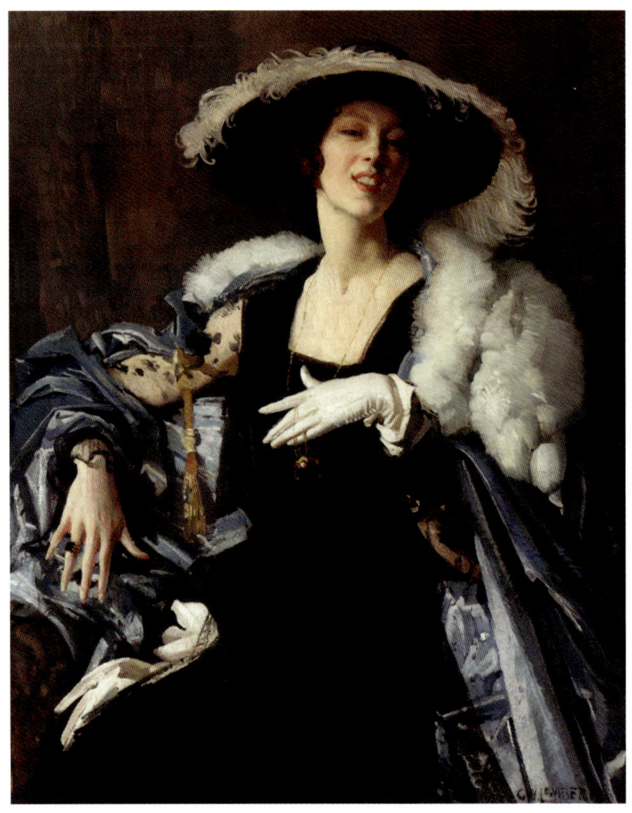

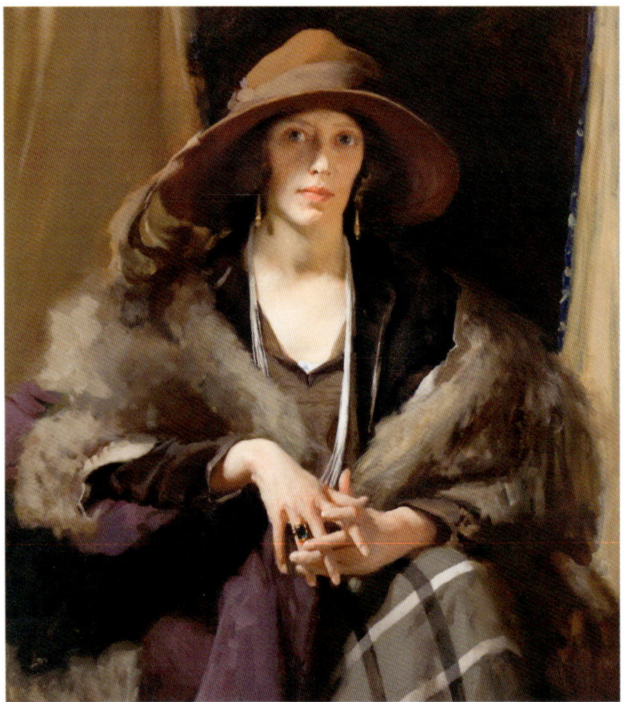

his health deteriorated. When compared with other portraits of the 1940s, such as Albert Tucker's *Self-portrait* 1941 [38] or Sidney Nolan's *Self-portrait* 1943 (AGNSW, p 120), Dobell's portrait of Smith was 'tame'. It merely tweaked at the boundaries of representational likeness.

Debates over the judges' decisions have continued on and off over the years and have given the Archibald Prize a notoriety. In 1952, when the prize was awarded for the seventh time in succession to William Dargie, some of the younger artists revolted. They were irate about the predictability of the judgment, as well as the academic nature of the winning portrait of Essington Lewis. John Olsen exclaimed: 'We've got artists but they don't get a chance.'[52]

1940s and 1950s

Because of the predictability of the decisions of the Archibald Prize judges, many of the leading artists in the 1940s and 1950s who did paint portraits, such as Russell Drysdale in Sydney, and Arthur Boyd and Albert Tucker in Melbourne, were not interested in competing for the prize. But other significant artists like Sidney Nolan, John Brack and Fred Williams did enter the competition, with Brack showing his *Barry Humphries in the character of Mrs Everage* 1969 (AGNSW) and Williams his *Portrait of Rudy Komon* 1978. Nolan submitted *Arthur Boyd* 1988, but this was rejected on a technicality—that the artist had not been resident in Australia for twelve months preceding the date of entry. Nonetheless, all these major Australian artists of the 1940s and 1950s produced strong portraits. Indeed, Tucker's portraits of 1945–47, with their lack of strain, greater subtlety and less frenzied expressionist impulse are some of his most impressive works.[53]

By and large, Arthur Boyd, Albert Tucker and Sidney Nolan, like the Modernists of the 1920s and 1930s, preferred to depict family, friends and colleagues rather than 'important people'. Some of their subjects became well-known figures in Australian society, but at the time they were painted, they were just 'mates'. Sometimes the artists chose distinctly disreputable subjects, with Tucker and Nolan depicting criminals, such as the murderer Sydney Fox [44] and outlaw Ned Kelly [43]. This was by no means a new subject in Australian art; colonial artists such as Thomas Bock, Charles Rodius and Thomas Mitchell had depicted the heads of convicted murders. They were all interested in conveying the character of their subject, but the earlier artists were interested in phrenology. Tucker and Nolan on the other hand wanted to create expressive psycho-portraits, painting expressively, applying their pigments rapidly and often using high-keyed colour. They were generally interested in conveying the inner minds of their subjects.

Ian Fairweather took painterliness to another level. In *Portrait of the artist* 1962 [54] Fairweather captured his large all-seeing eyes at the age of 71. In a characteristic manner, he transformed his face into broadly brushed, painted gestures; honest, instinctive and expressive. He used little colour to convey the aging self. But this is no image of a weak and decrepit man: it is strong, forceful, energetic. Fairweather turned himself into paint, an outer expression of an inner spirit; an exploration of the eternal mystery, 'who am I?'. For Fairweather painting was a personal thing, an inner compulsion, and this self-portrait is intensely personal. Yet like so many of his paintings it is a highly abstracted image.

Conclusion

From the 1940s Australia's foremost artists, except perhaps Dobell, did not specialise in portraiture as earlier artists had done. While Robert Dowling (1880s), Tom Roberts (1880s–1890s), George W Lambert (early twentieth century) and Stella Bowen (mid twentieth century) had devoted a greater part of their output to portraiture and earned their living from such work, the greatest Australian portraits of the late twentieth and early twenty-first centuries have been created by artists as an aside to their artistic practice. Indeed, many of Australia's most significant artists have produced remarkable portraits that can be ranked among their best work. These include Howard Taylor's *Double self-portrait* 1959 (AGWA),

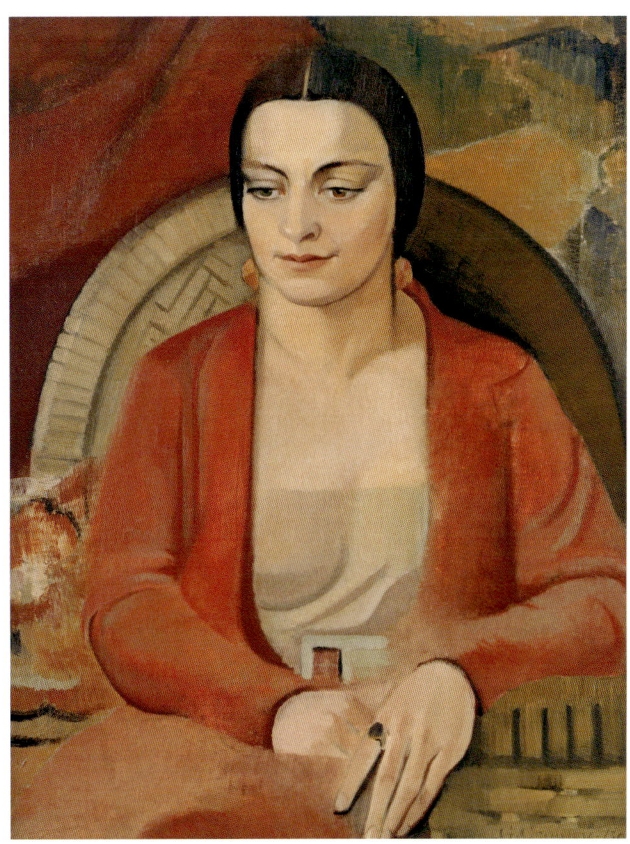

Grace Crowley
Miss Gwen Ridley 1930
oil on canvas on board
72 x 53 cm
Art Gallery of South Australia, Adelaide, purchased 1995 with the assistance of South Australian Government Grant

(opposite above) George W Lambert
The white glove 1921
oil on canvas
106 x 78 cm
Art Gallery of New South Wales, Sydney, purchased 1922

(opposite) W B McInnes
Miss Collins 1924
oil on canvas
91.4 x 73.6 cm
Art Gallery of South Australia, Adelaide, Morgan Thomas Bequest Fund 1930

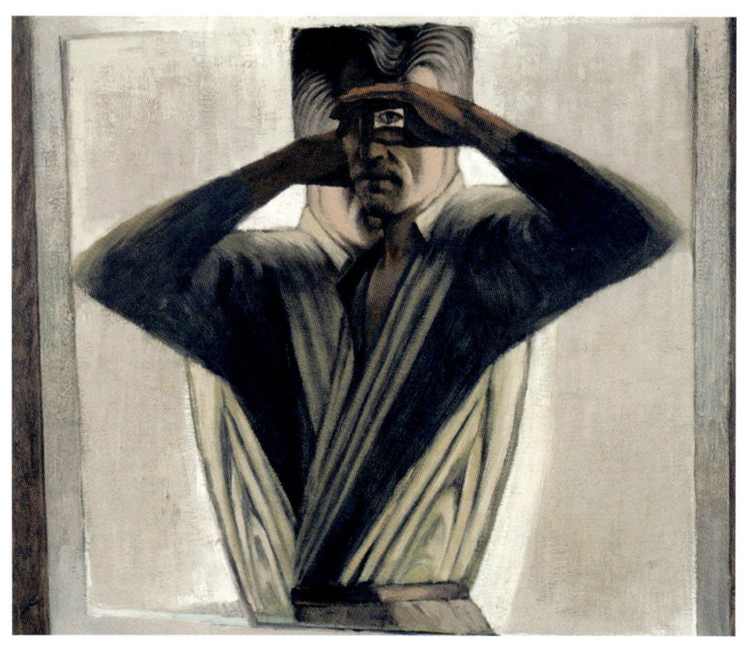

John Brack's *Barry Humphries in the character of Mrs Everage* 1969 (AGNSW) and Howard Arkley's *Nick Cave* 1999 (NPG).

Contemporary Australian artists have continued to explore current ideas in their portraits. In *Efficacy of medicine* 1995 (NGA), for instance, Guan Wei has expanded the concept of portraiture to explore what it is like being human in a society of mixed cultures. Liu Xiao Xian developed large-scale portraits such as *Reincarnation*: *Mao, Buddha and I* 1998 (NGA) in which each of the three portrait heads are made from tiny photographs of one of the other faces. The head of Mao in this portrait was constructed from a photograph of the artist; a single face multiplied many times to form a completely different face. As Australian art curator Deborah Hart commented, this 'suggests our human interdependence as well as our connections with the past and future reincarnations'.[54] Gordon Bennett questioned stereotypes and labelling in his self-portraits interrogating the narratives he had been taught at school about 'Australianness' and the racist attitudes towards Aboriginal Australians. Using his own family as subjects, Vernon Ah Kee has also explored the depth and complexity of modern Aboriginal life in his large charcoal portraits. In such ways portraiture continues to be renewed and refreshed—and to have an ongoing relevance to society.

Although some have assumed that portrait painting is a dying art and that since photography was invented the genre has been exhausted, this exhibition and publication show that nothing could be further from the truth. Indeed, some artists like Nolan and Tucker have worked from photographs and used them to create imaginative and imaginary portraits. Rather than painted portraiture becoming displaced by photography, portrait painters have assimilated photography and have continually come up with new ways of creating portraits—moving away from 'literal' likeness to images with a greater emphasis on aesthetic style, form and expressiveness, and from the external physical appearance of the body to the interior self. But photography *has* had a crucial impact on painted portraits. As the Director of the National Portrait Gallery, London, Sandy Nairne has observed, photography has 'changed the encounter between subject and artist, altered the context in which painted portraits are created'.[55]

This exhibition and publication cannot be either definitive or comprehensive of Australian portraiture. Instead it covers a range of works by some of the most famous Australian artists who produced portraits between 1880 and 1960. It includes work by artists from all states around Australia. Moreover, it attempts to give a broad coverage of most of those approaches and trends in painted portraiture during this period. The selection has consciously focused on the quality of the work rather than the subject of the portrait.

With only 54 portraits covering just 80 years of Australian art from the collection of the National Gallery of Australia, there are bound to be omissions. We would have liked, for instance, to include Ambrose Patterson's *Self-portrait (La fenêtre de l'atelier)* c 1902 and Hilda Rix Nicholas's *Les fleurs dédaignées* 1925,

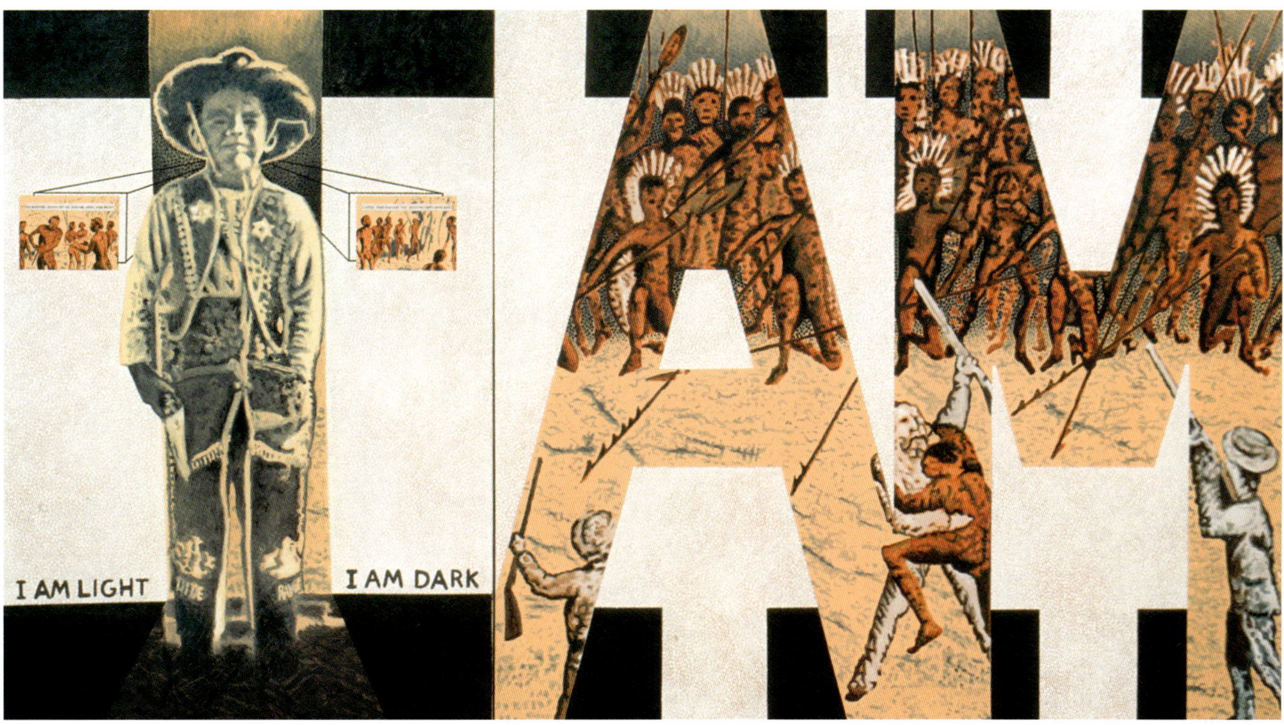

Gordon Bennett
Self-portrait (but I always wanted to be one of the good guys) 1990
oil on canvas
150 x 260 cm
private collection

(opposite) Howard Taylor
Double self-portrait 1959
oil on composition board
71.8 x 84 cm
Art Gallery of Western Australia, Perth, purchased 1985

but these arresting works are too fragile to travel. For a similar reason there are no portrait sculptures or portraits on paper. Images of women and by women are well represented, and there are a number of works which reflect Australia's postwar immigration, such as Meldrum's *Poland (Madame de Tarczynska)* 1917 and Dušan Marek's *My wife* c 1952 [22, 48]. Regrettably no portraits of Australia's Indigenous people are included, reflecting a weakness in the collection. Tom Roberts and Arthur Murch, for instance, painted important images of Aborigines, but none of these are in the collection of the National Gallery of Australia.

Portraiture has been a vital force in Australian art and promises to remain so. A fascination with the human face and body is, after all, one of the basic interests of human beings. If viewing many of the portraits in the Archibald Prize exhibition, for instance, has been a disheartening experience at times, it is not because artists are not creating good portraits, or that portraiture is dead.

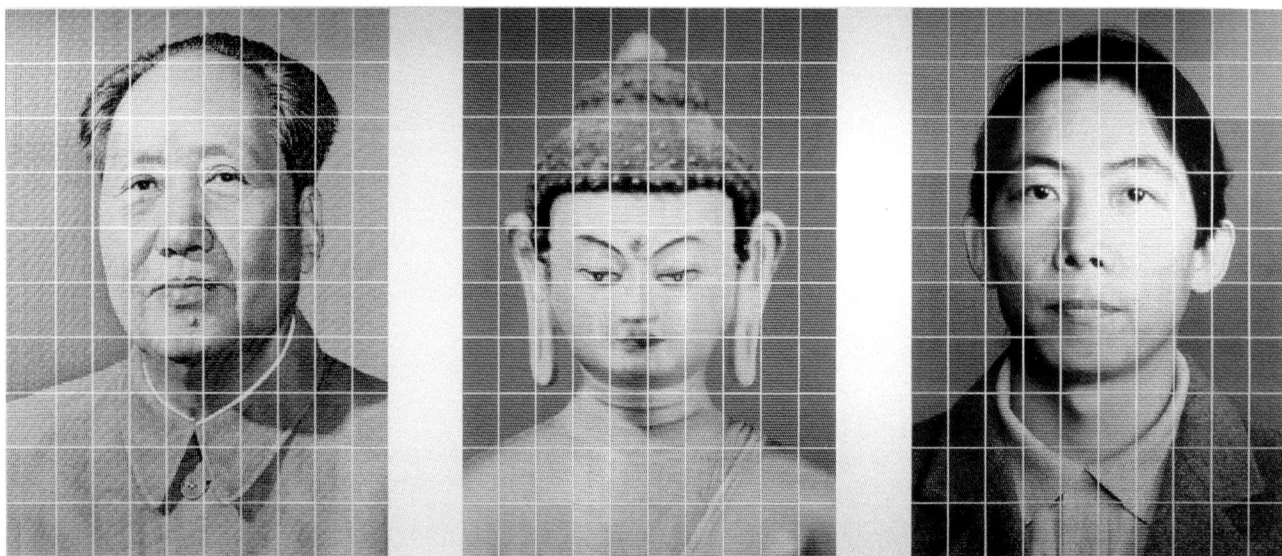

Liu Xiao Xian, *Reincarnation—Mao, Buddha and I* 1998
computer-generated digital image printed in black ink from inkjet printer on 300 sheets of thin board
overall 275 x 625 cm
National Gallery of Australia, Canberra, purchased 1999

It is, rather, that prize competitions do not attract or engender the best art in any form, at any time.

Australian artists have often challenged the possibilities of portraiture, rejected the predictable and pushed boundaries in both their choice of subject and their painterly approach, creating controversy and debate. At the same time they have created portraits that reveal what it is to be an Australian—and to be human. There is every reason to suppose that they will continue to break new ground in the expanding field of portraiture.

Notes

1 R Brilliant, *Portraiture*, Reaktion Books, London, 1991, p 9.
2 Degas to Walter Sickert, quoted in L Cumming, *A face to the world: on self-portraits*, Harper Press, London, 2009, p 4.
3 See A Sturgis, *Faces*, National Gallery, London, 1998, pp 62–6.
4 en.wikipedia.org/wiki/Portrait, viewed 23 March 2010.
5 www.abc.net.au/tv/facepainting, viewed 25 March 2010.
6 J Reynolds, *Discourses on art*, IV. Reynolds observed that 'if a portrait painter is desirous to raise and improve his subject, he has no other means than by approaching it to a general idea. Reynolds leaves out all the minute breaks and peculiarities in the face, and changes the dress from a temporary fashion to one more permanent, which has annexed to it no ideas of meanness from its being familiar to us. But if an exact resemblance of an individual be considered as the sole object to be aimed at, the portrait painter will be apt to lose more than he gains by the acquired dignity taken from general nature'. www.authorama.com/seven-discourses-on-art-6.html, viewed 12 March 2010.
7 Tom Roberts to Frederick McCubbin, 30 June 1912, Frederick McCubbin Papers c 1900–c 1915, MS 8525, State Library of Victoria.
8 P G Konody, 'Art notes: the "Fair Women" exhibition', *Observer*, London, 25 February 1908, p 5.
9 R Gibson, *20th century portraits*, National Portrait Gallery, London, 1978, p 8.
10 'The Royal Academy. Second notice. Review of the portraits', *The Times*, London, 3 May 1911, p 7.
11 L Housman, 'The International Exhibition', *Manchester Guardian*, 8 April 1911, p 9.
12 Sir George Reid to George W Lambert, 15 May [1914], Lambert Family Papers, MS 97/2, Mitchell Library, State Library of NSW.
13 George W Lambert to George Pitt Rivers, 31 July 1929, Lambert Family Papers, MS 97/10, Mitchell Library, State Library of NSW.
14 Sergius, 'Farewell advice', *Undergrowth*, Sydney, July–August 1926.
15 R Fry, 'The French Group', in *Second Post-Impressionist exhibition*, exhibition catalogue, Grafton Galleries, London, 1912, p 16.
16 'Why call it a portrait? Roi de Mestre at the Students' Club', *Undergrowth*, Sydney, October–November 1927.
17 Helen Brack, quoted in A Sayers, *Portraits by John Brack*, National Portrait Gallery, Canberra, 2007, p 17.
18 Albert Tucker, quoted in J Mollison & N Bonham, *Albert Tucker*, Macmillan, Melbourne, 1982, p 42.
19 Albert Tucker, quoted in Mollison & Bonham, p 42.
20 www.artquotes.net/masters/freud-lucian-quotes.htm, viewed 29 March 2010.
21 A Sayers, *Possibilities of portraiture*, National Portrait Gallery, Canberra 1999, p 5.
22 William Dobell, quoted in R Corbell, 'Points of view', in *Possibilities of portraiture*, p 6.
23 M Friedlander, *Landscape, portrait, still life: their origin and development*, Schocken Books, New York, 1963, pp 247–8.
24 H Wilson, 'G W Lambert, ARA, painter', *Australian Quarterly*, Sydney, no 7, September 1930, p 93.
25 J Miller, *On reflection*, National Gallery Publications, London, p 176.
26 M de Montaigne, quoted in L Cumming, pp 80, 97.
27 S Grishin, 'The enigma of John Brack: notes towards a portrait of the artist', in K Grant et al, *John Brack*, National Gallery of Victoria, Melbourne, 2009, p 158.
28 A Sayers, *Portraits by John Brack*, p 5.
29 L Frued quoted in R Gibson, *20th century portraits*, p 15.
30 R Gibson, *20th century portraits*, p 17.
31 R Gibson, *The face in the corner: animals in portraits from the collections of the National Portrait Gallery*, National Portrait Gallery, London, 1998, p 15.
32 R Gibson, *The face in the corner*, pp 19, 52–3.
33 A Tucker quoted in Mollison & Bonham, p 42.
34 R Radford, *Australian Colonial art 1800–1900*, Art Gallery of SA, Adelaide, 1995, pp 42–3.
35 Jones observed that 'Dowling's painting shares Tissot's awareness of chic, with the inclusion of a Japanese cushion and tea service, then the height of fashion'. See J Jones, *Robert Dowling: Tasmanian son of Empire*, National Gallery of Australia, Canberra, 2010, pp 159–60.
36 R Radford, *Tom Roberts*, Art Gallery of SA, Adelaide, 1996, p 12.
37 H McQueen, in A Gray, *Australian art in the National Gallery of Australia*, National Gallery of Australia, Canberra, 2002, p 82.
38 Roberts had admired this painting in London in 1885, describing it as 'the finest painting he had seen by any living man'. See Humphrey McQueen, quoting Tom Roberts to Anning Bell, 5 October 1885, ML MS A2480/69.
39 Hugh Ramsay to Bernard Hall, 19 June 1902, Bernard Hall Archive, National Gallery of Australia Research Library, Canberra, 2BH343.
40 Hugh Ramsay 1902, quoted in P Fullerton, *Hugh Ramsay: his life and work*, Hudson Publishing, Hawthorn, 1988, pp 98–9. Tom Roberts was, on the other hand, critical of Sargent's work, writing to Frederick McCubbin on 23 May 1905: 'there's a man at the Chelsea Art Club doing some copies of Sargent's "Sir – Swettenham" quite deceptively. He says they're easy to do, because the original hasn't any "method" or finesse of painting.' See Frederick McCubbin Papers c 1900–c 1915, MS 8525, State Library of Victoria.
41 Australian art historian Mary Eagle suggested that the portrait is 'too vulnerable and soft for an era—and a nation—that promoted the self-reliant tom-boy'. See M Eagle, *The oil paintings of E Phillips Fox in the National Gallery of Australia*, National Gallery of Australia, Canberra, 1997, p 35.
42 British art historian Joanna Woodall observed that this trend in modernist portraiture 'enhanced the authority of the artist by making worthiness to be portrayed dependent upon one's relationship to him or her', and implied a 'lively intimacy between painter and sitter'. See 'Introduction', J Woodall (ed), *Portraiture: facing the subject*, Manchester University Press, Manchester, 1997, p 7.
43 W Moore, quoted on a Rupert Bunny exhibition text panel, Art Gallery of NSW, Sydney, 2010.
44 R Radford, *Island to Empire: three hundred years of British art, 1550–1850*, Art Gallery of SA, Adelaide, 2005, pp 119–20.
45 C Moore, 'Self-portrait', in D Edwards, *Margaret Preston*, Art Gallery of NSW, Sydney, 2005, p 148. Curator Roger Butler noted that the young girl's aspiration (to be 'advanced') is set against the artist's actual 'modernist' sophistication. See his submission to the Australian National Gallery Council re the purchase of *Flapper* 1925, 8 March 1988, p 2.
46 D Edwards, quoting 'Women's news: women painters' exhibition at the Art Gallery', *The Sydney Morning Herald*, 5 August 1946, p 6.
47 P Ross, *Lets face it*, 2nd rev edn, Art Gallery of NSW, Sydney, 2005, p 31.
48 Ross, p 31
49 http://en.wikipedia.org/wiki/Archibald_Prize, viewed 26 Oct 2009.
50 M Proust, *The remembrance of things past*, quoted in Brilliant, p 32.
51 D Thomas, 'Grace Adela Williams Crowley (1890–1979)', *Australian dictionary of biography*, vol 13, Melbourne University Press, Carlton, 1993, pp 539–40.
52 J Olsen, *The Sydney Morning Herald*, 1952, quoted in D Hart, *John Olsen*, Craftsman House, Sydney, 2000, p 16.
53 C Uhl, *Albert Tucker*, Landsdowne, Melbourne, 1969, p 42.
54 D Hart, email to A Gray, 4 April 2010.
55 S Nairne, 'Why do painted portraits still matter?', *Portrait*, no 20, p 6.

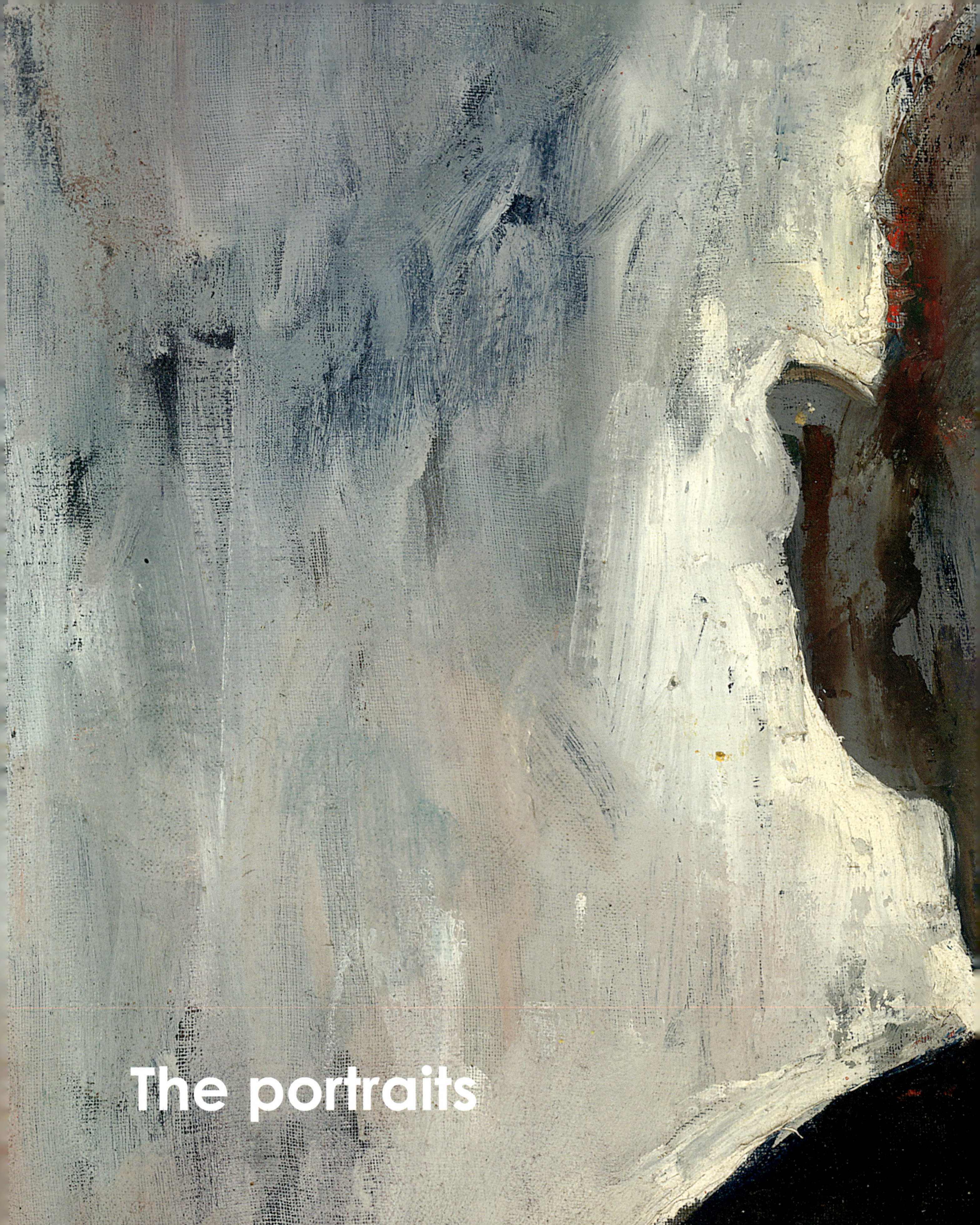

The portraits

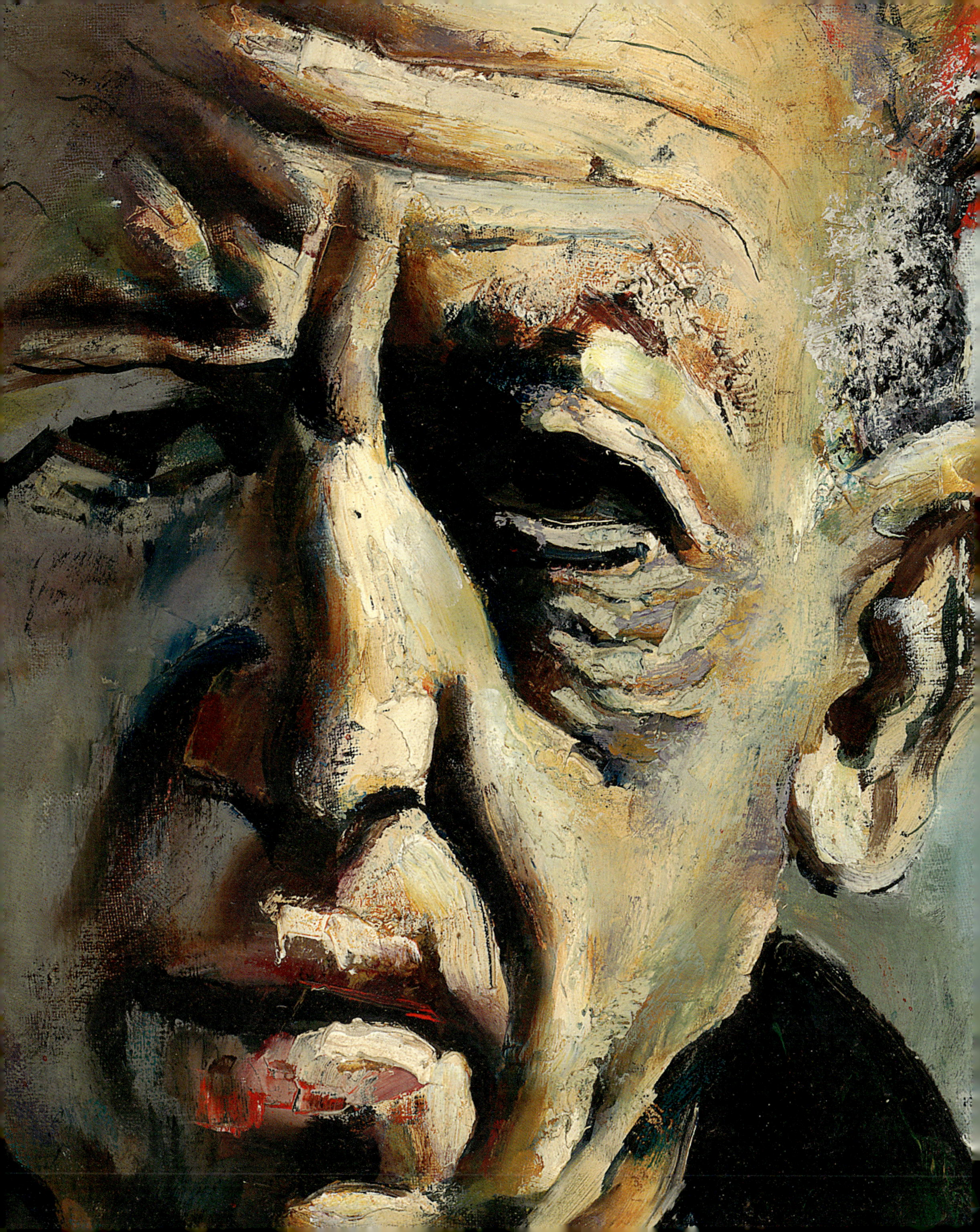

1 **Bernard Hall** (1859–1935)

Self portrait as a young man c 1880

painted in Munich, Germany
oil on canvas, 112 x 63 cm
National Gallery of Australia, Canberra, purchased 1977

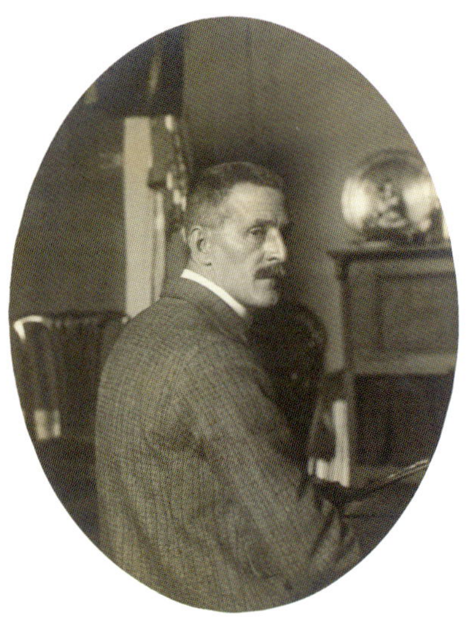

Bernard Hall, c 1900s
National Gallery of Australia Research Library, Canberra

Born in Liverpool in 1859, Lindsay Bernard Hall followed a career as an artist that would take him to Europe and eventually to Melbourne as the Director of the National Gallery of Victoria and Head of the Art School.

In 1874 at the age of fifteen, Hall began his art studies in London at the National Art Training School, later to become the Royal College of Art. From there he completed his training in Europe, attending colleges in both Antwerp and Munich. These studies gave him a solid grounding in drawing and a keen appreciation of technical mastery, which became his hallmark as an art educator.

In 1880 when Hall painted this work he was a young man of about twenty, living in Germany. While anecdotally described as shy, this portrait conveys a certain serious confidence. Hall has placed himself full-length at the centre of the canvas. This, together with the muted tones, brings to mind the formal aristocratic portraiture by artists such as Velasquez.

Hall enjoyed affluence in life and has deliberately placed himself within this grand tradition. We see him pictured as a modish young gentleman complete with the accoutrements of that station—cane, hat and fashionable shoes.

Rather than depicting himself as the artist, Hall has defined himself in terms of his social status. He has chosen an outdoor setting, which, while anonymous, conjures the image of a gentleman on his estate. This image is further substantiated by Hall's country attire, suitable for walking or hunting. Yet despite such affectations of status and style Hall retains an air of mystery and reserve, his face in the shadows.

Bernard Hall had an uneasy relationship with his adopted homeland and this work, which travelled with him from Germany to England and from England to Australia was possibly a reminder of Europe and his youth. The painting was still a feature in his studio in 1899 when he was photographed beneath it with his wife.

Dominique Nagy

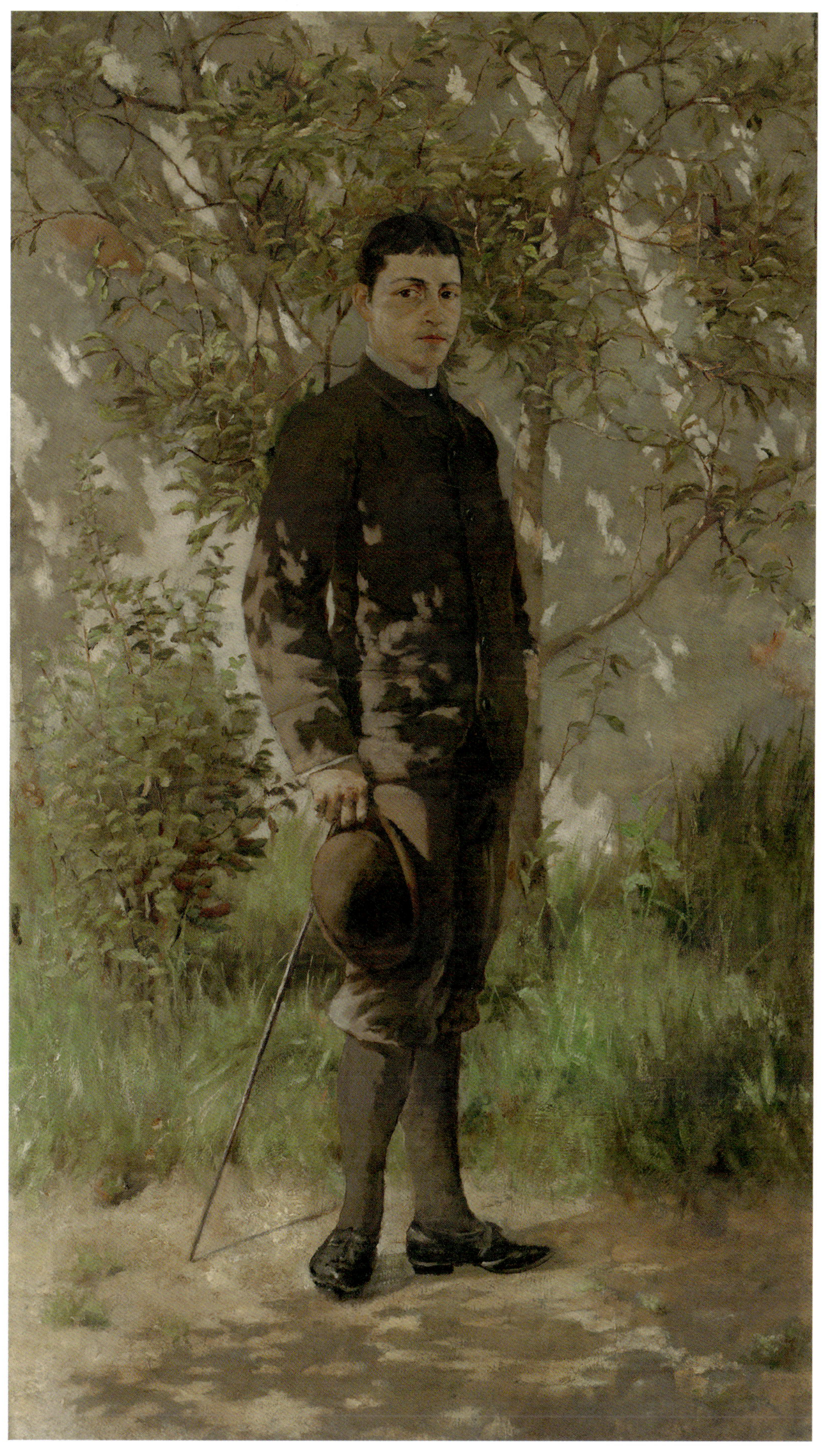

2 **Bernard Hall** (1859–1935)

J Montgomery, Esquire 1885

painted in London, England

oil on wood panel, 32.9 x 23.5 cm

National Gallery of Australia, Canberra, purchased 1977

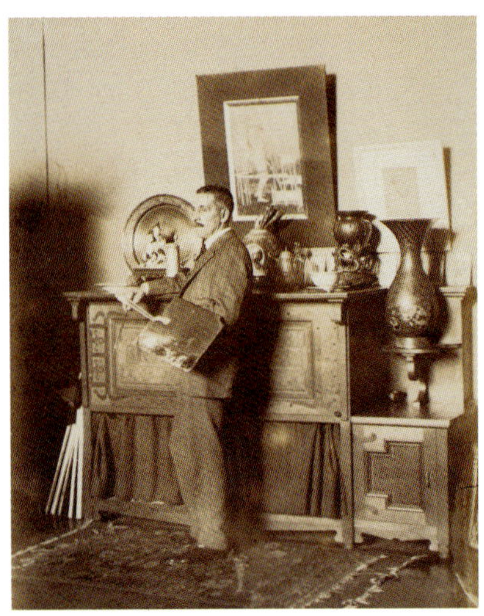

Bernard Hall standing in front of a dresser, c 1900s

National Gallery of Australia Research Library, Canberra

At just over thirty centimetres high the portrait of J Montgomery Esquire is an intimate study. Inscribed in German '*meine frende*', this work is far less formal than Hall's self-portrait and conveys a personal rapport between artist and sitter. Yet it could be said that Montgomery's appearance of relaxation—one leg crossed, one hand in his pocket, the other holding a burning cigarette and resting on the edge of a brown sofa—is undoubtedly posed.

From the fleshy pink wall to the glass and painting positioned behind him and the sensuous animal skin at his back, this scene is like a stage set constructed by the artist for Montgomery's timeless painted monologue. He stares out of the work with heavy lidded eyes and though he seems to be looking directly at the painter and therefore at us, he gives little away. His mind is elsewhere.

Montgomery is certainly a man of fashion, with natty striped waistcoat and colour-matched socks and shirt but the painting suggests that he has ventured in his imagination far beyond the confines of this room—perhaps to join an African safari or an archaeological dig in Samarkand. Whatever his dreams, the set of Montgomery's mouth communicates something we cannot know: a sense of frustration, perhaps, with certain aspects of his life that he shares with the artist. For despite Hall's technical flair and the fluidity of the paint, this portrait remains a private and personal conversation between friends.

Bernard Hall returned to England in 1882 after studying abroad, progressing his career as a painter and illustrator. The following year saw the Royal Academy exhibiting one of his works. An active participant in the London art circle, Hall also exhibited with the Society of British artists and in1886 was a founding member of the New English Art Club. This portrait was painted as part of a series of 'late-night' images of various friends, which were exhibited at intervals from 1886.

Hall migrated to Australia in 1892 following his appointment as Director of the National Gallery of Victoria. He was to remain in Melbourne until 1934 when he returned to London, where he died the following year.

Dominique Nagy

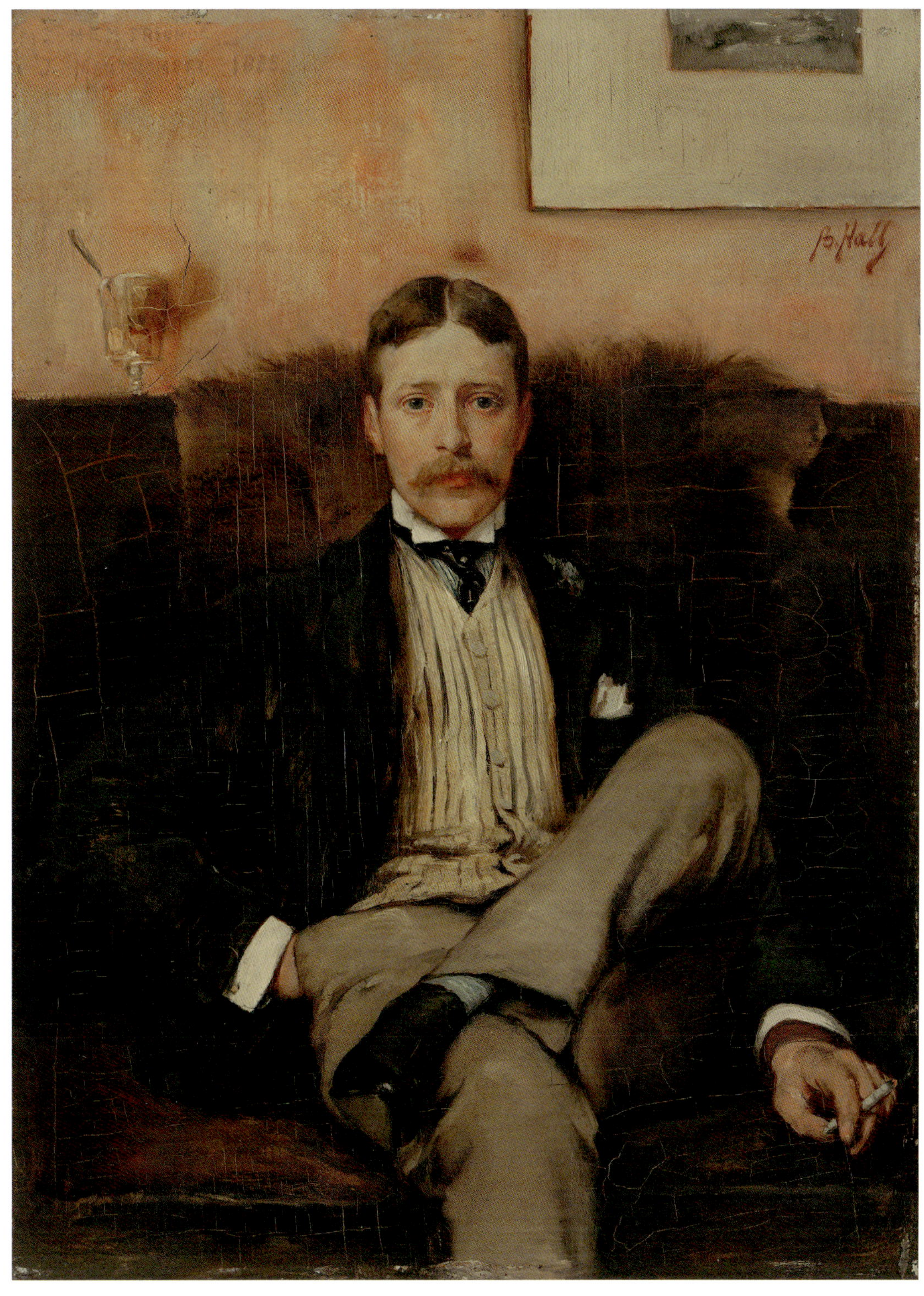

3 **Robert Dowling** (1827–1886)

Miss Robertson of Colac (Dolly) 1885–86

painted in Colac and Melbourne, Victoria
oil on canvas, 103 x 127.6 cm
National Gallery of Australia, Canberra, acquired with the assistance of the Masterpieces for the Nation Fund 2010

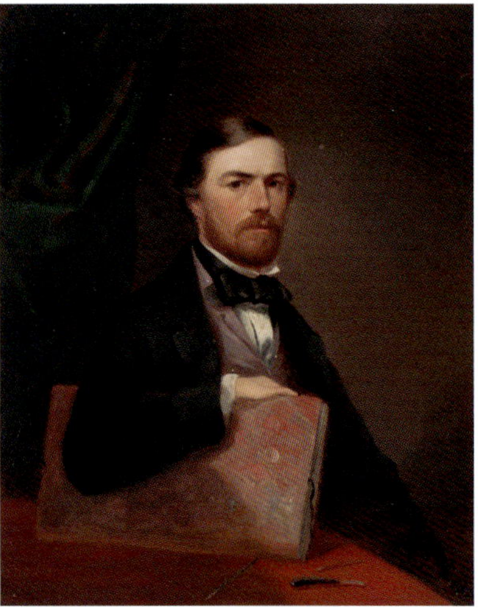

Robert Dowling
Self-portrait c 1852
oil on board, 30 x 25 cm
private collection

'If I am never to marry', Miss Robertson of Colac is reputed to have stormed, 'then I will be in mourning for the rest of eternity'.[1] Although she was courted by a number of suitors, her strict father considered none good enough for his daughter, so she never married.

Dolly (1866–1939), or Elise Christian Margaret Robertson, was the eldest daughter of William and Martha Robertson of 'The Hill', a country property near Colac in Western Victoria. Unhappy with Robert Dowling's first version of her commissioned portrait, showing her wearing a white dress, Dolly requested him to repaint her wearing a dark brown dress, which he did in 1886. Family tradition has it that Dolly insisted that she be repainted to make her look more grown up. Tradition also suggests that the dress was changed after Dolly's father rejected one of her most recent and dearly loved suitors. She was nineteen at the time.

One of Dowling's very last paintings, *Miss Robertson of Colac (Dolly)* is an impressive work which conveys Dolly's latent sensuousness—with the toe peeping out beneath the dress, the steam rising from the teapot, and the flowers in full bloom behind her. Dowling painted this portrait in a naturalist manner, yet it is a carefully constructed work. When repainting the portrait Dowling added other elements: he depicted Dolly with a cushion behind her and a favourite Japanese tea service on a tea table with vanilla slices. Her faithful brown-and-white spotted spaniel at her side provides companionship.

The artist of this portrait, Robert Dowling, holds a special place in the history of Australian art. He was Australia's first locally trained colonial artist. He was the most successful portrait painter in Australia in the 1880s. And he was the first Australian to achieve success at the Royal Academy in London. To get such a highly successful artist—with a large demand for his portraits—to repaint her portrait, must have taken some persuasion. Many other portrait painters would have refused. It is evidence that Dowling was a kindly man, and as James Smith, the critic for the *Argus* remarked on 14 July 1886, 'genial and sympathetic'. But it also suggests that Dolly had considerable charm, and may even have won the heart of the elderly painter.

Anne Gray

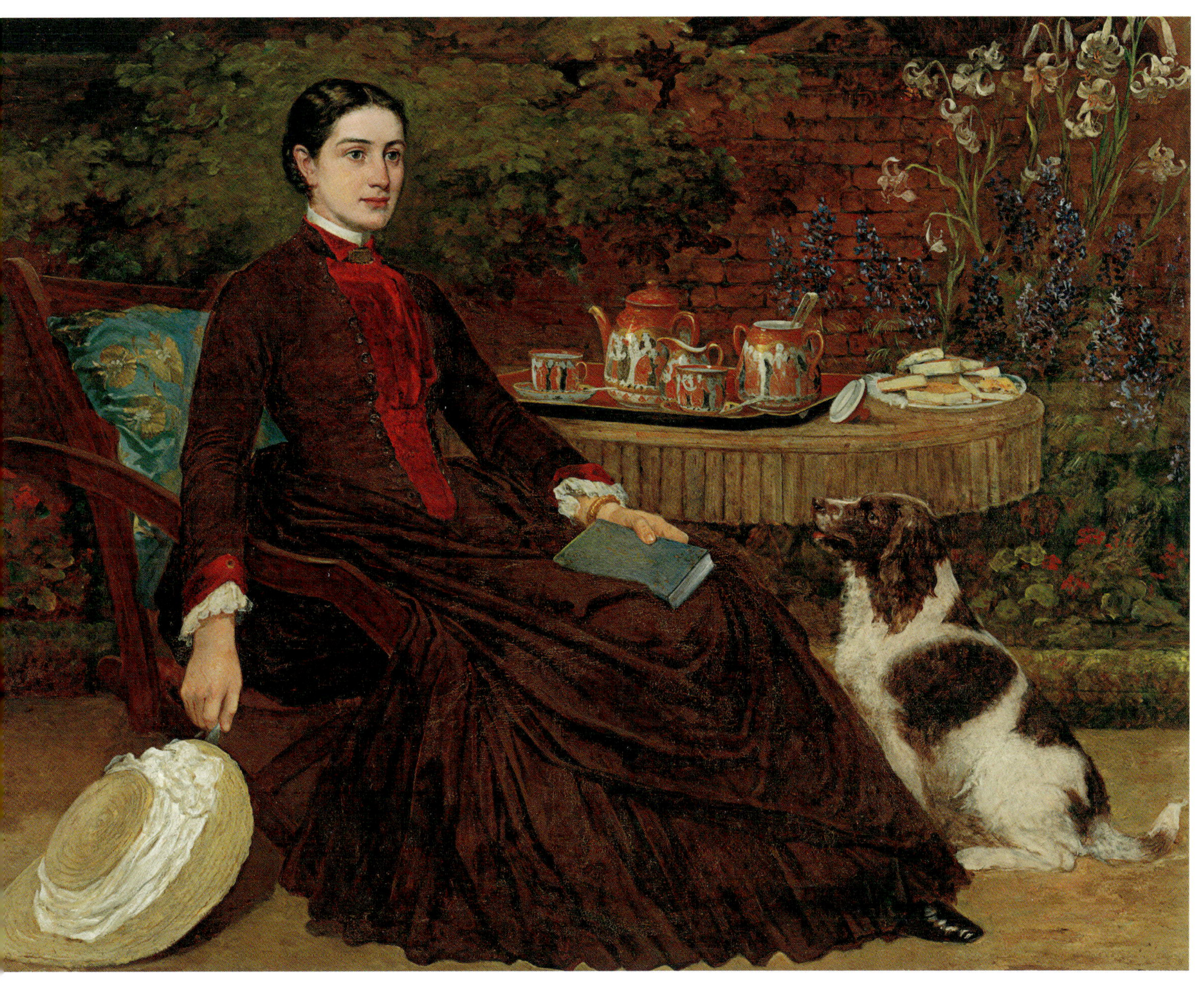

4 **Girolamo Nerli** (1860–1926)
Miss Myra Kemble 1888

painted in Sydney, New South Wales
oil on canvas, 145.5 x 79.3 cm
National Gallery of Australia, Canberra, purchased 1978

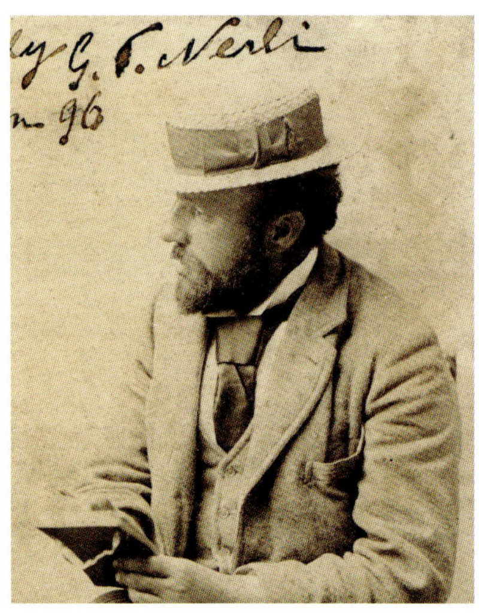

Girolamo Nerli, c 1889
Hocken Collections, Uare Taoka o Hakena, University Of Otago, New Zealand

Myra Kemble was one of Australia's best-loved stage actresses. She arrived in Australia with her family in 1864 from Sligo, Ireland and ten years later made her acting debut at age seventeen in the pantomime *Twinkle twinkle little star* at the Theatre Royal, Melbourne. Kemble was a talented actress, adept at performing a wide variety of roles. She was particularly successful in musical theatre and light comedy, and was also noted for her performances as Lady Macbeth and Ophelia in Shakespearean productions. The combination of talent, natural charm and phenomenal beauty secured her a special place in the hearts of the Australian public.

In *Miss Myra Kemble*, Girolamo Nerli conveys to the viewer a sense of Kemble's character, flair and beauty. She appears as if on a spot-lit, darkened stage. Playfully peeking out from behind a flamboyant pink ostrich-feather fan, she may be about to break into song or deliver a flirtatious monologue. Kemble appears stylish, her luxurious mantle draped open to display a chic, neatly corseted and bustled green day-dress. One wonders, what is costume and the actress and what is really Miss Kemble's character and her own sense of style?

Nerli sought to reject class distinction in academic portraiture by simplifying his backgrounds and eliminating any objects or settings that might reveal the social status of his sitter. His portraits featuring such simplification carry a more casual air than many of the same era, and concentrate our focus on the sitter's face and body. In this way, *Miss Myra Kemble* can be seen as an example of Nerli's egalitarian desire to free his sitter from a class-conscious setting.

J F Archibald, founder of the Archibald prize for portraiture, commissioned this portrait of Myra Kemble for the Criterion Theatre in Sydney, where it hung for many years. It is one of the larger and more ambitious portraits painted by Nerli during his time in Australia. The work was first exhibited in the 9th Annual Exhibition of the Arts Society of NSW in September 1888, and won critical praise for its rich colouring and Nerli's bold originality as a painter.

Italian born, Nerli was the son of an aristocrat. He travelled to Australia in his mid-twenties and while in Sydney in the 1890s associated with Australian painters Charles Conder and Tom Roberts. Nerli returned to Europe in 1904 and died in Nervi, Italy in 1926.

Miriam Kelly

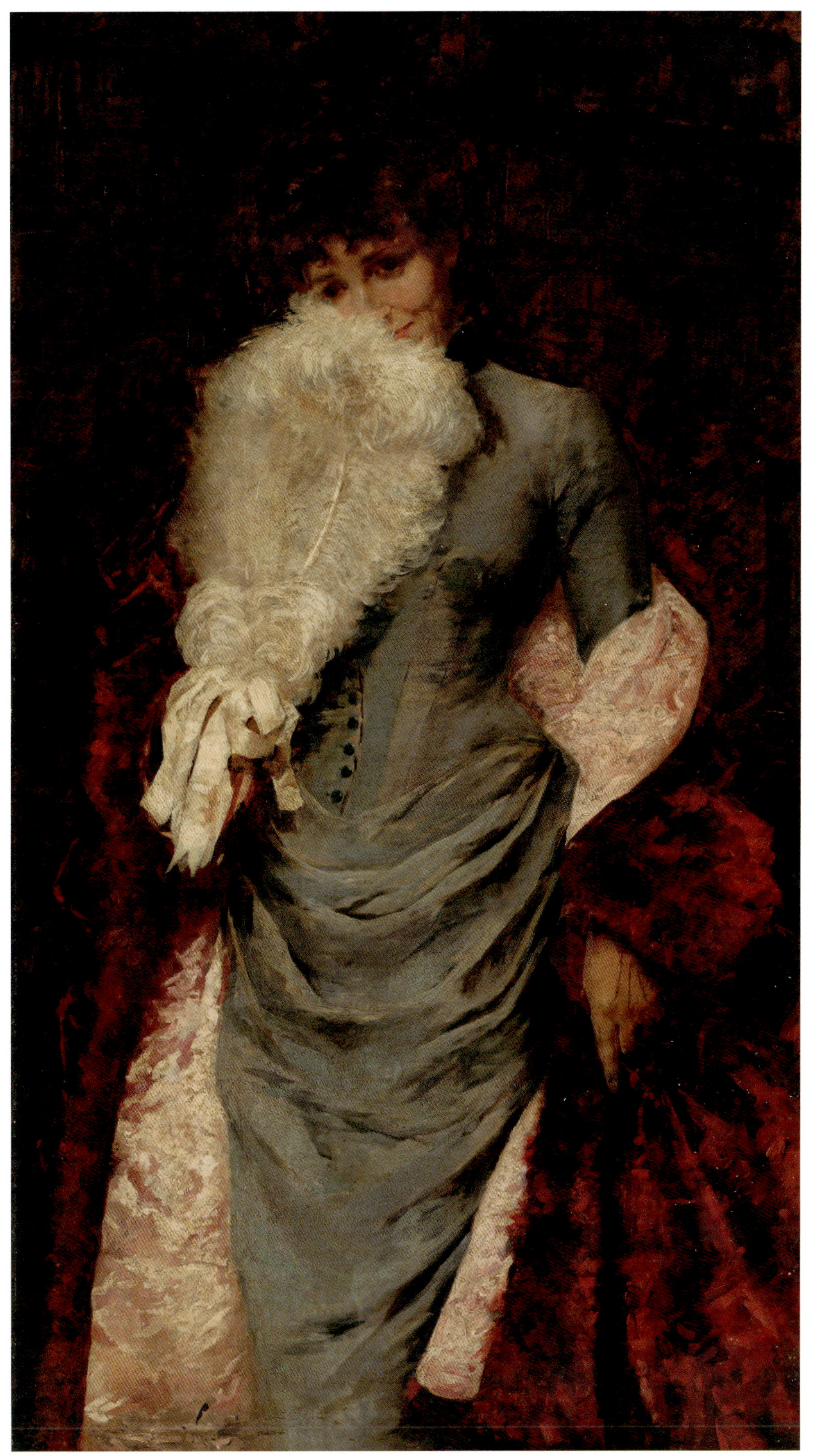

5 **Tom Roberts** (1856–1931)

An Australian native 1888

painted in Melbourne, Victoria
oil on canvas, 127.2 x 76.2 cm
National Gallery of Australia, Canberra, purchased through the Joseph Brown Fund 1979

'A native of Australia, a beautiful girl in a pink gown'; so Madame Elmhurst Goode described Tom Roberts's *An Australian native* in her reminiscences.[2] Roberts was Australia's foremost portrait painter in the late 1880s and 1890s. He was the leader of the group of artists who exhibited '9 by 5 Impressions' in 1889 and became known as the Australian Impressionists, and the painter of patriotic images of 'heroic masculine labour' such as *Shearing the rams* 1890. He exhibited *Australian native* at an open day in his studio in July 1888, and later at the Centennial International Exhibition of 1888–89.

Roberts's title, 'An Australian native', suggests he considered his subject to be a type, a young 'native-born' woman of Anglo-Celtic descent. In the years immediately before Federation, when Australia was still a group of colonies, there was a degree of national fervour. As Humphrey McQueen has observed, in portraiture this manifested itself through 'the creation of a physical type: healthy and vigorous young Australian-born men and women, capable of producing strong children'.[3] In 1885 Roberts returned to Melbourne after having studied and travelled abroad. He was particularly interested in promoting a national 'home-grown' culture and in the 1890s he painted a series of informal portraits on wood panels. He regarded these as being 'Australian' types or characters, 'familiar faces and figures' from the arts and society.

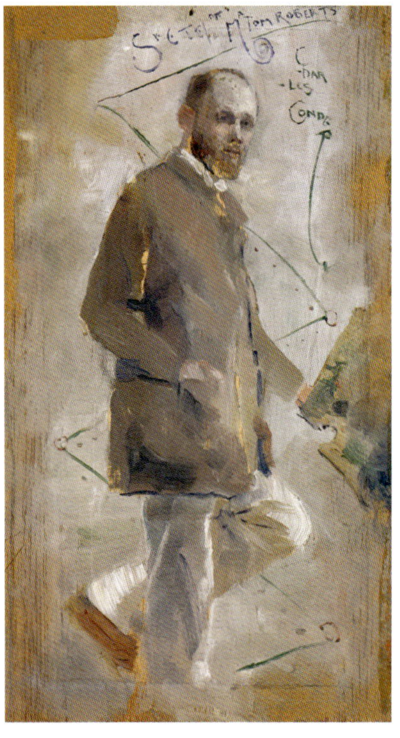

Charles Conder
An Impressionist (Tom Roberts) c 1889
oil on cedar panel, 28.5 x 23.4 cm
Art Gallery of New South Wales, Sydney, purchased with funds provided by the Art Gallery Society of New South Wales, 1997

But *An Australian native* is more than an image of a type, it presents an individual with a distinctive character, and demonstrates Roberts's 'wondrously tender manner with women'. This slim, dark-haired woman is dressed in her best clothes; soft pink gown, brown gloves and feather hat. She has a sweet face and a pensive, almost wistful, expression.

Among the many possible models for the portrait is the Australian contralto singer, Ada Crossley (1871–1929), who was a member of the Austral Salon of Music, Literature and the Arts, from whom the portrait was purchased.[4] What is more, photographs support this attribution. Ada Crossley had auburn-brown hair and dark eyes, a long nose, full cheeks and smiling mouth, and would have been aged seventeen at the time. She was just at the beginning her career. She described herself as 'a regular bush youngster', and was later described in the *Evening Post*, Wellington, New Zealand (1903) as 'an Australian native'.

Anne Gray

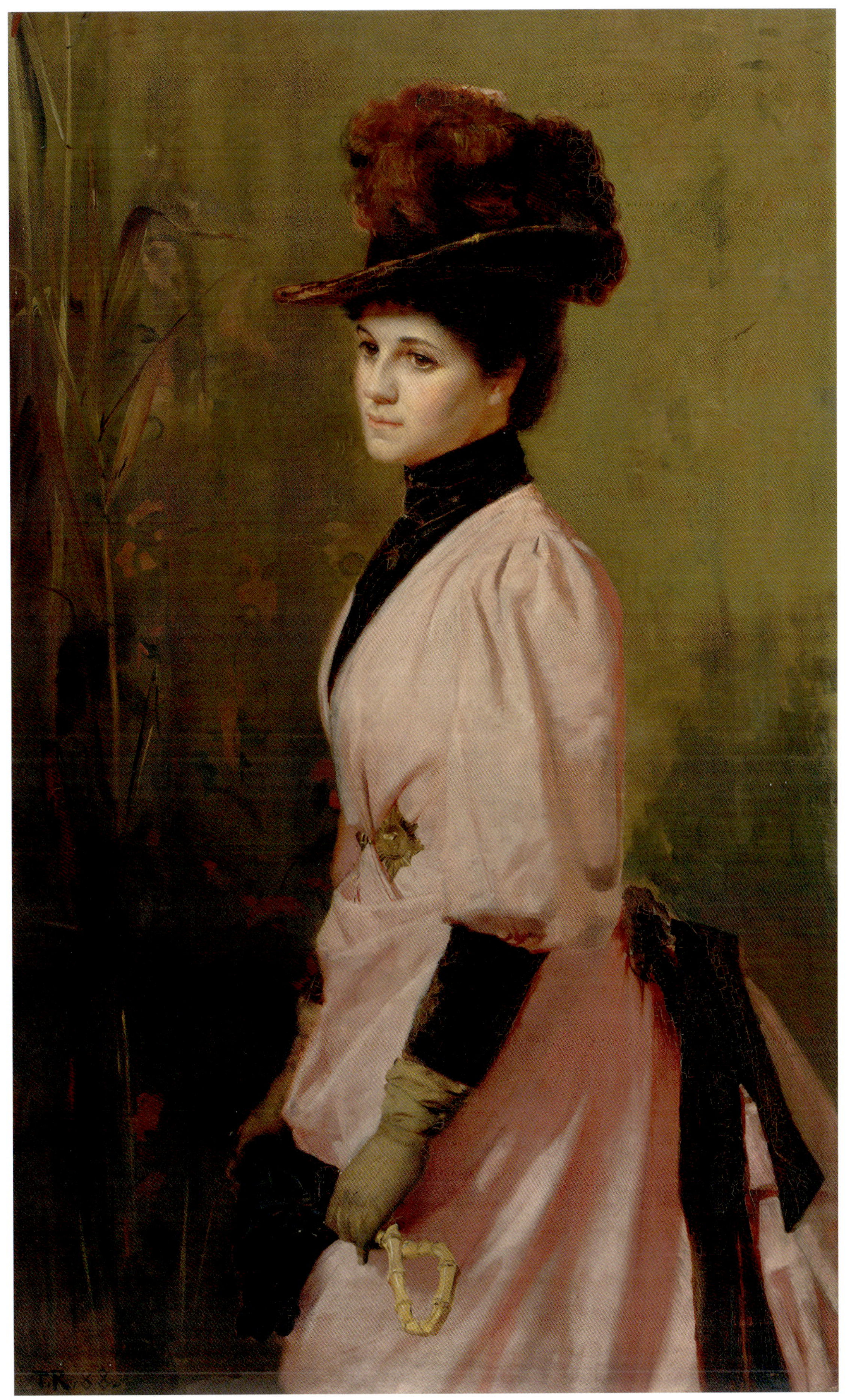

6 **Tom Roberts** (1856–1931)

Mrs Leonard Dodds c 1893

painted in Sydney, New South Wales
oil on canvas, 50.8 x 40.7 cm
National Gallery of Australia, Canberra, purchased 1959

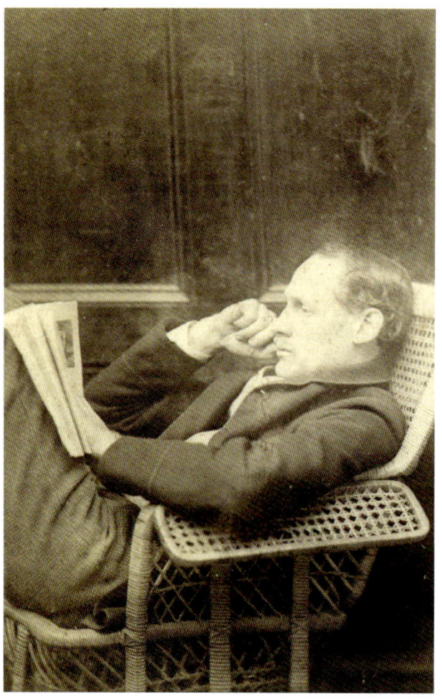

Tom Roberts in the early days, Melbourne, 1890s
La Trobe Library, State Library of Victoria, Melbourne

Parting her lips in a serene smile, Mrs Dodds sits seemingly unposed and unaffected. A gentle glance over her shoulder is captured with casual elegance. Not possessing the formal airs of many portrait sitters, she is pictured at ease in the company of her artist friend Tom Roberts.

The leg-o-mutton sleeve of her crisp white blouse dominates the composition, its copious volume and energetic articulation a counterpoint to the delicate modelling of the sitter's features. The simplicity of the shallow background focuses our eye on her warm, luminous skin and natural bearing. With unadorned hair swept up in a simple bun, Roberts effortlessly portrays her quiet effervescence.

Daughter of Henry and Harriet Dodds, Winifred Dodds (1866–1946) married her cousin Leonard Dodds in 1887. A beautiful and intelligent society lady, she participated in flower shows, community events and hosted lunches and afternoon teas accompanied by music programs. These occasions were often associated with the Society of Artists' exhibitions. Leonard and Winifred lived on Wycombe Road in Neutral Bay, near Roberts's digs at Curlew Camp in Little Sirius Cove on Sydney Harbour. Both steadfast patrons of the arts, they took an active interest in the artists' camp and established a considerable collection including works by Roberts and Arthur Streeton.

By October 1891, a month after arriving in Port Jackson from Melbourne, Roberts had settled happily at Curlew. Frederick McCubbin remarked in a letter to him: 'I am so glad you feel in sympathy with Sydney: I think you must get more sun than we do, and it makes you feel chirpy.'[5] Though many of the artists at the camp, including Roberts and Streeton, survived on a minor stipend, they did not neglect the luxuries of late Victorian middle-class life. Housed in extensively furnished tents complete with Oriental rugs, they enjoyed the company of an itinerant Italian seaman as manservant and Old Jules as cook.

Roberts came to the camp optimistic of Sydney's prospects and despite a deepening Depression sold two portraits to the Art Gallery New South Wales. During his four and a half years at Curlew, the 'Society Bohemian' became one of Sydney's most fashionable portrait painters.[6] In *Mrs Leonard Dodds* the artist reveals this celebrated aptitude for realising the subtle nuances of the sitter's personality, with Streeton remarking that the portrait is 'a rare one, & she'll never have better'.[7]

Emma Colton

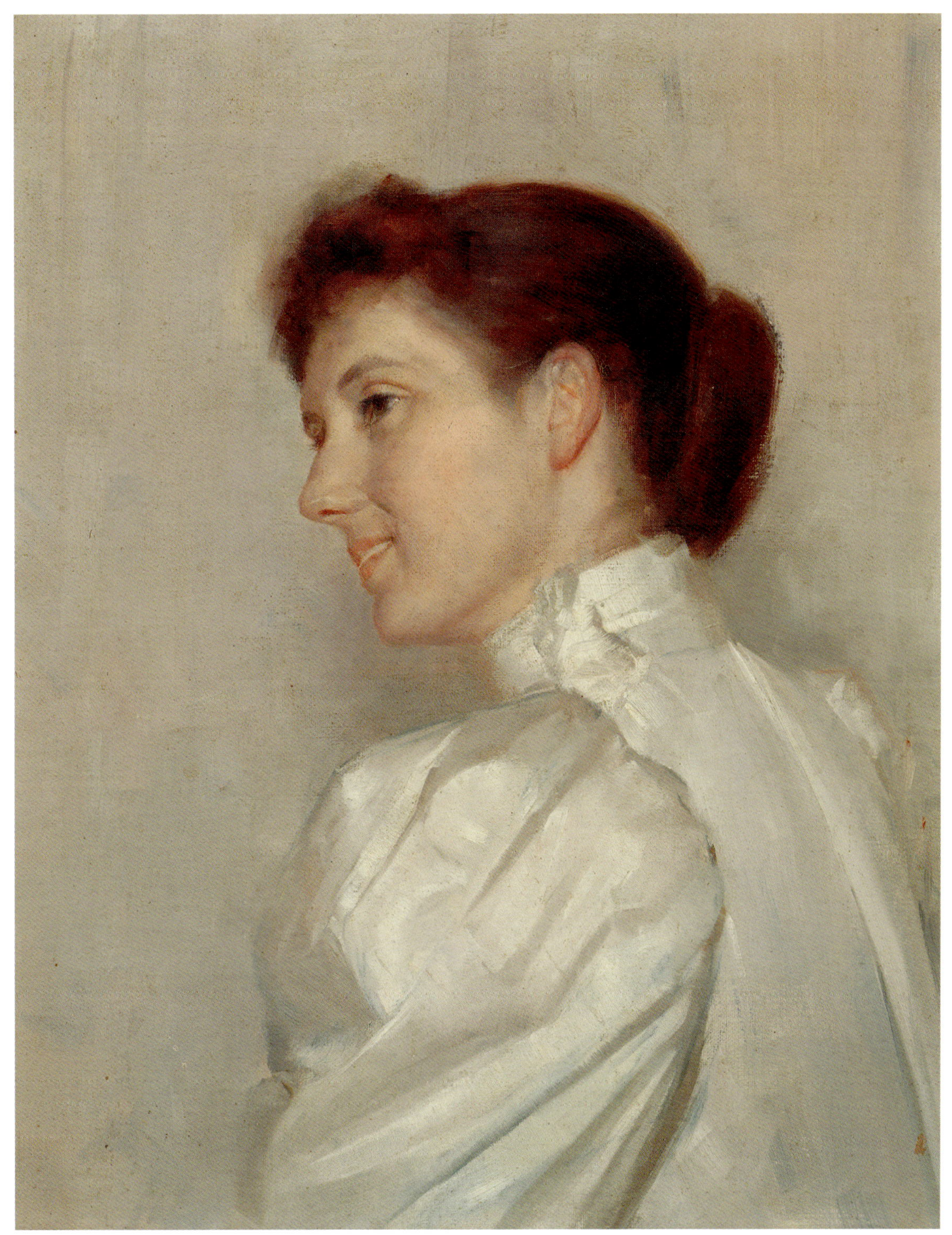

7 **Tom Roberts** (1856–1931)

Portrait study of Lena Brasch c 1893

painted in Sydney
oil on canvas, 61.2 x 51 cm
National Gallery of Australia, Canberra, purchased 1966

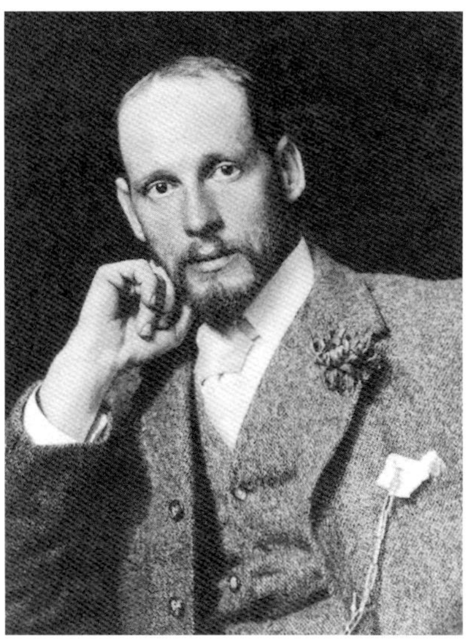

Tom Roberts, early 1890s
private collection, Melbourne

Tom Roberts first met Selina Venus (Lena) Brasch in 1888 at her sister's wedding in Melbourne, where Roberts was best man. They were reacquainted in 1891 when Roberts travelled to Sydney, staying at Curlew Camp at Sirius Cove. Established by her brother Reuben Brasch, she became a regular visitor to the Camp and to Roberts's and Arthur Streeton's fortnightly 'Studio Thursdays'.[8] The extent of the relationship between Roberts and Brasch is unknown but it seems that the artist had a respectful fascination with her; *Portrait study of Lena Brasch* is the first of a number of paintings by Roberts for which she modelled.

This portrait study captures a woman of great beauty and fine features, yet she is reserved, drawing away, her posture stiff and her large grey eyes hidden. Sitting for Roberts for the first time, she appears shy, hesitant to reveal too much. Roberts worked on her face and added the vibrant red in her hat but left the portrait unfinished. He covered it with a new canvas and re-figured her as *An eastern princess* c 1893 (NGA), a portrait of an exotic woman.

Of the paintings for which Brasch modelled for Roberts, this is one of only a few where she is not dressed in costume but has been painted as herself. Here it is her downcast eyes that intrigue most; in her reluctance to look at the artist, and at us, the painting captures a mood rather conveying a personality.

Portrait study of Lena Brasch wasn't discovered until 1975 when Gallery staff removed *An eastern princess* from its stretcher and found the study underneath.

Tom Roberts was born in England, and moved to Australia in 1869. With Frederick McCubbin, Charles Conder and Arthur Streeton, he set up artist camps in Melbourne and Sydney where painters could capture the Australian landscape *en plein air*. In a nostalgic letter to Frederick McCubbin dated 31 December 1914, Roberts wrote:

> I saw Mrs Abrahams, & [one] of the dear old Don's children at Mrs Wyatt's (Lena Brasch) a little while ago—it brought back old times to me. You remember the evenings we sat at the Camp, the last light of the sun on the ti tree in the creek—the smell of the chop—& the gum twigs—the mopoke. a happy time.[9]

Georgia Connolly

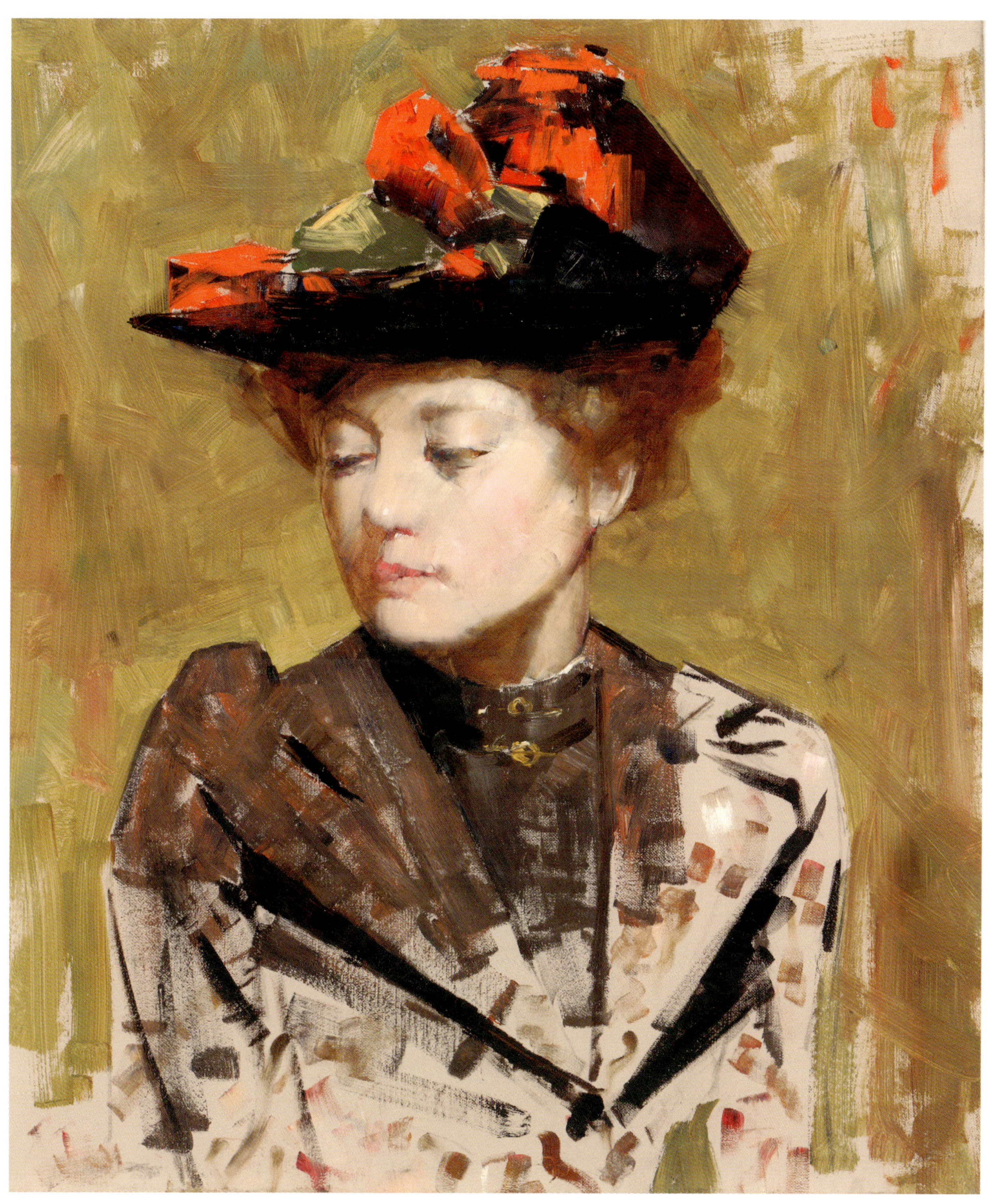

8 **E Phillips Fox** (1865–1915)
Mrs James Pirani 1893

painted in Melbourne, Victoria
oil on canvas, 102.2 x 75.6 cm
National Gallery of Australia, Canberra, purchased 2010

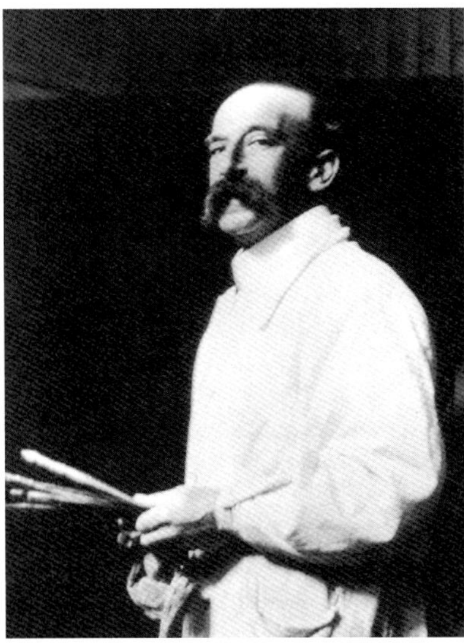

E Phillips Fox, c 1915

Mrs James Pirani appears to be sitting, watching, waiting calmly for life to flow to her. She is shown to be a stately, elderly woman, whose patience might be equalled by her confidence. She looks out of the picture with a steady gaze, and gentle smile. Her neat hair, dress and glint of jewellery suggest that she was mindful of her appearance. Mother of ten children, she is portrayed here as an archetypal dignified matriarch. Clothed in black, emerging from a dark background, with a large white handkerchief in her right hand, we might ask whether she was in mourning. Or does the black dress indicate her sobriety or piety? Certainly the solidity of the composition suggests a steady character.

Abigail Davis (1821–1897) was the daughter of Gabriel Davis, a Jewish optician of Leeds and his wife Ann Aaron. In 1842, at the age of 21, she married the clothier James Cohen Pirani from London. They migrated to Melbourne in 1858, with their five children Frederick, Sophia, Regina, Annie and Samuel. After their arrival in Australia, James worked as the manager of a men's clothing and outfitting business and later as a bank manager. They had five more children. This portrait was commissioned by Abigail's son Samuel, when she was aged 72, perhaps in gratitude to his mother and for her dedication to her children. She lived with him during her last years. Samuel was a pianist and a friend of the artist E Phillips Fox; he frequently socialised with Fox and the commission may also have been to express his support of the artist.

Fox painted this sensitive portrait soon after his return to Melbourne in 1892, after studying in Paris and France and working at the artists' colony at St Ives in Cornwall. He achieved a reputation for his sensuous and stylish works celebrating light and colour. However, while in Madrid, Fox copied Velasquez's works. *Mrs James Pirani* reflects Fox's admiration of Velasquez's paintings in the way he captured the flesh tones of Abigail Pirani's face and hands, as well as the manner in which he offset her silvery hair against the dark dress. The portrait is a work of great clarity that evokes the presence of a strong and gracious woman.

Anne Gray

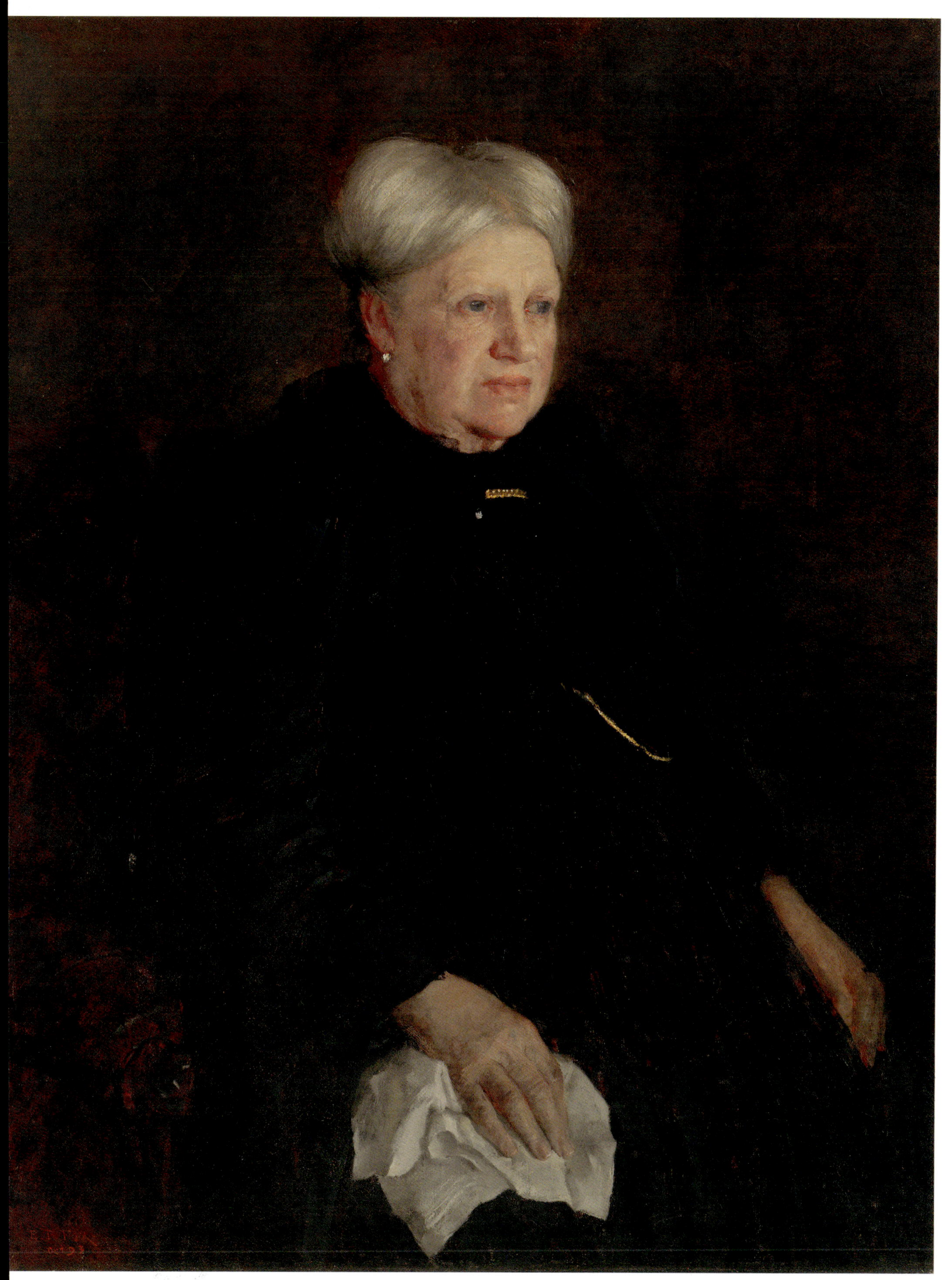

9 **Tom Roberts** (1856–1931)

Sketch portrait—Senator JT Walker 1901

painted in Sydney, New South Wales
oil on canvas mounted on cardboard, 9.2 x 7.9 cm
National Gallery of Australia, Canberra, purchased 1976

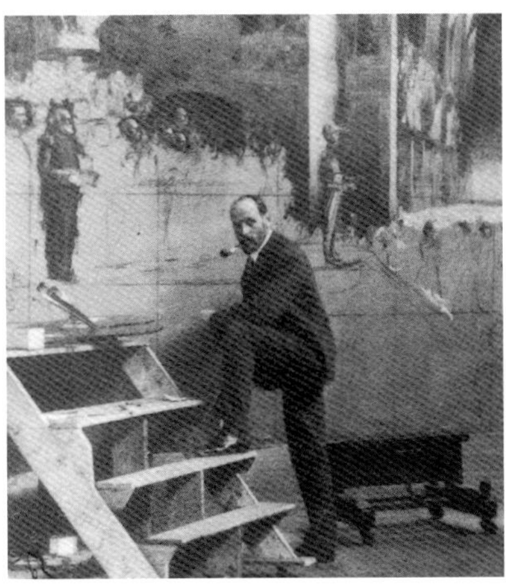

Tom Humphrey
Tom Roberts in front of 'The Big Picture' 1902

At the turn of the twentieth century, Tom Roberts won the portrait commission of a lifetime—to capture the first Commonwealth Parliament of Australia, convened in Melbourne in May 1901. The artist was required to represent accurately the 269 people in attendance, providing a grand and realistic pictorial record of the most momentous occasion in Australia's history. The portrait of Senator James Thomas Walker, measuring only 9.2 by 7.9 cm, was undertaken as a primary study for the commission, which Roberts was to nickname 'The Big Picture'.

Scottish-born Walker was a Liberal and Free Trade senator from 1901 to 1913, and a long-term director of the Bank of New South Wales. Roberts painted him in profile, looking straight ahead, dressed for the Opening in tones of brown and black. The study is sketched with economical brushstrokes and includes an indistinct portrait looming above Walker's right-hand shoulder; by contrast, the engaging energy of this little portrait study is lost on the figures of Walker and others in the finished commission, which appears more formal and stilted.

Tom Roberts was one of Australia's most talented painters and portraitists, but he still yearned to prove himself, especially in England. At the time he welcomed the commission but the painting, ultimately spreading over fifteen square metres of canvas, was to occupy him for more than two years in Sydney, Melbourne and London. The stress, eyestrain and exhaustion it brought on nearly broke him, and the work failed to boost his profile or enhance his reputation at the time.

For the finished *Opening of the first Parliament of the Commonwealth of Australia, May 9 1901* 1903 (Parliament of Australia). Roberts received the sum of 1000 guineas, increased from the contracted fee of 650 guineas because he had to enlarge the canvas to include all the attendees. For all his toil, he did not sign the finished picture, which hangs in Parliament House, Canberra. He did, however, place his initials on the study of Senator J T Walker, made while the project was still fresh and the artist was filled with hope for it.

Simon Elliott

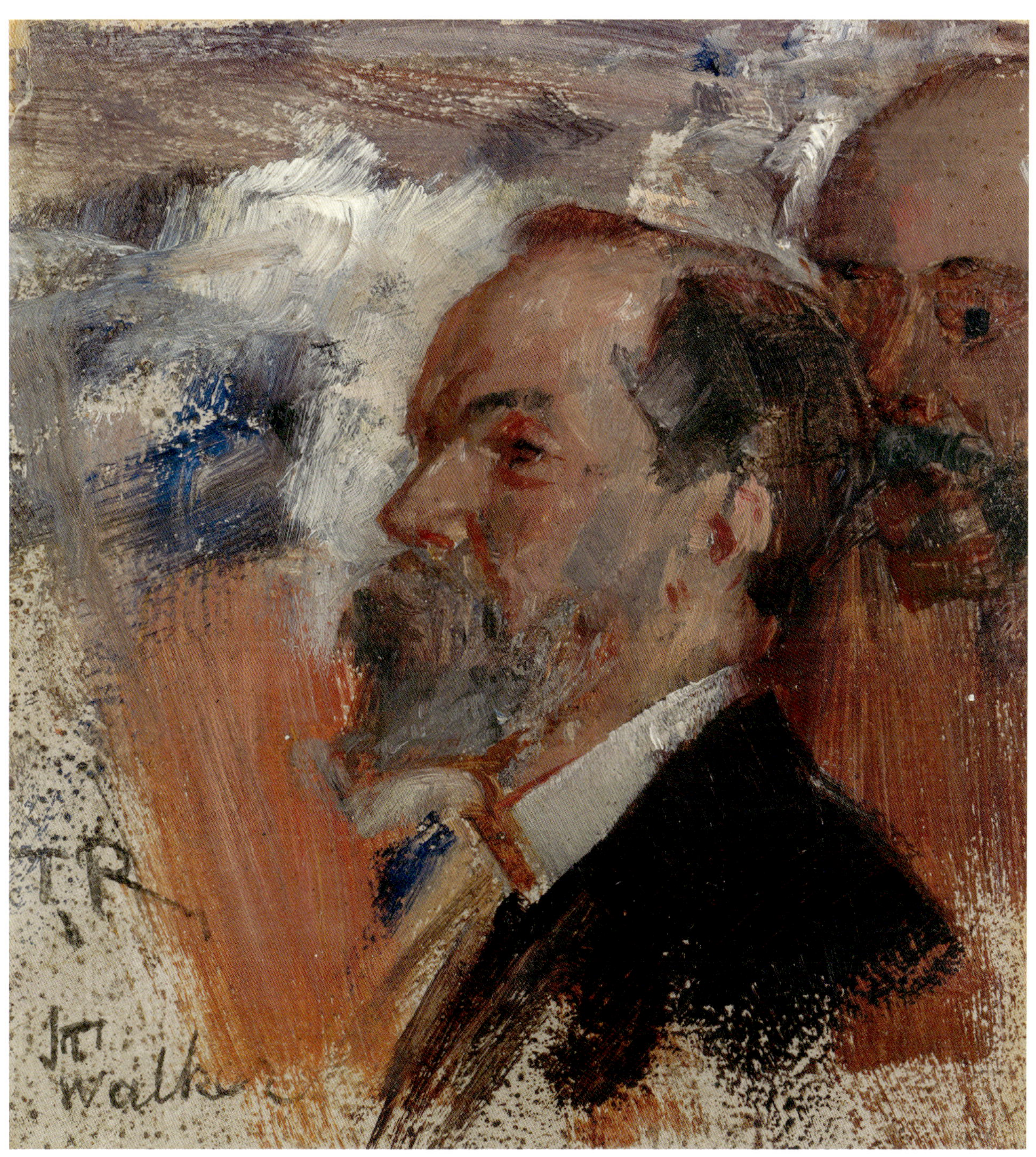

10 **Hugh Ramsay** (1877–1906)
Self-portrait: bust showing hands 1901–02

painted in Paris, France
oil on canvas, 36 x 46 cm

National Gallery of Australia, Canberra, bequest of William Stewart McDougall

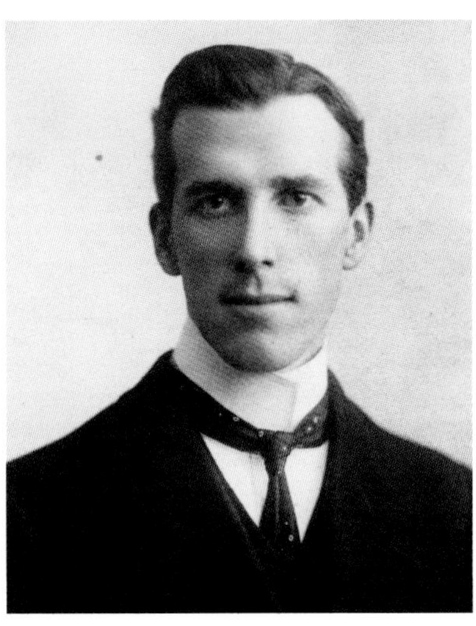

Hugh Ramsay, c 1900

Hugh Ramsay's self-portraits painted in his Paris studio are some of the most important works by an Australian expatriate artist at the turn of the twentieth century. Ramsay was a prolific painter, producing over 25 self-portraits in oil and pencil, as well as studio interiors and portraits of fellow artists, friends and commissioned subjects.[10]

Self-portrait: bust showing hands shows Ramsay, possibly at the end of an enjoyable evening, his handsome features flushed and his tie loosened. This is a relaxed moment shared with the viewer—the sense of intimacy accentuated by the painting's horizontal format and the close cropping of the sitter's face and hands.

A smaller self-portrait than was usual for the artist, this work nonetheless shows his accomplishment as a portrait painter. Taking on the role of sitter liberated Ramsay from the expense of hired models and allowed a degree of critical self-analysis and introspection. Working from a mirror image, the painting reveals an artist who is fascinated by character and personality. His quizzical eyes see us, without too much intent, but enough to engage our interest. The paintbrush in his left hand seems like an unlit cigar while the right hand betrays the artist's rather foppish, demeanour.[11]

The lighting in the work is dramatic. With his face in half darkness, we see Ramsay, the model, glowing in subdued light. The tonal composition reduces the background detail to subtle patterns on the armchair and in the light reflected off his smooth skin. The starched white collar strikes a note of contrast. This work would have been painted at night by oil lamp, hinting at Ramsay's impoverished Parisian lifestyle.

Born in Glasgow, Scotland, Ramsay's family migrated to Australia in 1878, settling in Melbourne. He studied painting under Bernard Hall at the National Gallery School, Melbourne and travelled to Europe in 1900 with George Lambert. In Paris, Ramsay studied at the Académie Colarossi. In 1902, four works were selected for display at the New Salon in Paris; a remarkable achievement for such a young and relatively unknown Australian artist.

Tragically, Hugh Ramsay's potential to become a major Australian artist was cut short. Falling ill with tuberculosis, he returned to Australia in 1902 where he painted with even greater urgency. His health worsened and he died just before his 29th birthday.

Georgia Connolly

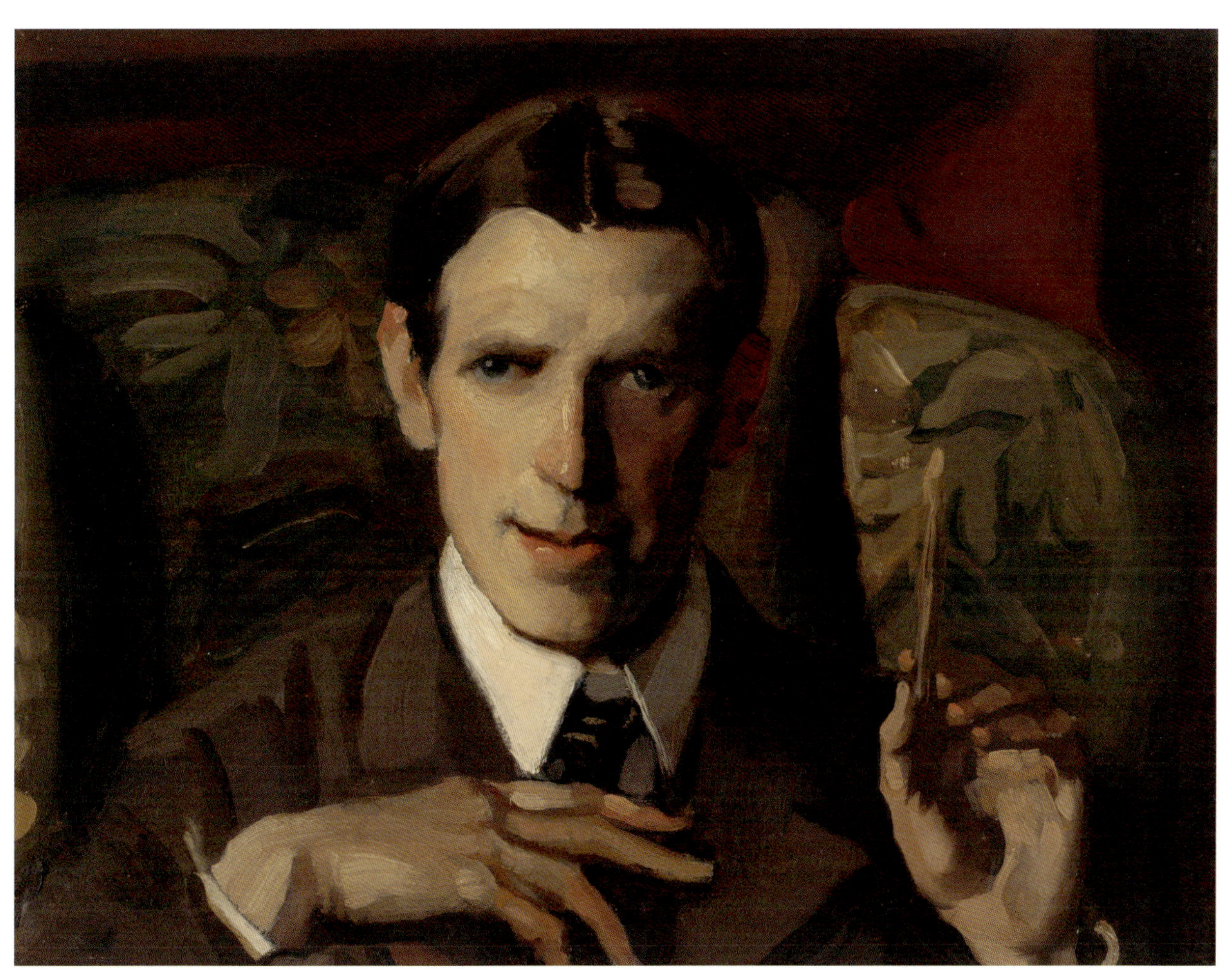

11 Hugh Ramsay (1877–1906)

Rosenthal at the piano 1902

painted in Paris, France

oil on canvas, 30.3 x 46.6 cm

National Gallery of Australia, Canberra, given in memory of Sir James McGregor 1974

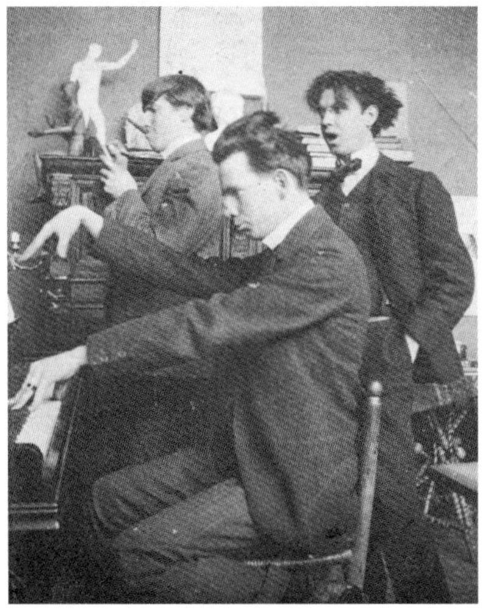

Ramsay playing the piano in his studio at 51 Boulevard St Jacques, Montparnasse with James McDonald and Frederick Frieseke, 1901–02

Hugh Ramsay painted this portrait of Polish pianist Moriz Rosenthal (1862–1946) after attending his recital at the Salle des Agriculteurs in Paris on 23 January 1902, the first anniversary of Queen Victoria's death.

Ramsay had arrived in Paris a year earlier, just before the momentous event that marked the end of an era. Perhaps, back in his wintry studio after the excitement of escorting Amy Lambert—wife of friend and fellow-artist George W Lambert—to hear the celebrated pianist, the artist sensed his own passing in the shadows.

Rosenthal's repertoire at the time included works by Chopin, Liszt and Schubert; and he would almost certainly have played his own composition, 'Papillons', at the recital. Yet his genius at the keyboard—a touch keen enough to set butterflies dancing—is not felt in Ramsay's portrait.

Music was almost as important as painting to Ramsay and within two months of arriving in Paris he had cut his food budget to hire a piano.[12] He played well and entertained his friends with gusto, especially when spirits were low. In the same way, he would fill his letters home with anecdotes and sketches of his wonderful new art-life and the success of his work in the Salons. Small as it is, however, *Rosenthal at the piano* has none of the liveliness of a sketch. The paint is thick and deliberately applied, more with palette knife than brush; the colours are subdued.

The horizontal composition of Ramsay's painting is similar to Whistler's 1859 work, *At the piano* (Taft Museum, Cincinatti). But whereas Whistler shows a sumptuous golden room where a young girl in white gazes enraptured at the beautiful pianist, Ramsay's painting is bleak, the grand piano almost like a grave. And this toughness is the source of its power.

Hugh Ramsay was a 'bright star' at the centre of his family but he readily identified with the short-lived Romantic poet John Keats and became something of a soul mate of Dame Nellie Melba, who lost her mother when young. The warmth of this connection is no better expressed than in Ramsay's portrait of her niece Nellie Patterson [12], painted around 1903. Within the context of the Rosenthal work it is a shimmering affirmation of life. But death stalked the artist, who passed away on 5 March 1906 at his childhood home in Melbourne.

Laura Murray Cree

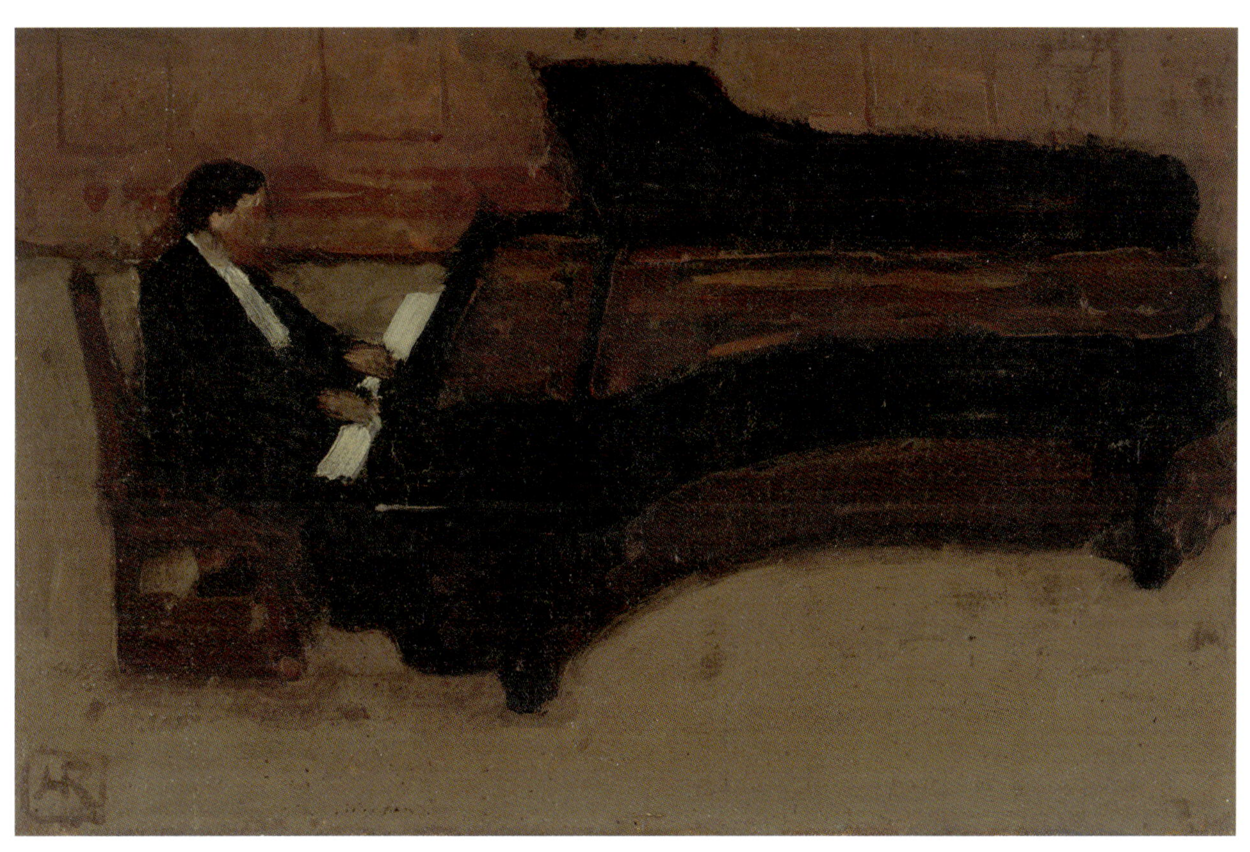

12 **Hugh Ramsay** (1877–1906)

Miss Nellie Patterson 1903

painted in Melbourne, Victoria
oil on canvas, 122.3 x 92.2 cm
National Gallery of Australia, Canberra, purchased 1966

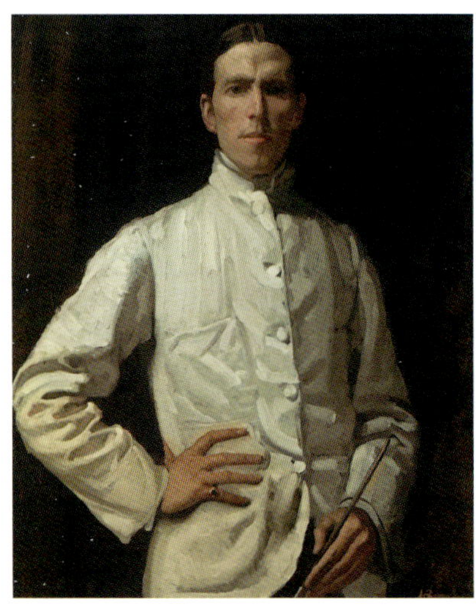

Hugh Ramsay
Self portrait in a white jacket 1901–02
oil on canvas, 92.3 x 73.5 cm
National Gallery of Victoria, Melbourne
presented through the NGV Foundation by Nell Turnbull, niece of the artist, and by her children John Fullerton, Patricia Fullerton and Fiona Fullerton, Founder Benefactors, 2002

Five-year-old Miss Nellie Patterson's large, deep brown eyes front a determinedly brave look. Yet there is a sense of wariness and unease, perhaps because of her somewhat precarious position atop an enormous, pink, velvety cushion from which she is said to have continually slipped while sitting for this portrait. One of two daughters of Tom Patterson and Isabella (née Mitchell), Nellie was also a beloved niece of Australian opera diva, Dame Nellie Melba. A doting aunt, Melba commissioned this portrait from Hugh Ramsay after she arrived back in Australia in late 1902, following over fifteen years touring Europe and the United States of America.

In this portrait, Ramsay has expertly captured the quality of light bouncing off Nellie's pink chiffon party frock, silk sash and matching pink shoes—an expensive French gift from her aunt. Nellie appears in stark contrast to the dim studio interior in which she sits, angelic and glowing. Ramsay has emphasised the textures and luminosity of her outfit with his bold use of white and high-sheen paint. These technical developments were inspired by the bravura style of American artist John Singer Sargent.

While Nellie's exquisite young face and fresh skin have been rendered with utmost delicacy, softness and tender realism, large areas of the work are painted with much wider, looser brushstrokes. Patricia Fullerton has surmised that this less detailed brushwork reflects a sense of urgency that developed in Ramsay's painting as the severity of his illness worsened in the years leading to his death.[13]

Ramsay first met Melba in Paris after he achieved great success in the competitive *Société Nationale des Beaux-Arts* earlier in 1902. Melba was well known for her patronage of fellow artists and in particular fellow Australians. In December 1902, when both Ramsay and Melba were in Australia, Melba staged an exhibition of 38 works by Ramsay at her Toorak home in Melbourne. This was the only solo exhibition of Ramsay's works during his lifetime.

Miss Nellie Patterson remained in the collection of the Patterson family until it was purchased for the national collection in 1966.

Miriam Kelly

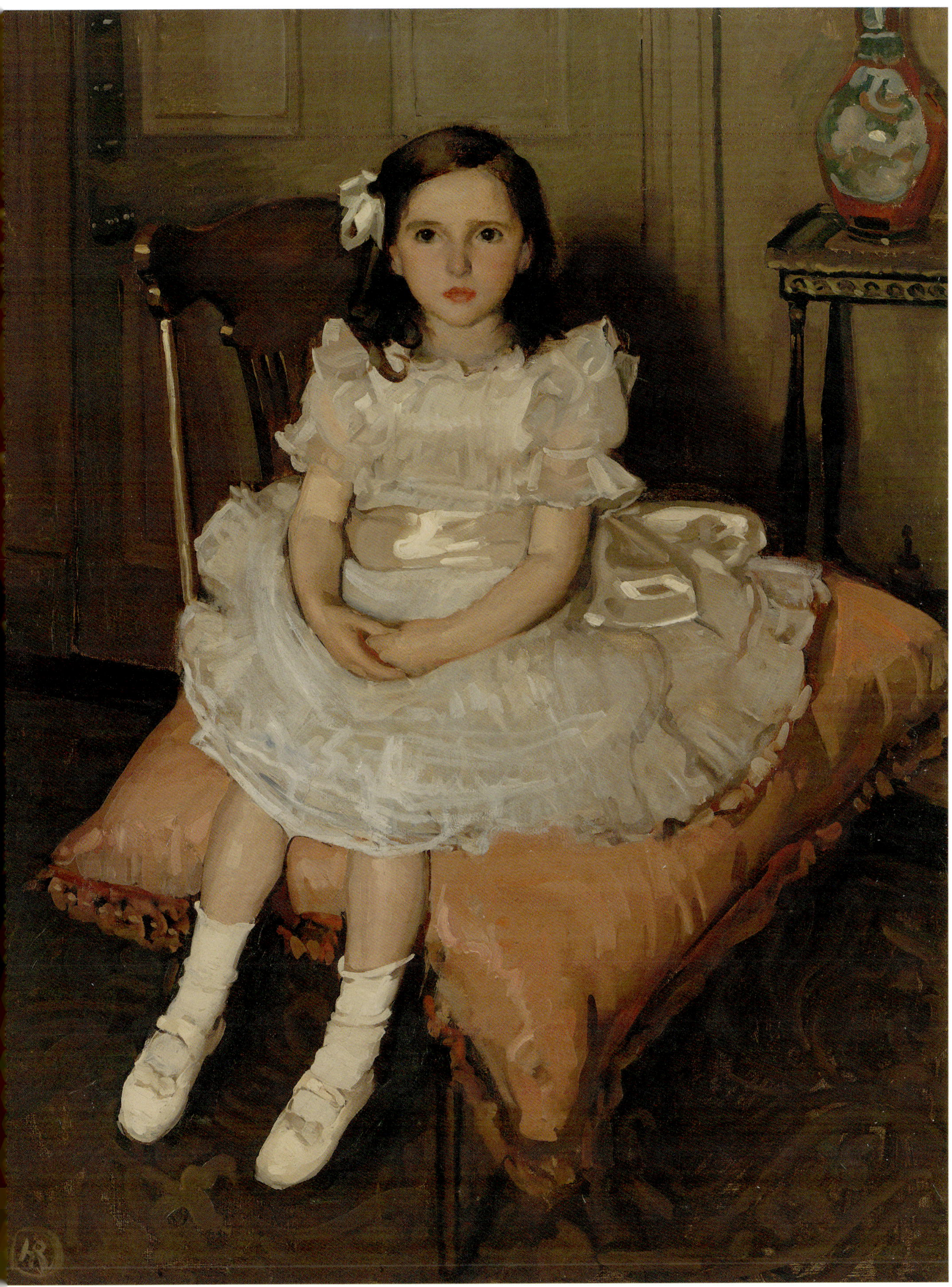

13 E Phillips Fox (1865–1915)

Elsie, daughter of H W Brooks, Esquire 1904

painted in London, England
oil on canvas, 136.5 x 71.3 cm
National Gallery of Australia, Canberra, purchased 1963

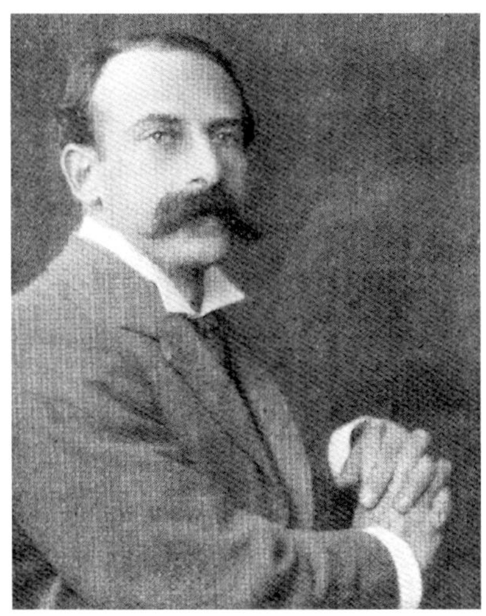

E Phillips Fox, c 1901

Elsie Brooks sits passively, her hands lightly resting in her lap. At nine years of age, modelling in Fox's studio in 1904, she is a child of the Edwardian age. This was the time when childhood was becoming recognised as a separate state of being; a new social concept in the late nineteenth century and Edwardian eras.[14]

Elsie was the daughter of Harry Wilkinson Brooks, an industrialist from Melbourne living with his family in London. Brooks was a successful businessman who commissioned this portrait of his daughter. In the painting, Elsie is a symbol of her family's stature, depicting new industrialist wealth. However, in the simplicity of the sitter's environment and less ornate nature of her dress and accessories, Fox shifts this reference. Elsie is still an Australian child who affects fewer of the Edwardian characteristics than does her contemporary Nellie Patterson, as captured by Hugh Ramsay in his portrait, *Miss Nellie Patterson* 1903 [12].[15]

The figure of Elsie is firmly structured and modelled, combining freshness and childlike innocence within a semi-formalised setting.[16] Framed by a dark background, Elsie sits modestly on a low bench, her expression demure. The tenderness of her form, however, belies her age. Her rosy cheeks, soft skin and chubby arms and hands show her to be younger than her years. Fox uses a warm colour palette and rounded brush to highlight her fair skin and soft shadow lines. Nevertheless, Elsie's gentle face and small hands are secondary. The focus of the painting is the light emanating from the folds and frills in her dress; its dainty floral pattern, golden sash and fine bonnet with translucent ribbon in contrast to the rich 'leafy' patterns in the background.

In 1901, with the support of the Gilbee Bequest for which he was commissioned to paint *Landing of Captain Cook at Botany Bay 1770* 1902 (NGV), Fox moved to London. From then until 1905, he was a central figure within a substantial London-based community of Australian artists. It was through this community and his exposure to works by European contemporaries that Fox became a keen follower of French Impressionism. He married fellow artist Ethel Carrick in 1905 and relocated to Paris, where they lived until their return to Melbourne in 1913. Fox continued to exhibit in Australia until his death in 1915.

Georgia Connolly

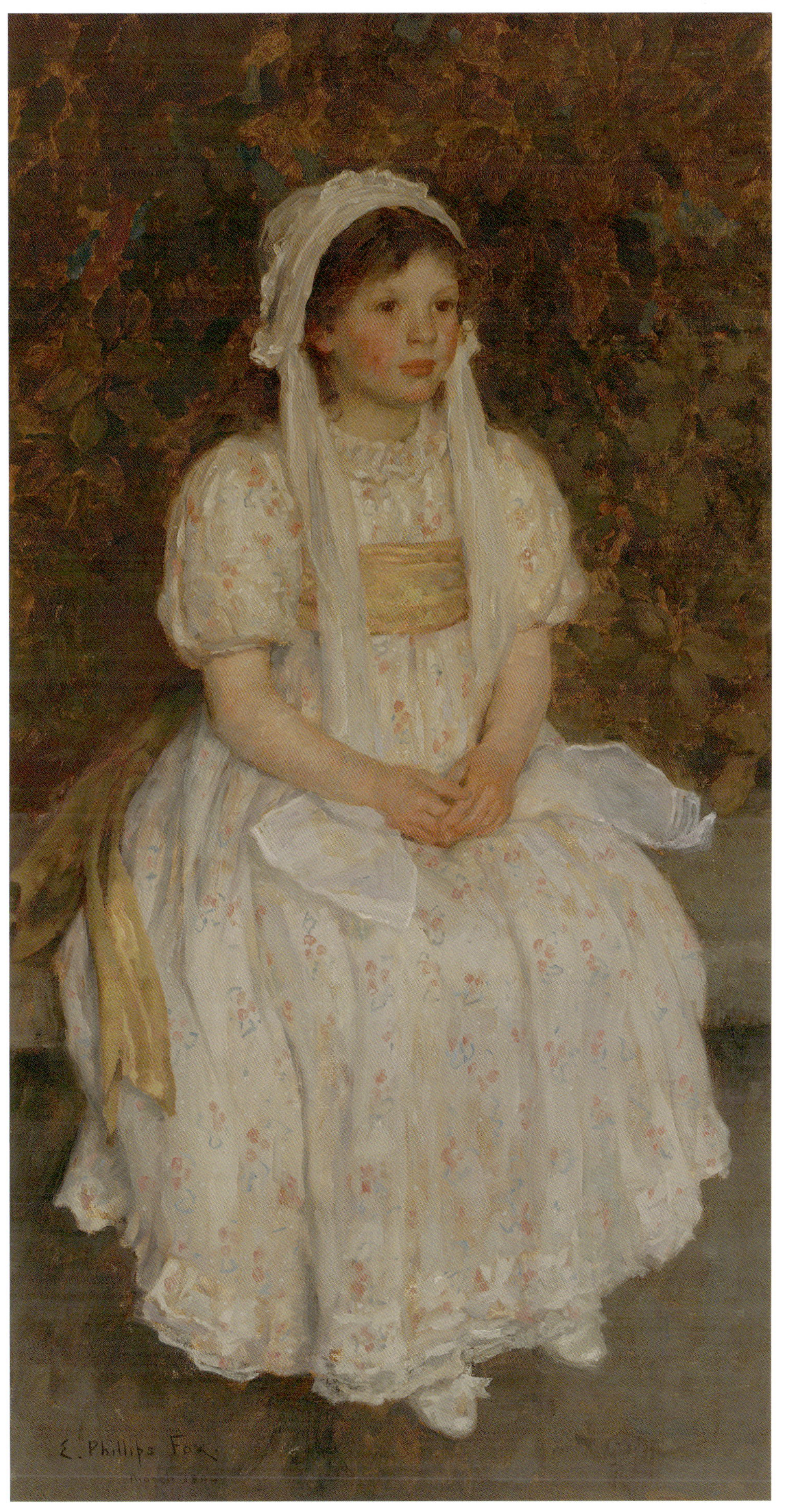
E. Phillips Fox

14 **George W Lambert** (1873–1930)

The old dress 1906

painted in London, England
oil on canvas, 206 x 143.7 cm
National Gallery of Australia, Canberra, purchased 1974

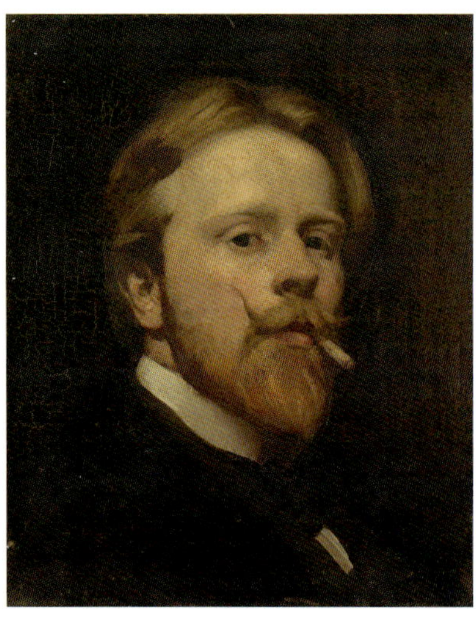

George W Lambert
Self-portrait c 1906
oil on canvas, 46.3 x 38.2 cm
National Gallery of Victoria, Melbourne
The Joseph Brown Collection, presented through the NGV Foundation by Dr Joseph Brown AO OBE, Honorary Life Benefactor, 2004

'"Well, what do you think of me?" she cried; and with a hand at her waist she spun about as if to show off some miracle of Parisian dressmaking'. So Edith Wharton's impoverished character explains how she transformed an old dress into a new one, by simply twirling around and asking, 'Well, what do you think of me?'[17] Proverbially clothes have been said to make the man—or the woman. Certainly, they have indicated a person's wealth and position in society. They have equally been used as a disguise and as fancy dress.

The young woman was probably Kitty Fallon, one of Lambert's favourite models at this time, who also took lessons in drawing from him. The dress is from the early Victorian era and was probably from his costume box. Kitty is portrayed 'dressing up' and posing for the painting in a rather artificial manner. Her facial expression is pleasantly bland, and Lambert may have intentionally sought to reduce the importance of her expression to emphasise the dress.

Lambert was one of Australia's most brilliant, witty and fascinating artists, who produced a diverse range of work, including a number of celebrated portraits. He lived and worked in London for about twenty years, and returned to Sydney in 1921 as the most successful Australian artist of the era. He painted *The old dress* during his early years in London, before he had achieved significant recognition.

Like other Edwardian artists, Lambert often painted generalised portraits, and gave his works generic titles rather than those of the sitters. And like other Edwardians, he also referred to the paintings of earlier artists in his work. In this study in white, grey, grey-green and black Lambert may have been exploring Whistler's approach to painting in *Harmony in grey and green: Miss Cicely Alexander* 1872–74 (Tate, London), which had been exhibited in Whistler's 'Memorial Exhibition' at the New Gallery, London in 1905. Like Miss Alexander, Lambert's model is dressed in a tiered white dress and shown turned in three-quarter view, with her hands by her sides. And, in a Whistlerian manner, Lambert has used the ornate furniture to provide a kind of decorative frieze behind his subject.

Anne Gray

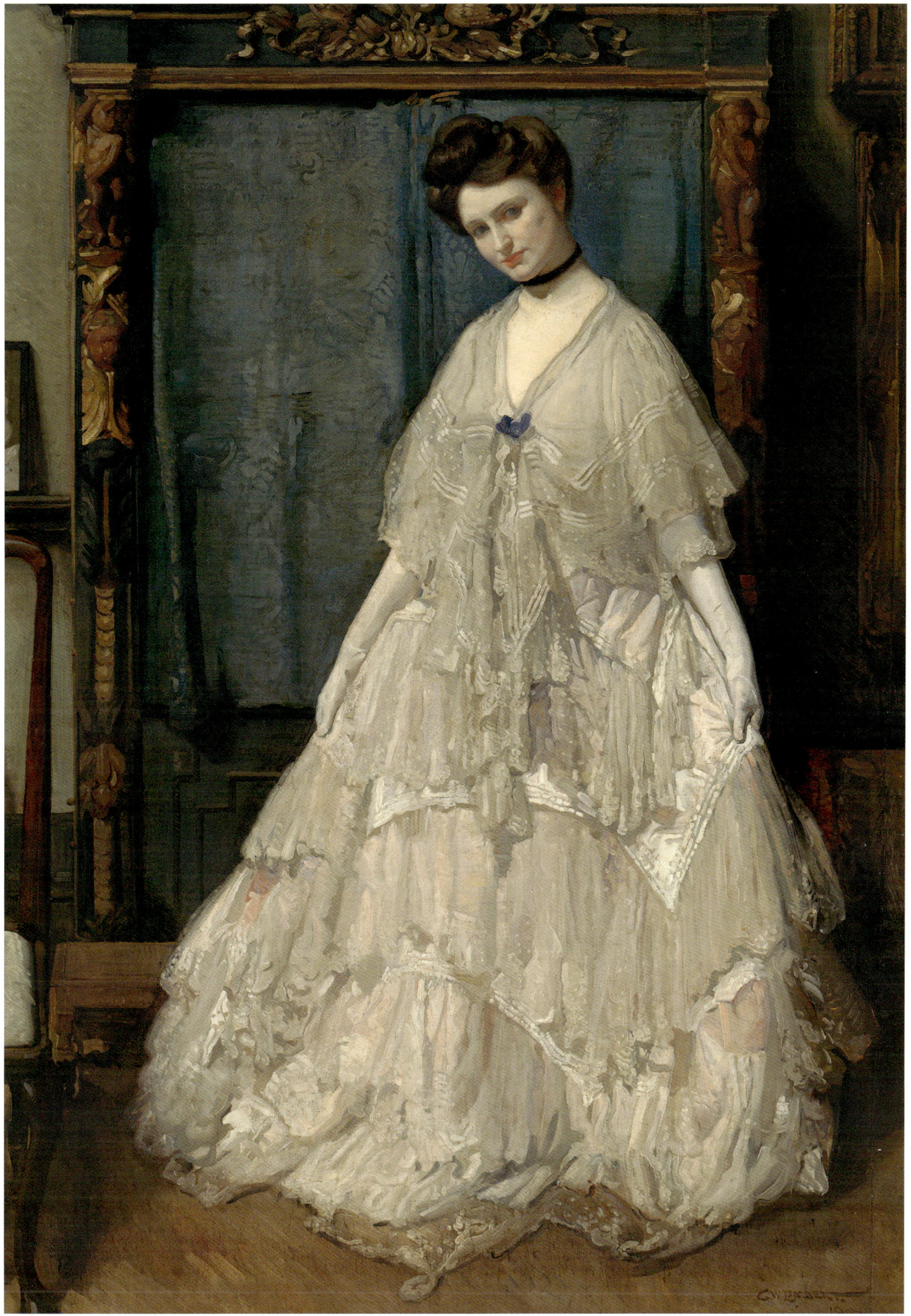

15 **Frederick McCubbin** (1855–1917)

Self-portrait c 1908

painted in Melbourne, Victoria
oil on canvas, 48.5 x 41 cm
National Gallery of Australia, Canberra, purchased 1977

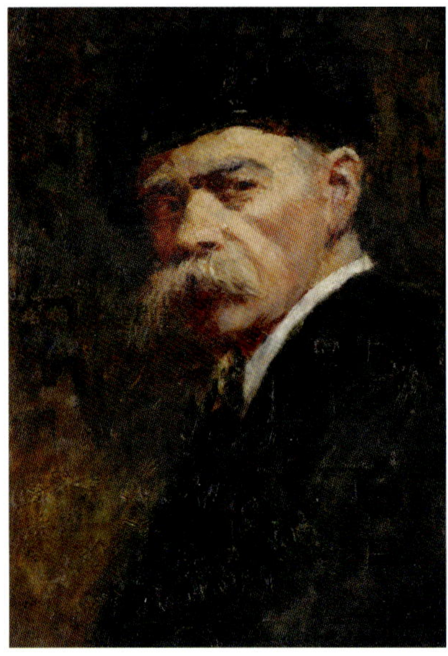

Frederick McCubbin
Self-portrait 1916
oil on canvas mounted on plywood,
50.3 x 35 cm
Art Gallery of Western Australia, Perth, purchased with funds from the Great Australian Paintings Appeal, 1981

'Love' is the key to his whole life. He loved swearing (a dinkum Aussie), loved a good story, even against himself; made his students realise his love of art.[18]

A kind and sincere man, Frederick McCubbin was much loved. He had a gentle presence, and the air of a poet and dreamer. He could also be energetic, fun, warm and gregarious—and would gesticulate freely with his arms and hands. He was a thinking man, and he liked to make others think and laugh. He was an extensive and discriminating reader, particularly of biography and high fiction, and enjoyed talking on a wide range of topics.

McCubbin was a son of Melbourne. He was born and brought up in working-class Melbourne, trained at the National Gallery of Victoria's art school from 1872 to 1886 and was drawing master there from 1886 to 1917. No other Melbourne artist was better known than he during his lifetime. Working together with Tom Roberts, Arthur Streeton and Charles Conder, between 1885 and 1890, McCubbin was part of the legendary group, the Australian Impressionists. He made his name with his national naturalist images of Australian bush life such as *Down on his luck* 1889 (AGWA), but painted his most brilliant works in his last years, from 1907 to 1917, sparkling impressions filled with light and colour.

This work, painted at the age of 53, is one of at least six self-portraits. It is among the most intimate and searching. McCubbin adopted a spare composition and created an image that is convincing in its subtle modelling of the head. He applied his paint thinly, building up the flesh tones carefully, especially on the left side of the face.

McCubbin may well have based this head-and-shoulders portrait on Rembrandt's *Self-portrait at the age of 34* 1640—which he could have viewed in detail in the National Gallery, London in 1907—in which Rembrandt depicted himself in a similar self-assured pose, looking directly out of the picture. As in the master's painting, the eyes and the mouth in McCubbin's self-portrait are keenly alive and reveal something of the artist's mind and soul.

Anne Gray

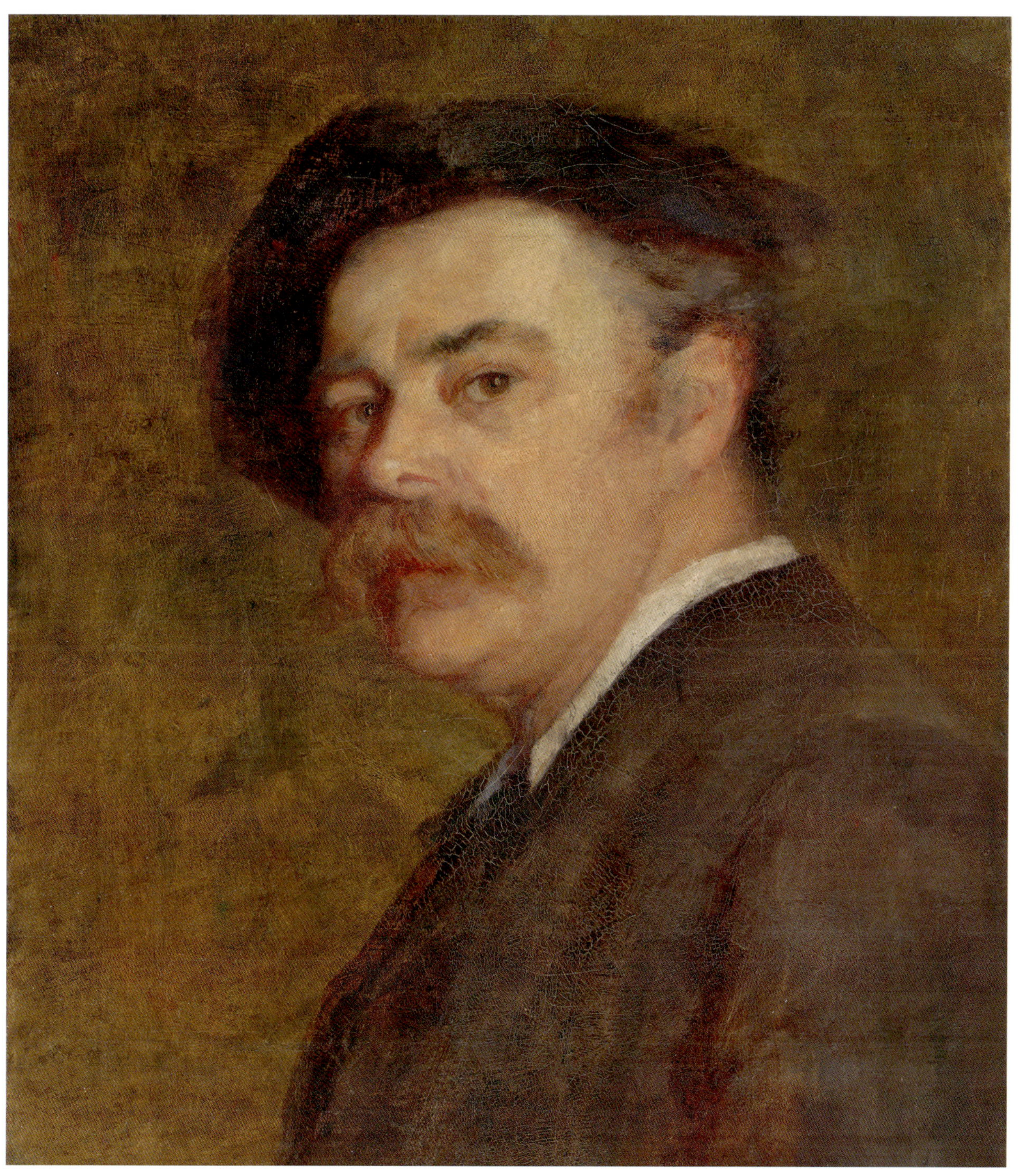

16 **Tom Roberts** (1856–1931)

Madame Hartl c 1909

painted in London, England
frame carved by Lillie Williamson, the artist's wife
oil on canvas, 114.5 x 76.4 cm
National Gallery of Australia, Canberra, purchased 1969

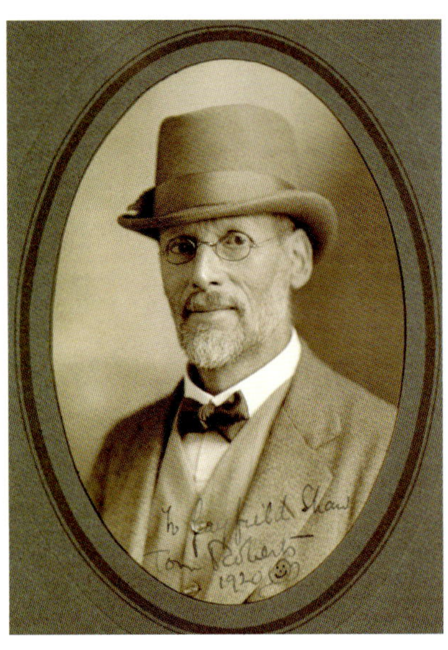

Alice Mills
Tom Roberts 1920
National Portrait Gallery, Canberra, gift of Gerard Vaughan 2001 donated through the Australian Governments Cultural Gifts Program

With no knowledge of the subject, one could assume that *Madame Hartl* is the portrait of an opera singer caught backstage before or after a performance. This is not the case. It is a staged portrait of Madame Ruby Hartl as she had appeared in fancy dress at the Chelsea Arts Club Annual Costume Ball at the Royal Opera House in Covent Garden on 18 February 1909. Roberts and his wife had also attended, with other artist friends. During the Edwardian period many artists and socialites were drawn to such spectacle and it is not surprising that Roberts asked Madame Hartl to pose for him in her costume as 'La Tornabuoni', the oft-painted wife of the fifteenth-century Florentine arts patron Giovanni Tornabuoni.

In this re-enactment, Madame Hartl appears much more casual than one imagines she would have been at the ball. The portrait has a soft, sleepy quality, as if she has just arisen or is going to bed in her night attire (albeit very glamorous). The creamy fullness of her exposed skin, verging on titillation, reveals an intimacy with the subject.

Roberts's treatment of Madame Hartl's strange, partly concealed hand is at odds with her softness and doleful expression. She looks away from the painter and the viewer as if about to turn and leave; or perhaps something else has caught her attention.

There is another possible explanation for Roberts's posing of the figure in this work. He may have been aware of the famous portraits of Giovanna Tornabuoni by Domenico Ghirlandaio, one of which shows a beautiful young woman clothed in gold-braided fabric of soft pink, her head turned slightly from the viewer; and another where the subject is shown in full profile and wearing a gown richly embroidered in autumnal colours.[19] Roberts's portrait seems to be a fusion of the two. The composition also has references to 'the grand manner of Velasquez', whose paintings Roberts had studied closely in the National Gallery in London.[20]

Roberts painted *Madame Hartl* during his second extended stay in England and Europe from 1901 to 1923. It is an assured work and was shown at the Royal Academy in 1910 in this frame carved by Lillie Williamson, the artist's wife.

Julie Donaldson

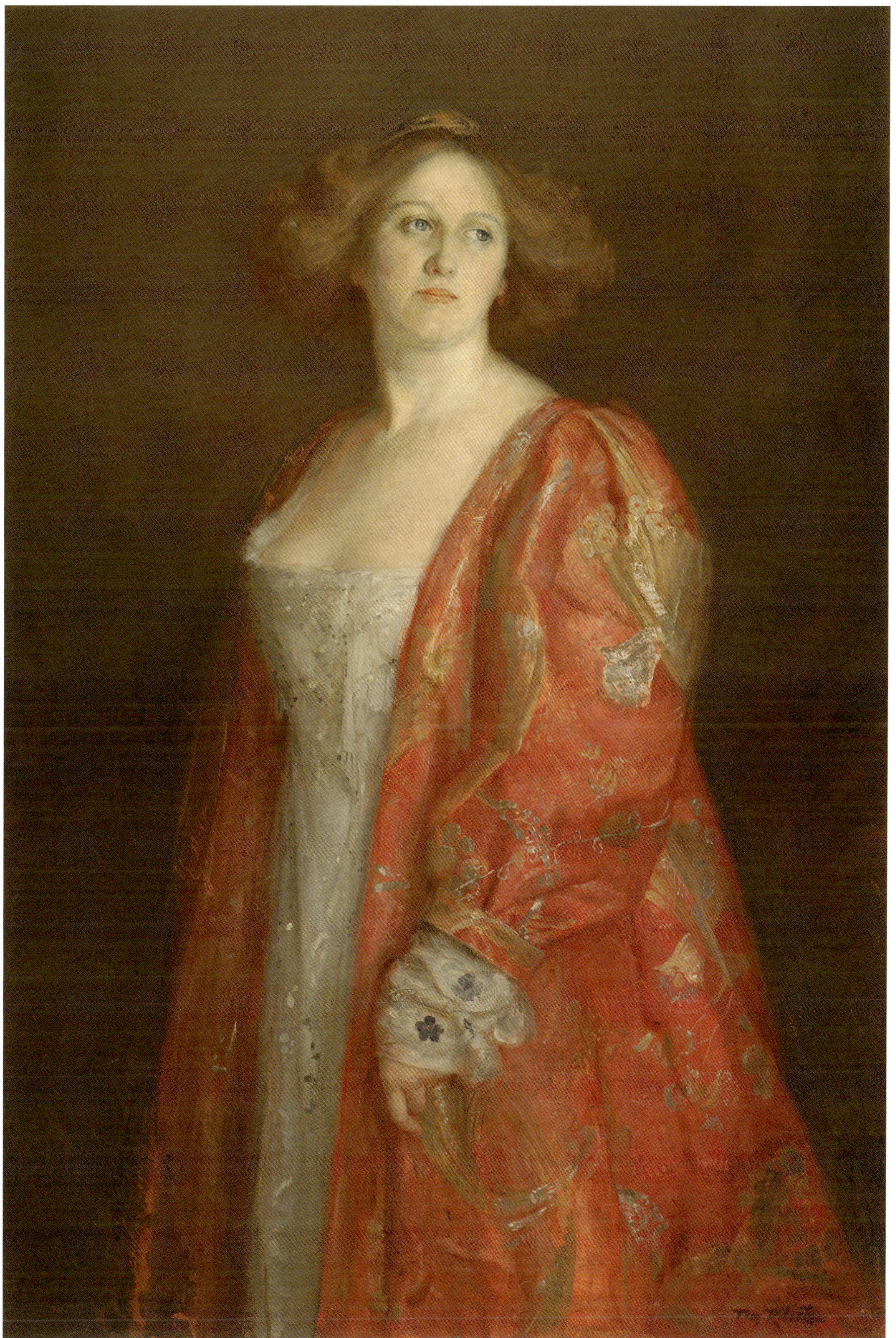

17 Charles Wheeler (1880–1977)

After the ball (Après le bal) 1910

painted in Melbourne, Victoria
oil on canvas, 43.4 x 43.7 cm
National Gallery of Australia, Canberra, purchased 1976

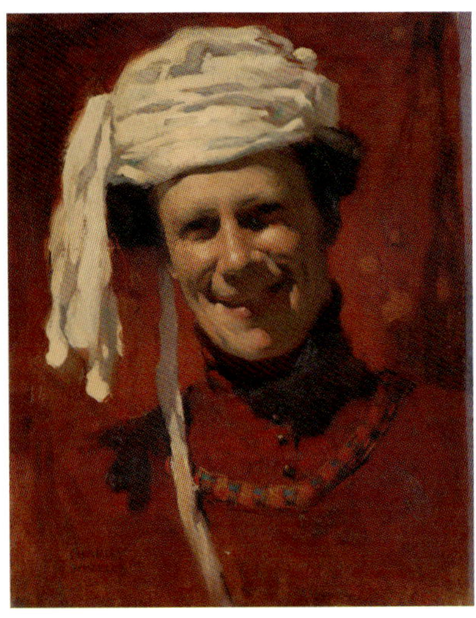

Charles Wheeler
Before the ball (Avant le bal) 1910
oil on canvas, 43.7 x 34.6 cm
National Gallery of Australia, Canberra, purchased 1976

After the ball by Charles Wheeler is a self-portrait of the artist at thirty years of age. The painting is one of a pair. Its brother painting, *Before the ball* 1910, is more what one might expect from a portrait. It is the face of a handsome young man. He is smiling, as though he were checking his costume in the mirror or posing for a picture before a fancy dress party.

'[N]o matter how fine as a painting', Wheeler once said of portraiture, 'if it is a bad likeness it is a bad portrait, as I understand that term.'[21] In *After the ball*, Wheeler flaunts his abilities as a painter, creating an accomplished likeness of his own face contorted in an exaggerated yawn.

Wheeler was born in Dunedin, New Zealand in 1880. He began his artistic career as an apprentice lithographer, with further studies at the Working Men's College and the National Gallery School in Melbourne. When war broke out in 1914, Wheeler was already in Europe studying painting. He enlisted and ceased artwork until the war ended.

One of Wheeler's great champions was art critic J S MacDonald, who wrote:

> His canvases give one the impression that, once decided on, he never doubted in his mind as to what their eventual appearance would be, and, that point settled, straightway set himself to embody it in a way that should technically be, as far as he could ensure it, immune from criticism.[22]

Wheeler's paintings, however, were often criticised for their loyalty to nature, the very quality which others so admired in his work. He has been called old-fashioned, conservative, a traditionalist, and was accused of 'passionless naturalism' by some art critics. Well into his eighties and still painting in his Melbourne studio every day, Wheeler remarked: 'I may be old-fashioned, but I feel there is more to painting than an ability to shriek louder and longer than the next man.'[23]

Melanie Beggs-Murray

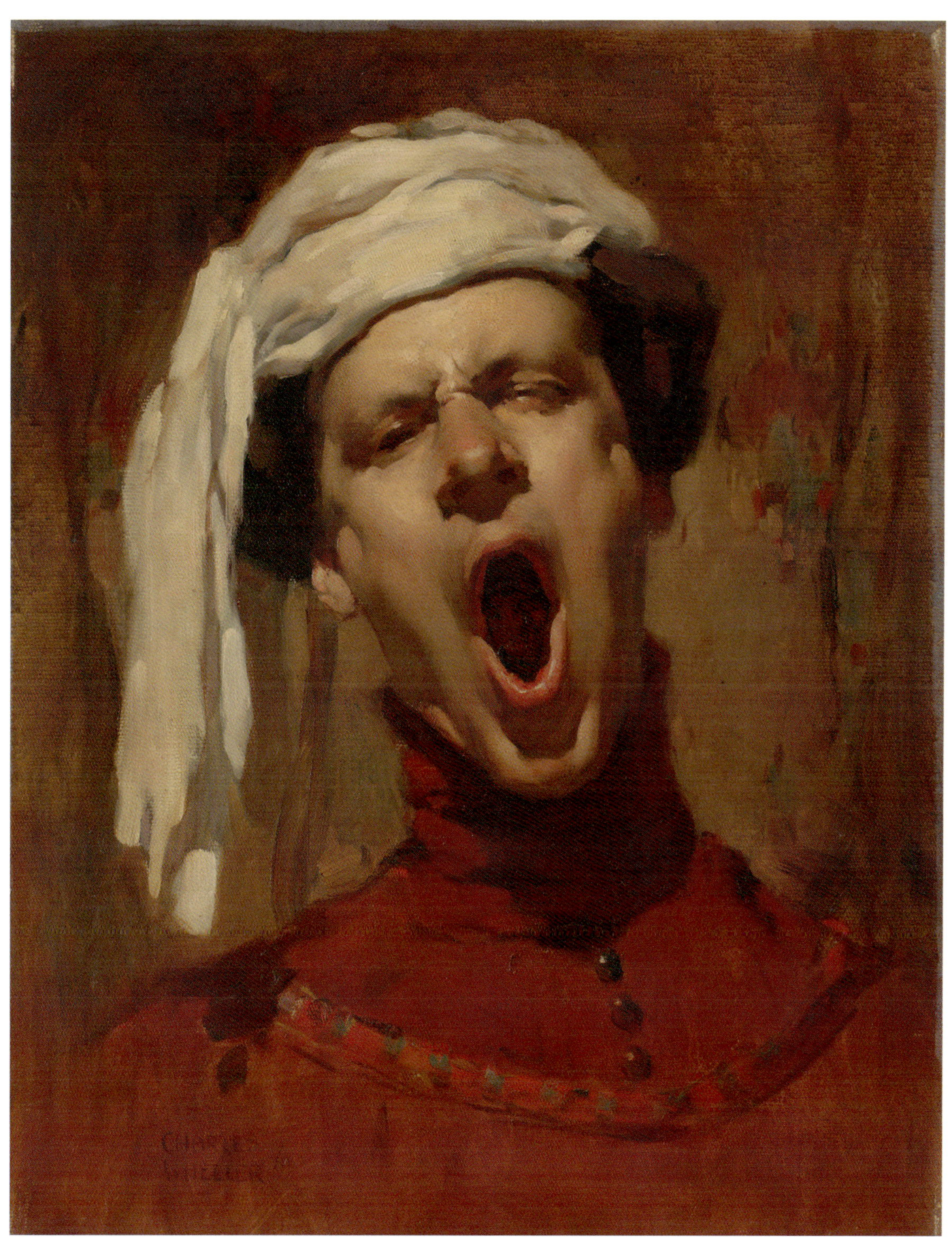

18 **Violet Teague** (1872–1951)

The boy with the palette 1911

painted in Melbourne, Victoria
oil on canvas, 175.5 x 108.5 cm
National Gallery of Australia, Canberra, gift of US Teague 1976

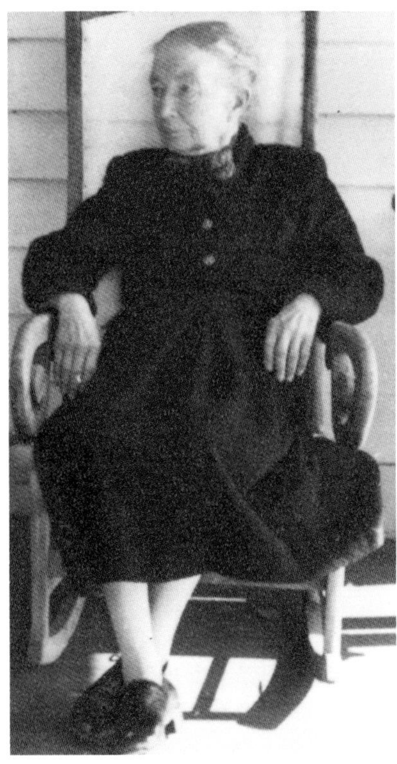

Violet Teague, c 1940s
State Library of Victoria, Melbourne

'The boy artist works with the same facility in oil, water, black and white, and the etching needle, the latter, if anything, showing his artistic powers at their best'.[24] So Theo Scharf (1899–1907), the child prodigy, was described in 1914. He was the son of a prominent Melbourne family, and often painted with Violet Teague. In 1914, he migrated to Munich to further his training, where he became a painter, printmaker and illustrator. In the early 1920s, he produced his best-remembered work, *Night in a city*, a portfolio of twenty etchings—a satirical account of a typical European city between early evening to dawn, revealing the dark underside of society.

In *The boy with the palette*, Teague portrayed the artist as a twelve-year-old young man. By depicting him with an assertive gaze and studied stance, using a bold composition, she showed him as conscious of his talent and confident of his future.

Teague was one of a group of financially independent middle-class Edwardian women who never married and devoted their lives to art. She began her art studies in Brussels and England and continued them in Melbourne. Her art was a blend of the traditional and the modern. Likewise, her life was a compromise between the somewhat daring existence of a serious female artist and the conservative existence of a dutiful daughter who interrupted her career to look after her ailing father. She was described in 1949, just before her death, as being: 'a small frail person … quiet of manner, yet with a surprising vitality and a more surprising sense of whimsy' she was direct 'in a mannered way and her eyes twinkle humorously'. She could talk on any subject 'from racehorses to the decline of Western Culture exactly and wittily'.[25]

The boy with the palette is only partly about Scharf and his prodigious talent; it is also a splendid painting of forms and colours, a melody in black, brown and gold. Teague's inspiration was a trio of artists who were much admired by the Edwardians: Velasquez, Whistler and Manet. She took from them the dramatic composition, with the crisply contoured, sinuous figure of the boy placed against the thinly painted background. To this extent, *The boy with the palette* is an aesthetic object first and a character study second.

Anne Gray

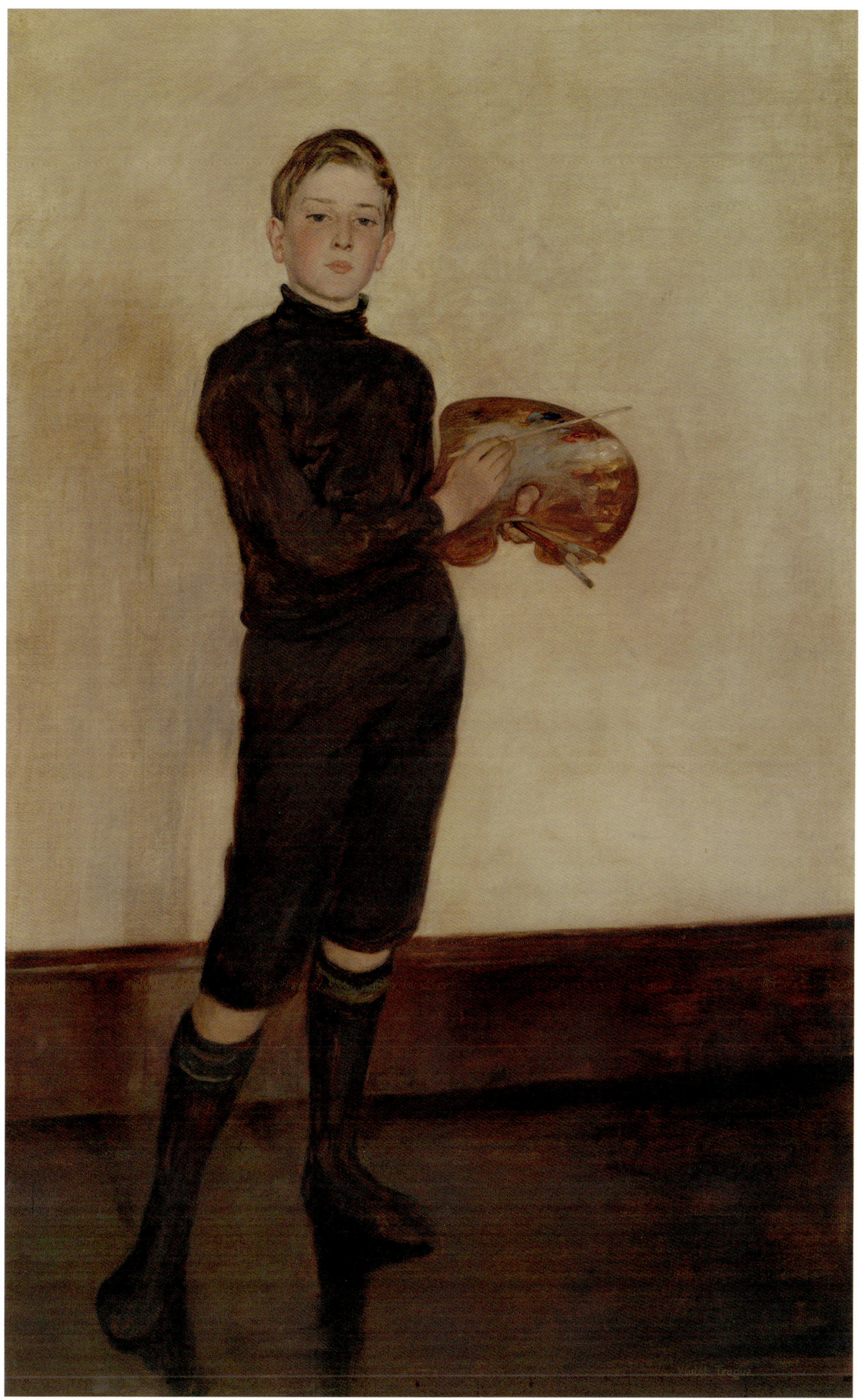

19 George W Lambert (1873–1930)

Chesham Street 1910

painted in London, England
oil on canvas, 62 x 51.5 cm
National Gallery of Australia, Canberra, purchased 1993

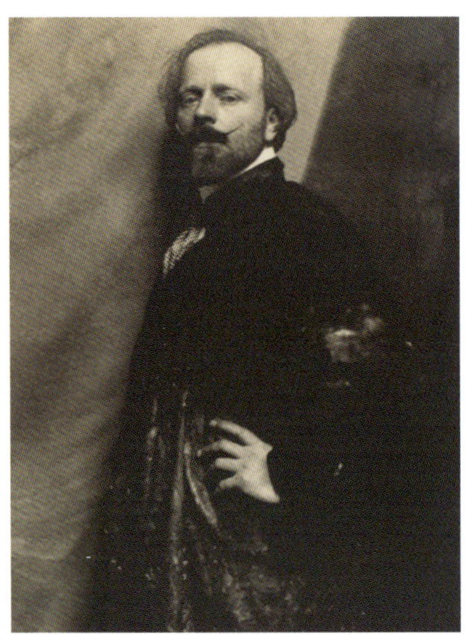

Lambert in London, 1911

George W Lambert liked to entertain, to have fun and to be the centre of attention. He once made his exit by cartwheeling across the centre of a room in a flowing cape. He enjoyed dressing up and acting out roles, and remarked that 'artificiality is the quality which makes man the master of the world'.[26]

In *Chesham Street* Lambert certainly showed off. It is a bravura work in which the artist displayed his considerable ability in depicting naked flesh. He also presented the physical prowess of his bare torso; taut and tense and gleaming in the light. He showed himself with head held high, lips closed and looking down on the viewer. Or did he?

It has been said that Lambert's model, Williams, posed for the nude figure.[27] But the features of the face resemble those of Lambert; so it may be that Williams posed for the kneeling man to the right and not the central figure. Or did Williams pose for the torso and Lambert place his own head on it? That would be a clever conceit. We will never quite know. Certainly, the central figure was intended as a self-portrait, whether Lambert used a model or not.

In 1910 Lambert was working in London, at the height of his powers, and receiving good notices in the press. A British critic linked Lambert's work to that of the successful artists Augustus John and William Orpen, 'painters of real strength, originality, and occasional charm'.[28]

Chesham Street has been read narratively as a scene in a consulting room in Chesham Street, London with a doctor examining the heart or lungs of his patient. This, however, is not the subject of the painting but the excuse for the composition; dramatically, it is about the psychological intrusiveness of such a physical examination. In 1901, Freud published his *Psychopathology of everyday life* and, during the decade, his ideas about exploring the psyche gained wider understanding. This painting appears to be a metaphor: this man seems to have nothing to hide, to be literally and metaphorically bearing his chest, exposing his heart and soul to the world in an outrageous fashion. And yet, as we have seen, it is also an artifice—Lambert may merely have pretended to display his body. Moreover, the drama of the body draws attention away from the face, and the identity and psyche of the subject.

Anne Gray

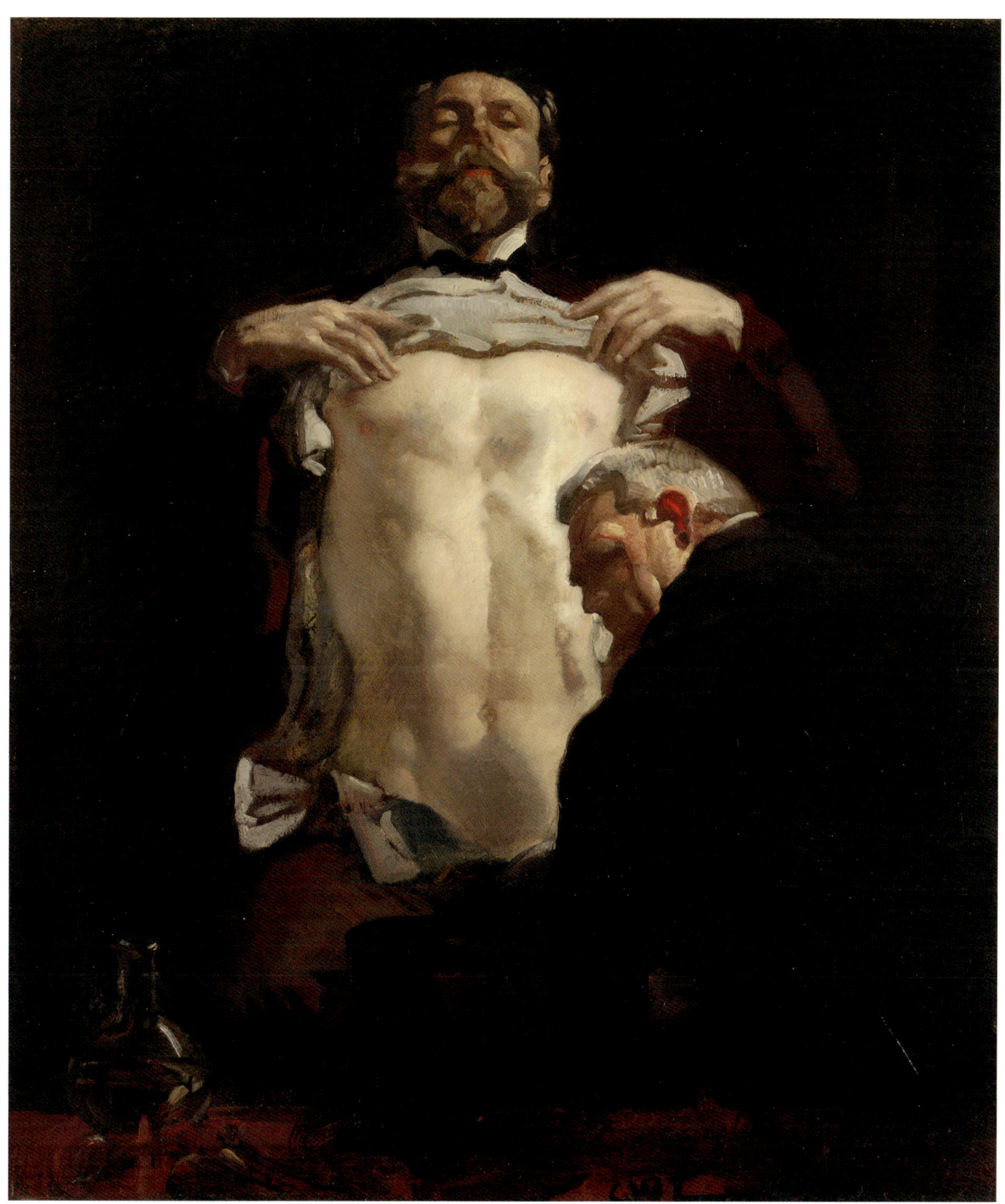

20 **E Phillips Fox** (1865–1915)
The green parasol c 1912

painted in Paris, France
oil on canvas, 117 x 89.5 cm
National Gallery of Australia, Canberra, purchased 1946

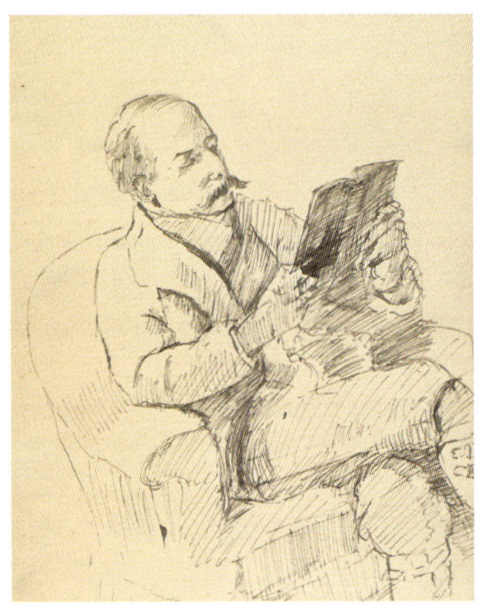

E Phillips Fox
Self-portrait from a sketchbook 1905
pencil, 35 x 26.5 cm
National Gallery of Victoria, Melbourne
presented by the Executors of the Estate of Mrs Phillips Fox, 1952

The green parasol, depicting friend and sometime student Edith Anderson, was painted in the idyllic surroundings of the Fox's home at 65 Boulevard Arago, Paris. Painted in the afternoon sunlight, the work emanates the warmth and glow of a relaxing summer's day in the garden. The painting reveals Fox's ability to create dappled and diffused light across the scene and demonstrates his position as one of Australia's Impressionists.

The pure, vibrant and juxtaposing colour and raw, unpainted patches crossing the canvas create both movement and quiet within the painting. The stirring of leaves and petals is sensed in the mass of trees and flowers; Edith's movement as she settles herself and her dog while holding her parasol in place brings a certain tension. But her face, seen in half-profile, is peaceful and untroubled. Edith looks fondly at her pet and is relaxed in the company of the painter. This is life in Edwardian Paris and an intimate moment revealing the friendship between sitter and artist.

The green parasol is also an example of Fox's desire to blur portrait and subject painting; to make a picture rather than paint a portrait.[29] Edith and the garden appear to become one. The green chiffon of Edith's dress melts into the surroundings while the middle- and background collapse, drawing us towards her as the central focus. We enter her calming space. Yet the garden, its movement and light, remain vividly present.

Edith Anderson (1880–1961) and her future husband, Penleigh Boyd, were close friends of the artist. Originally a painter from Brisbane, Edith studied in London and had been living in Paris for some time. Fox first asked her to model for *The green parasol* as well as a number of other paintings because he was attracted by her rich auburn hair and grey-green eyes—both fashionable at the time.[30]

Life in Paris for E Phillips Fox allowed him to paint as he wished. After his marriage to Ethel Carrick he was no longer reliant on commissions to support his career, as had been the case in London. Success in Paris was confirmed by his membership of the Société Nationale de Beaux Arts (1910) and the International Society of Painters, Sculptors and Gravers (1912).

The green parasol was the first portrait to be acquired for the national collection, purchased by the Commonwealth Art Advisory Board in 1946.

Georgia Connolly

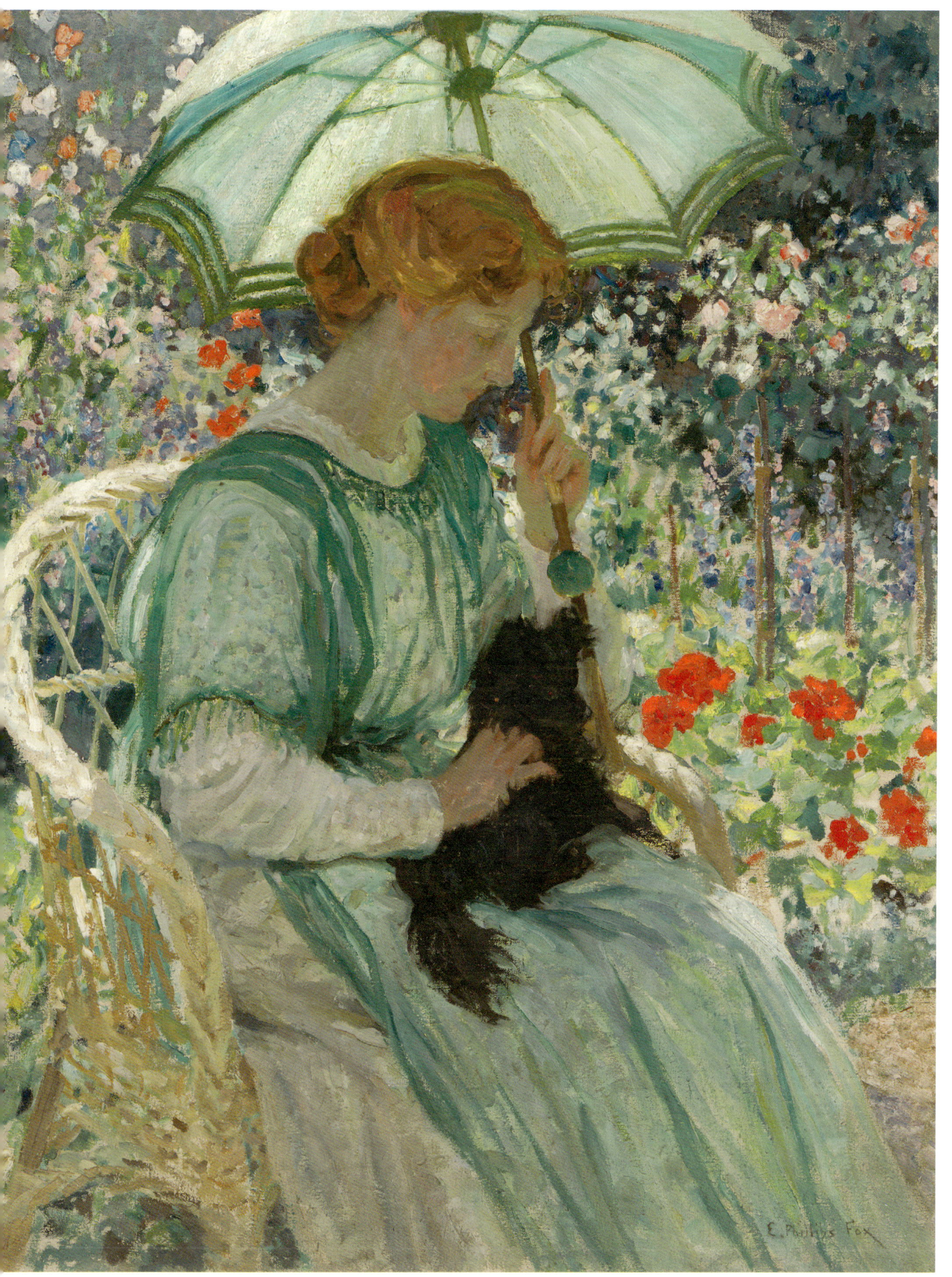
E. Phillips Fox

21 **Grace Cossington Smith** (1892–1984)

Study of a head: self-portrait 1916

painted in Sydney, New South Wales
oil on canvas, 26 x 21 cm
National Gallery of Australia, Canberra, purchased 2010

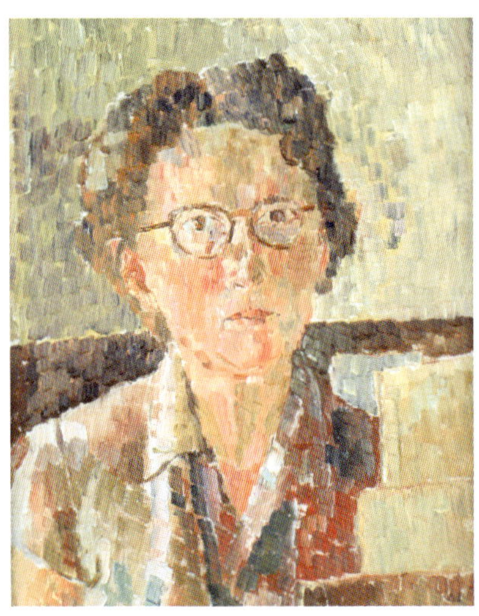

Grace Cossington Smith
Self-portrait 1948
oil on cardboard, 39.5 x 30.5 cm
National Portrait Gallery, Canberra

Art is about … expressing things unseen—the golden thread running through time.[31]

Grace Cossington Smith's jewel-like self-portrait shines with an external and inner luminosity. Painted while she was a student with Anthony Dattilo-Rubbo, the high-key palette of pinks, blues and greens and animated brushstrokes reveal the influence of British Post-Impressionists like Harold Gilman and Spencer Gore. It is possible that Cossington Smith had seen works by these artists while she was living in England between 1912 and 1914. Dattilo-Rubbo's classes and the Post-Impressionist images he showed them had certainly inspired her. Norah Simpson, a fellow student who studied in London, also brought reproductions back to the classes. Cossington Smith recalled Simpson saying that the students needed to attain an effect of light and colour, like 'crushed diamonds'.[32]

Vibrant colour began to feature early in Cossington Smith's art. When she returned to Australia in 1914, she was delighted to find that her father had built her a light-filled studio in the garden of their Turramurra home on Sydney's North Shore. It was a vote of confidence in her potential as an artist. It was a space of her own—a space to freely experiment. As the title *Study of a head: self-portrait* suggests, the work was a way of applying lessons taught at art school. More significantly it is a self-portrait of a dedicated, thoughtful, passionate young artist pushing the boundaries of convention.

Cossington Smith, Roland Wakelin and Roy de Maistre became known as Australia's first Post-Impressionists, praised and reviled in the 1920s for their inventive modern works. Cossington Smith's ravishing paintings of radiant flowers, trees, gardens and still-life subjects during this decade, along with her daring depictions of the Sydney Harbour Bridge under construction, are now widely recognised as among the most significant modernist works in Australia. Later in life she became well known for paintings of interiors of her Turramurra home, filled with mosaic-like touches of shimmering colour, like 'compressed sunlight'.[33]

The scene had been set from her student days. Around the time she painted her early self-portrait, Datillo-Rubbo said: 'I can't understand why you've kept off painting for so long, because you have such a wonderful colour sense.'[34] One might imagine her fired up by these comments when she painted her poignant, luminous self-portrait, gazing into the distance; a burgeoning artist on the threshold of her dream.

Deborah Hart

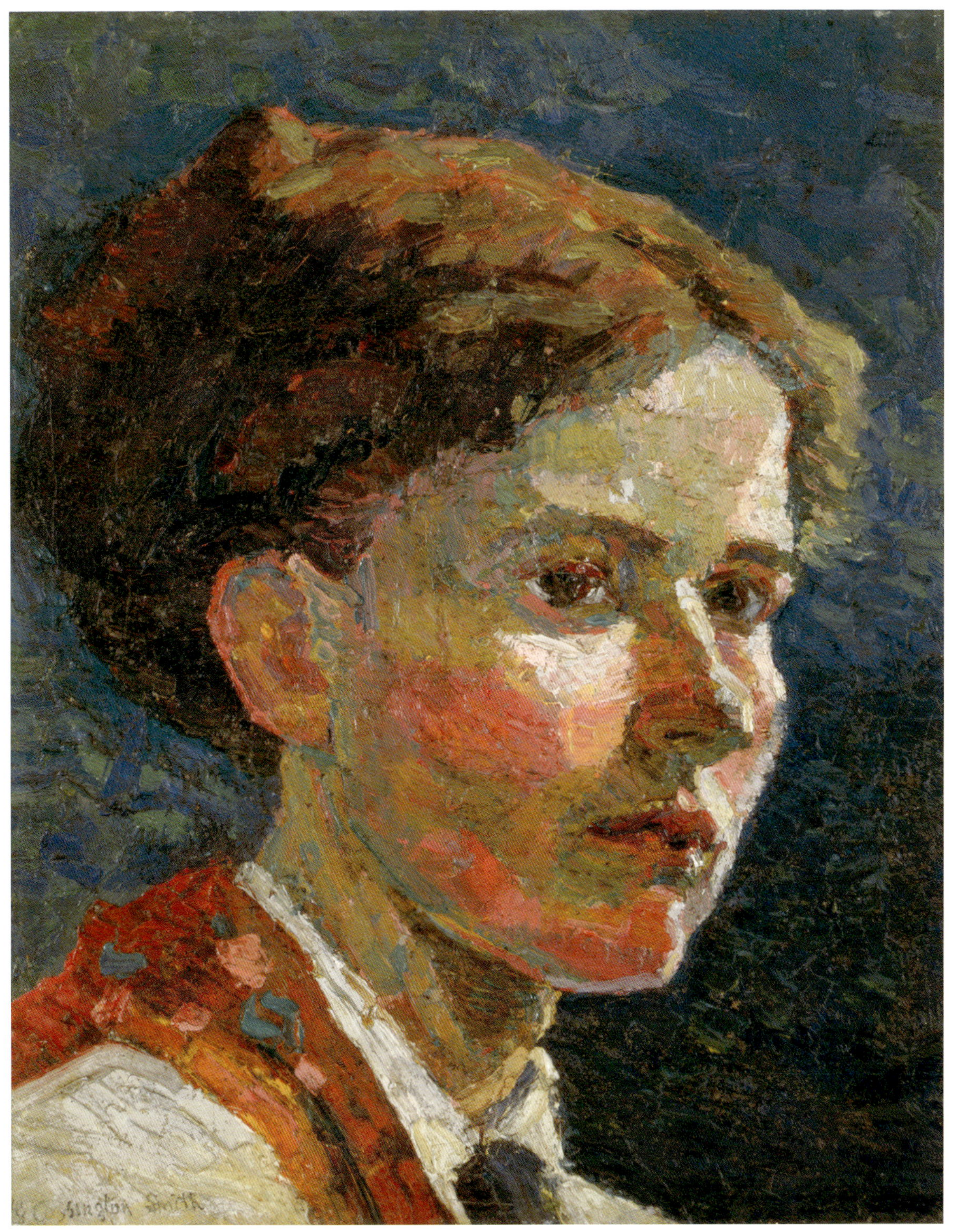

22 **Max Meldrum** (1875–1955)

Poland (Madame de Tarczynska) 1917

painted in Melbourne, Victoria
oil on canvas mounted on composition board,
154.4 x 89.2 cm
National Gallery of Australia, Canberra, purchased 1980

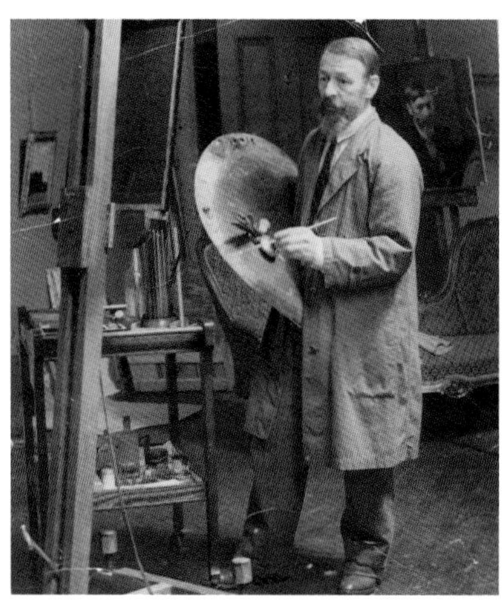

Percy Spiden
Max Meldrum in his studio c 1952
State Library of Victoria, Melbourne

Jadwiga de Tarczynska (neé Kilbach) arrived in Australia in 1912, on holiday with her close friend, concert violinist Stanislaw de Tarczynski. Jadwiga and Stanislaw married in Melbourne in early 1913. The outbreak of the war prevented their return to Europe and reluctantly they exchanged their tourist visas to become immigrants.

The young couple quickly emerged as active members of the Melbourne arts and cultural community; Stanislaw performed in Melbourne theatres, Jadwiga took up language teaching, and their grand Mont Albert residence became a cultural hub.

In *Poland (Madame de Tarczynska)*, Jadwiga is depicted in a costume from the Kraków region, its embroidered lace-up vest, long colourful ribbons, lace apron and cap later becoming the most recognised of all historical Polish costumes. She was dressed for one of many Polish Day celebrations the couple hosted at their home when Max Meldrum caught a glimpse of her. They had formed a close friendship with the outspoken Scottish-born artist, who was inspired to capture the vibrancy of her attire. Meldrum noted at the time that the portrait would have to be a sprint, an impression filled with nervous energy, as the ribbons might move at a second sitting.[35]

The human subject for Meldrum was less important than the act of painting. His broad, energetically applied brushstrokes quickly captured the light and shade of his subject, yet he paid minimal attention to facial expression. He produced a lively image with pure bright colours, contrary to his characteristically muted tonal palette, hoping it might silence criticism of his works as unfashionable and gloomy.

Meldrum came to Australia with his family in 1889, settling in Melbourne. After a long period of study and residence in Europe (1900–13) he returned to Australia, imbued with passion and ideas. He developed a theory of painting claiming it was a pure science of optical analysis. He believed tone (contrasting light and dark) to be the most important component of painting, and that it would provide the ultimate truth in representing nature. His Melbourne school of painting, established in 1917, soon proved popular but Meldrum attracted controversy throughout his career.

Madame de Tarczynska never owned the portrait. After being exhibited in Melbourne in 1922, the painting was displayed in the Meldrum family home until its acquisition by the National Gallery of Australia in 1980.

Miriam Kelly

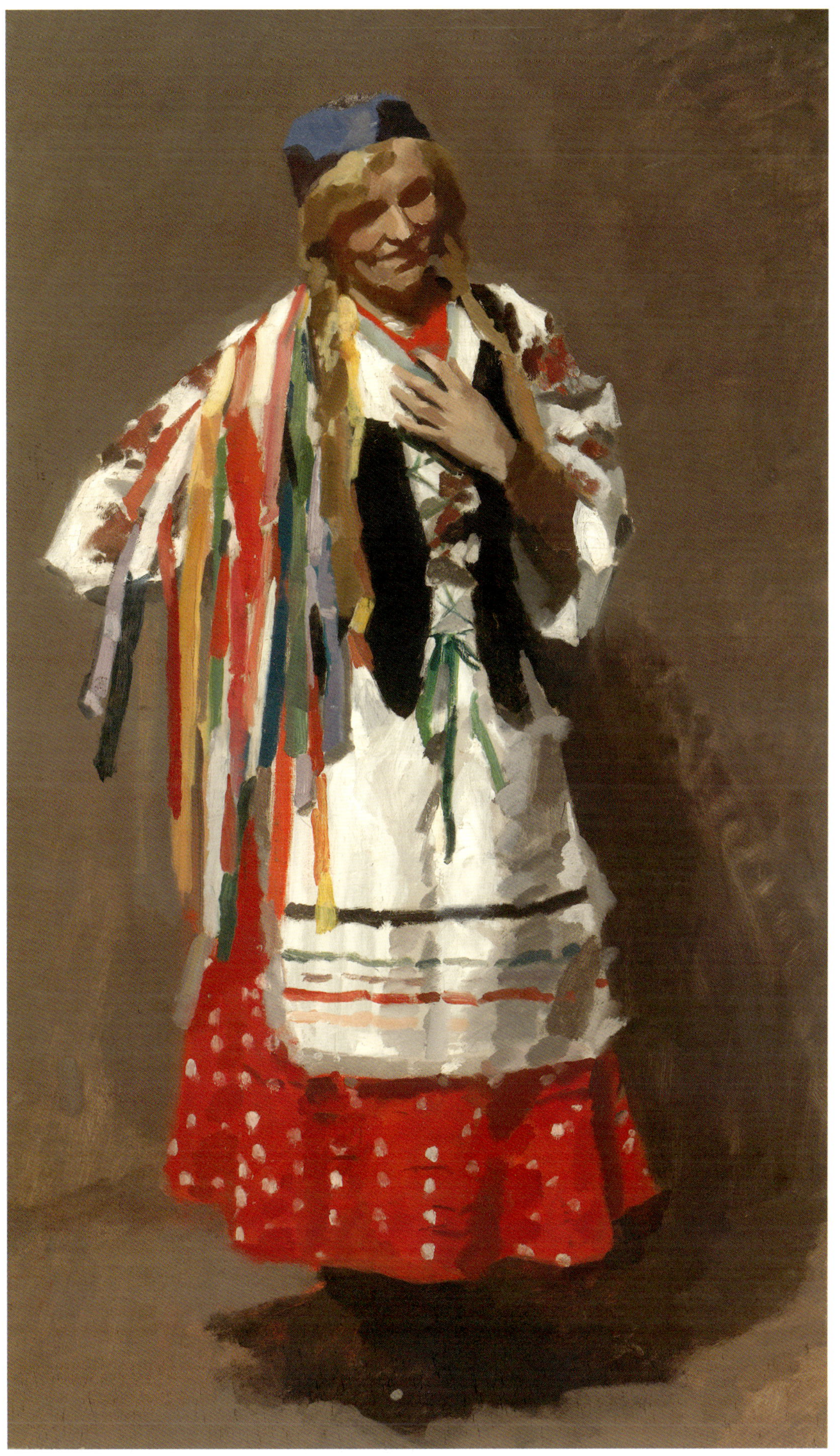

23 **Rupert Bunny** (1864–1947)

Woman in a brown hat
(Femme au chapeau brun) c 1917

painted in France
oil on canvas, 70.3 x 54.2 cm
National Gallery of Australia, Canberra, purchased 1976

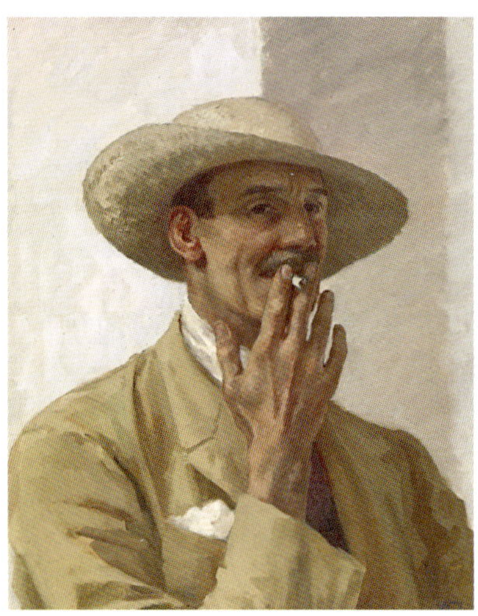

Rupert Bunny
Self-portrait c 1920
oil on canvas, 62.8 x 47.4 cm
National Gallery of Victoria, Melbourne, Felton Bequest, 1927

A woman in a brown straw hat is looking at you. Framed beneath the wide brim her gaze is steady yet imperturbable; the warmth of the day belied by a faint flush on her cheeks and chin. She is Jeanne Heloise Morel, wife and muse of the artist Rupert Bunny.

Jeanne had met Bunny over twenty years earlier at art school in Paris where she painted and modelled. Noted for her French beauty, she became his favourite sitter and they married in 1902. In his earlier paintings, Bunny often depicted her in romantic surroundings, wearing elaborate dresses and with her hair pinned up with flowers and ribbons. However, in this postwar portrait the carefree girl of *la belle époque* is now a middle-aged woman whose hair is contained under a practical sunhat. The impersonal title and domestic setting suggests that this painting was perhaps a formal exercise exploring the interplay between colour and pattern. Bunny echoes the blue-green of Jeanne's eyes in her looped beads and floral kimono-style jacket. The fabrics are thinly painted with deft brushstrokes, the canvas showing through in the cut-lace blouse at her throat. These textures evoke the smoothness of Jeanne's pale skin, painted in creamy opaque tones, with pale green highlights across her brow. She rests her arms on an embroidered tablecloth, while behind her is the shimmer of a woven grass wall.

Bunny painted an almost identical version of this portrait titled *In a summer house: portrait of the artist's wife* c 1917 (NRAG). While the composition shows a wider view of the domestic setting, it also includes more detail such as a white cuff at Jeanne's wrist and a patterned hatband.

Born in St Kilda, Melbourne in 1864, Rupert Bunny began studying civil engineering and then architecture before enrolling in 1881 at the National Gallery School. He sailed for Europe in 1884 where he continued his art studies in London and Paris. Over the next fifty years, Bunny established his career in France as a painter of elegant portraits and large-scale allegorical compositions drawn from myths and literature. Jeanne modelled for many of his paintings until she suffered a stroke in 1929. She died in April 1933 whilst Bunny was briefly painting and teaching in Melbourne; he returned permanently to Australia later that year.

Sarina Noordhuis-Fairfax

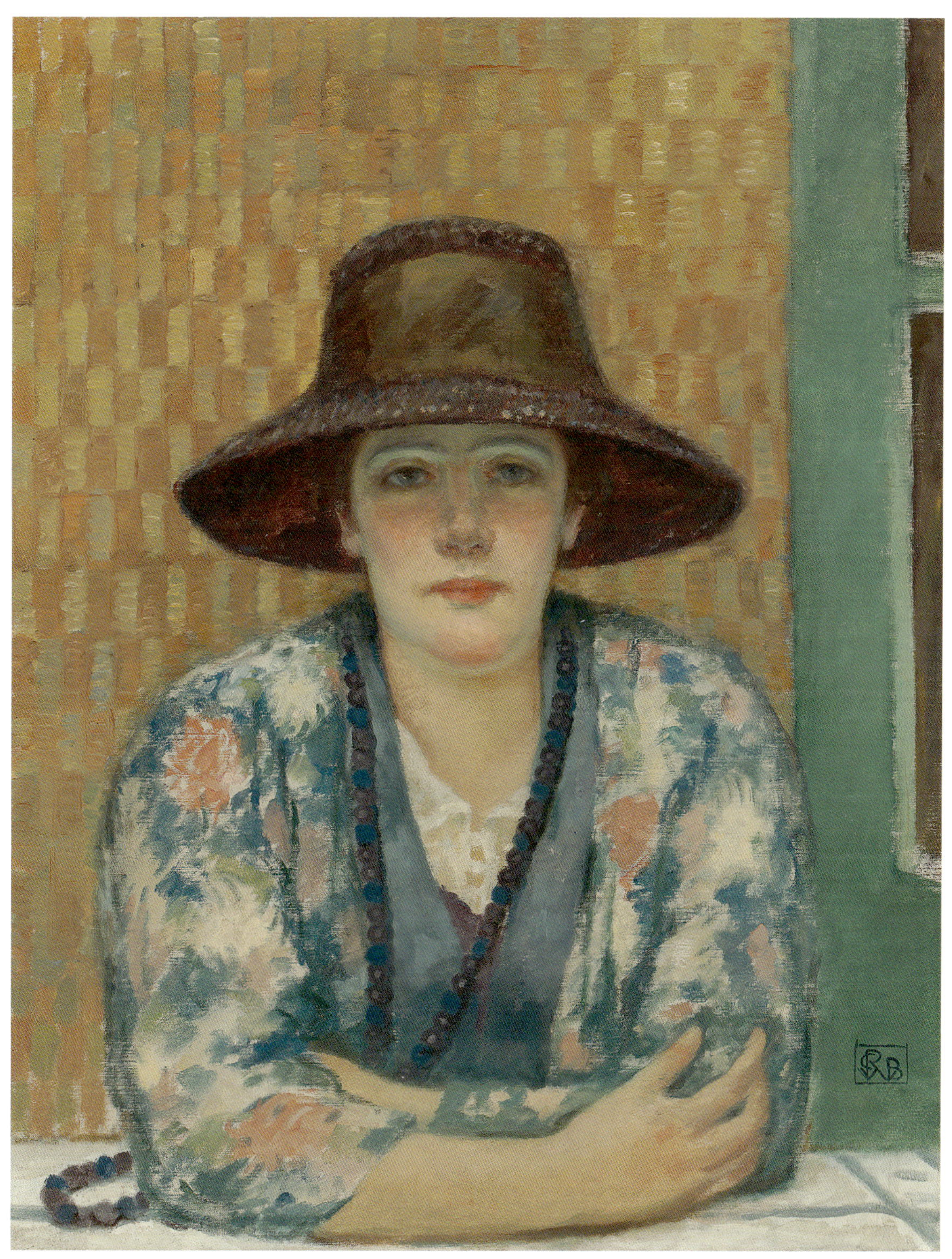

24 **George W Lambert** (1873–1930)
Weighing the fleece 1921

painted at Wanganella Estate, in Deniliquin, New South Wales
oil on canvas, 71.7 x 92.2 cm
National Gallery of Australia, Canberra, purchased 1966

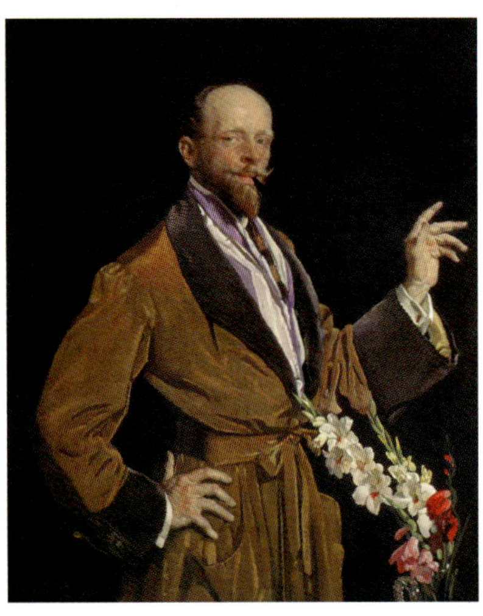

George W Lambert
Self-portrait with gladioli 1922
oil on canvas, 128.2 x 102.8 cm
National Portrait Gallery, Canberra
gift of John Schaeffer AO 2003, donated through the Australian Government's Cultural Gifts Program

'A masterpiece of small portrait grouping in a woolshed … a painting I've had in my mind for 25 years.'[36] So George W Lambert described his painting *Weighing the fleece*, one of the first major works that he painted after his return to Australia in 1921. He had arrived back with great acclaim after a successful career in London. And he wanted to paint images of Australia that would be 'for all times a record of bush life by one who really knows'.[37] Lambert painted the portraits of the successful grazier, Mr Leigh Sadleir Falkiner and his wife Beatrice, located in a brick-walled woolshed on the Falkiner's property, Wanganella Estate, near Deniliquin in the Riverina district of New South Wales. He emphasised their good fortune as woolgrowers by portraying them looking at an impressive record-priced fleece in the centre of the composition. He also included two further portraits, that of Falkiner's nephew, John Robert Carse, weighing the fleece, and their bookkeeper, Philip Darbyshire, holding a notebook in his hand. And Lambert might also be said to have painted a portrait of the merino rams, both champions.

Falkiner commissioned this work but did not purchase it because he did not like the way Lambert had portrayed himself and his wife.[38] This may have been because Lambert showed the couple as well-tailored observers on the edge of the scene, rather than as the main subjects of the composition. Moreover, Lambert depicted them statically, as if they were a tableau of modern life, figures on a stage set. Certainly, some contemporary Australian critics thought the image to be unemotional and lacking sympathy with the subject. But Lambert intentionally spurned a sentimental response and consciously sought to render his images more durable by focusing on structure and pattern. He was not willing, moreover, to change his portrait to suit those who commissioned it.

Lambert was, indeed, proud of his attention to detail in this painting, including his depiction of the interior of the shed, especially the 'beams and the swallow droppings on the beams, corrugated iron, oil drum, kerosene tin, wool bale, brand on the wool bale'. And this group portrait received acclaim from other contemporary critics who thought it a typical image of Australian life and a national subject.

Anne Gray

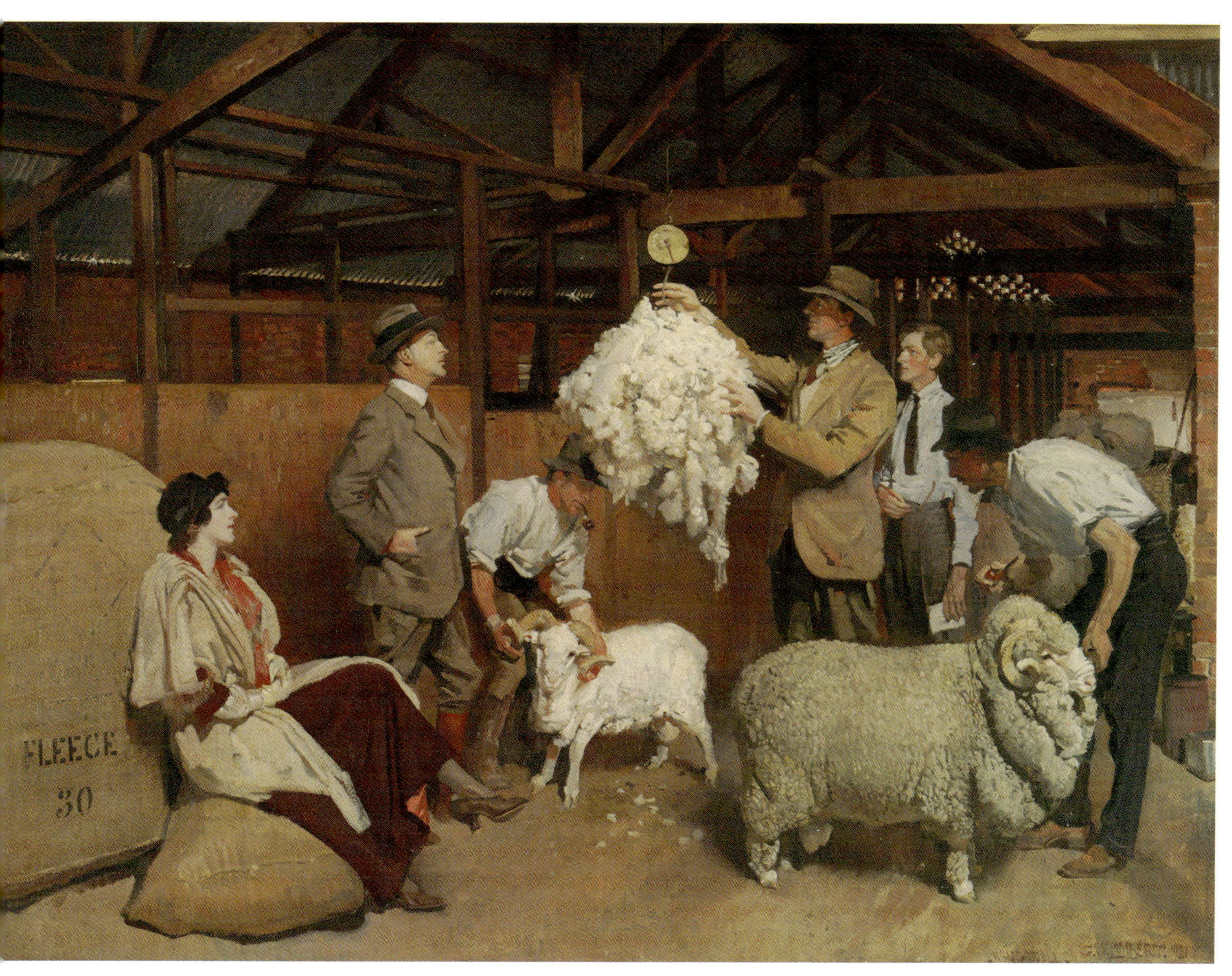
FLEECE
30

25 Margaret Preston (1875–1963)

Flapper 1925

painted in Sydney, New South Wales
oil on canvas, 77.3 x 58.5 cm

National Gallery of Australia, Canberra, purchased with the assistance of the Cooma–Monaro Snowy River Fund 1988

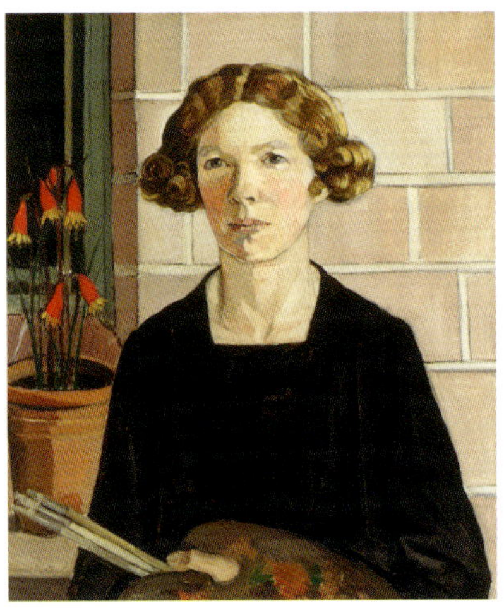

Margaret Preston
Self-portrait 1930
oil on canvas, 61.3 x 51.1 cm
Art Gallery of New South Wales, Sydney, gift of the artist at the request of the Trustees, 1930

Margaret Preston, one of Australia's great modernists, is best known for her portraits of flowers. She painted few portraits of people, noting that she gave it up because people used to 'grumble at their likenesses'.[39] The year before painting *Flapper* she completed a dramatic portrait of uncomplaining banksias with a similarly restricted palette and composition of bold, simplified shapes.

Despite her misgivings about more conventional portraiture, Preston advocated that women should paint good portraits as proof that they think for themselves. When she painted her thoughtful *Self-portrait* 1930 (AGNSW) she was the only woman and only modernist commissioned by the Trustees of the Art Gallery of New South Wales to paint a self-portrait.[40] It was confirmation of her growing reputation in the 1920s and she was thrilled to be asked.

During the first two decades of the twentieth century Preston had travelled and studied in Europe. She was inspired by the Second Post-Impressionist Exhibition organised by Roger Fry in London and by the Japanese print tradition of *ukiyo-e*. In the 1920s she was advocating an Australian ethos and in 1927 an issue of *Art in Australia* was dedicated to her work. By 1928 when she painted her striking *Flapper* she was distilling aspects of what she had learnt and pushing herself further.

The model for *Flapper* was Myra, Preston's maid. She looks out directly as if posing for the camera. At the time she would, of course, have been looking at Preston: face to face, artist and subject enmeshed in each other's gaze. It has been noted that Myra is not quite flash enough in her homely attire of woollen dress and knitted tights to be a bohemian flapper of the 1920s.[41] Firmly anchored in the composition, she doesn't appear as a shrinking violet either but rather as a self-possessed young woman.

The artist and sitter had come to know one another well and we might surmise that they discussed what Myra would wear for her sittings. Perhaps she had recently bought the lovely cloche hat, a common item of a flapper's apparel, setting the tone for the painting. The brim of the hat is pulled down to reveal only a glimpse of her up-to-date bobbed haircut, while the jaunty feathers animate the composition. Ultimately, as a painter of modern life, Preston reveals young rosy-cheeked Myra as an aspirational flapper in a thoroughly modern painting.

Deborah Hart

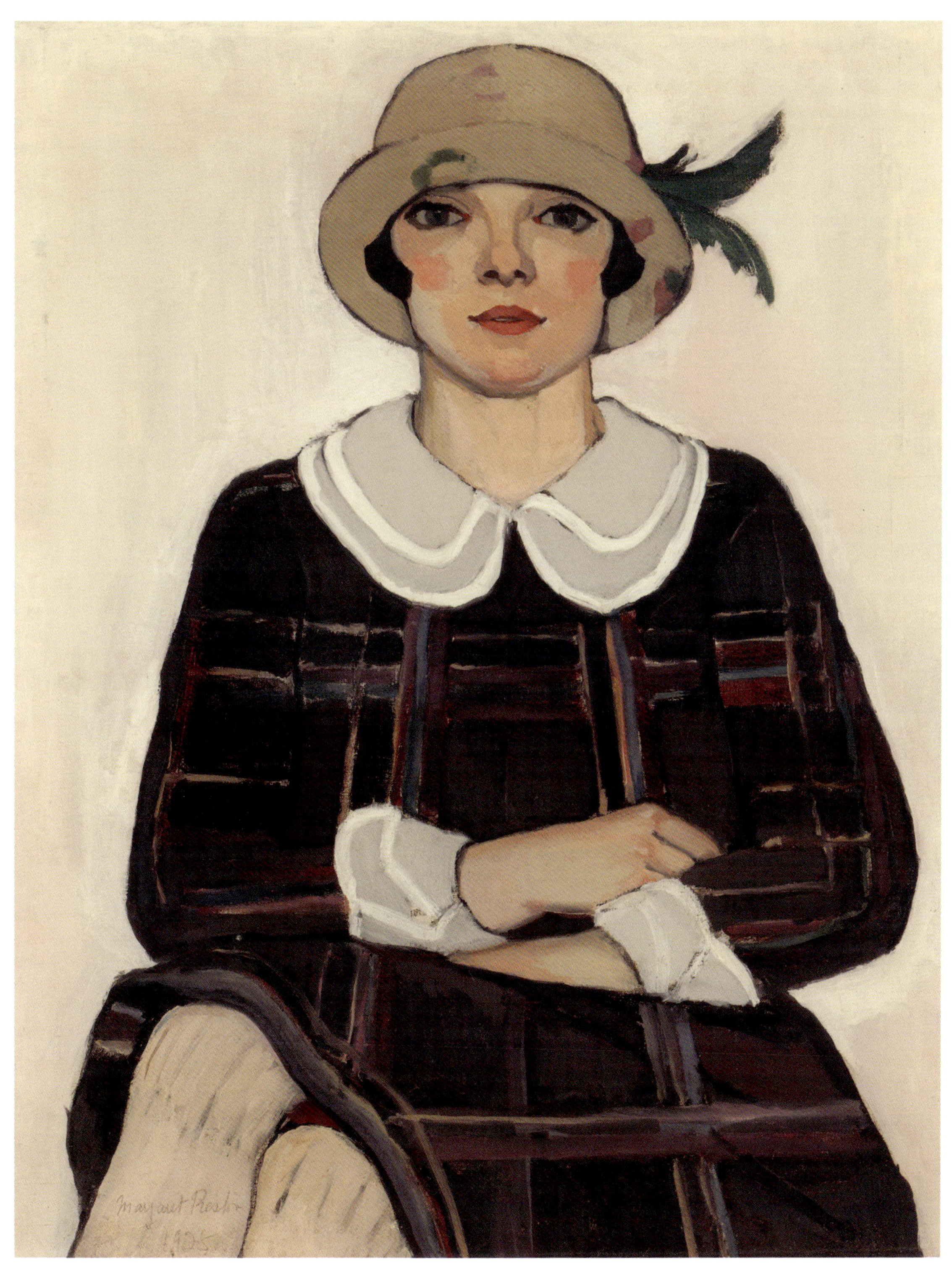
Margaret Preston

26 **Agnes Goodsir** (1864–1939)

The Parisienne c 1924

painted in Paris, France

oil on canvas, 61 x 50.1 cm

National Gallery of Australia, Canberra, purchased 1993

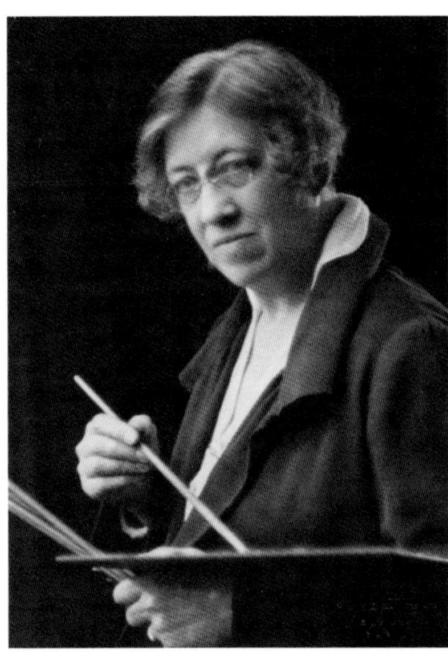

Agnes Goodsir, c 1927

Agnes Goodsir Archive, Bendigo Art Gallery

Paris was the place to be in the 1920s. This was especially true for adventurous artists, writers and performers, who flocked to this 'City of light' in the years following the First World War. Goodsir, an Australian by birth, had come to know Paris well. At the time of painting *The Parisienne* she was living in an apartment at 18 rue l'Odéon in Montparnasse. Sylvia Beach (1887–1962), the renowned American who established the English-language bookshop Shakespeare and Company in Paris and first published James Joyce's *Ulysses*, lived in the same apartment block with her partner Adrienne Monnier (1892–1955). The sitter in *The Parisienne* is another American, Goodsir's close companion Rachel Dunn, nicknamed Cherry. She had divorced and moved to Paris to be with Goodsir. The combination of propriety and a sense of adventure was integral to their lives in Paris, as it is to this gently seductive portrait.

Cherry sat for numerous portraits by Goodsir, although many of them are more conventionally feminine and more domestic in their settings. Here Goodsir captures a sense of Parisian style, combining theatricality with elegant restraint. The sitter is placed against a muted cream background and her garments are simplified in shape and colour, giving strength to the composition. The tonal palette and delicately modulated forms recall Goodsir's early training in contrast with modernist practices at the time. Yet a more subtle feeling of modernity pervades the sitter. Stylishly dressed in a high collared jacket with a contemporary flapper's cloche hat she is casually holding a cigarette (perhaps the brand known as the Parisienne![42]). Smoking was considered a sign of emancipation and the rather masculine style of dress epitomised modernity in the streets, cafes, bars and theatres of the Latin Quarter in the 1920s. The sitter's eyes are in shadow, adding to the sense of mystery, while her lips are bright cherry red. Her hands are relaxed with each bearing the glint of a ring, perhaps indicating past and present lives.

When Goodsir visited Australia on Valentine's Day, 1927, she was hailed as 'a portrait painter of international repute'.[43] Apart from Cherry, Goodsir painted numerous famous and well-connected people including Leo Tolstoy and Banjo Paterson. Yet her portraits and likenesses of Cherry are, by and large, her most intimate and confident works. Goodsir returned to Paris for good later in 1927. It was where her heart resided; she too had become a Parisienne.

Deborah Hart

Postscript: Rachel Dunn died in 1950 at 18 rue de l'Odéon, Paris, and was buried in the same grave as Goodsir in the Bagneux Cemetery, south-west of Paris.

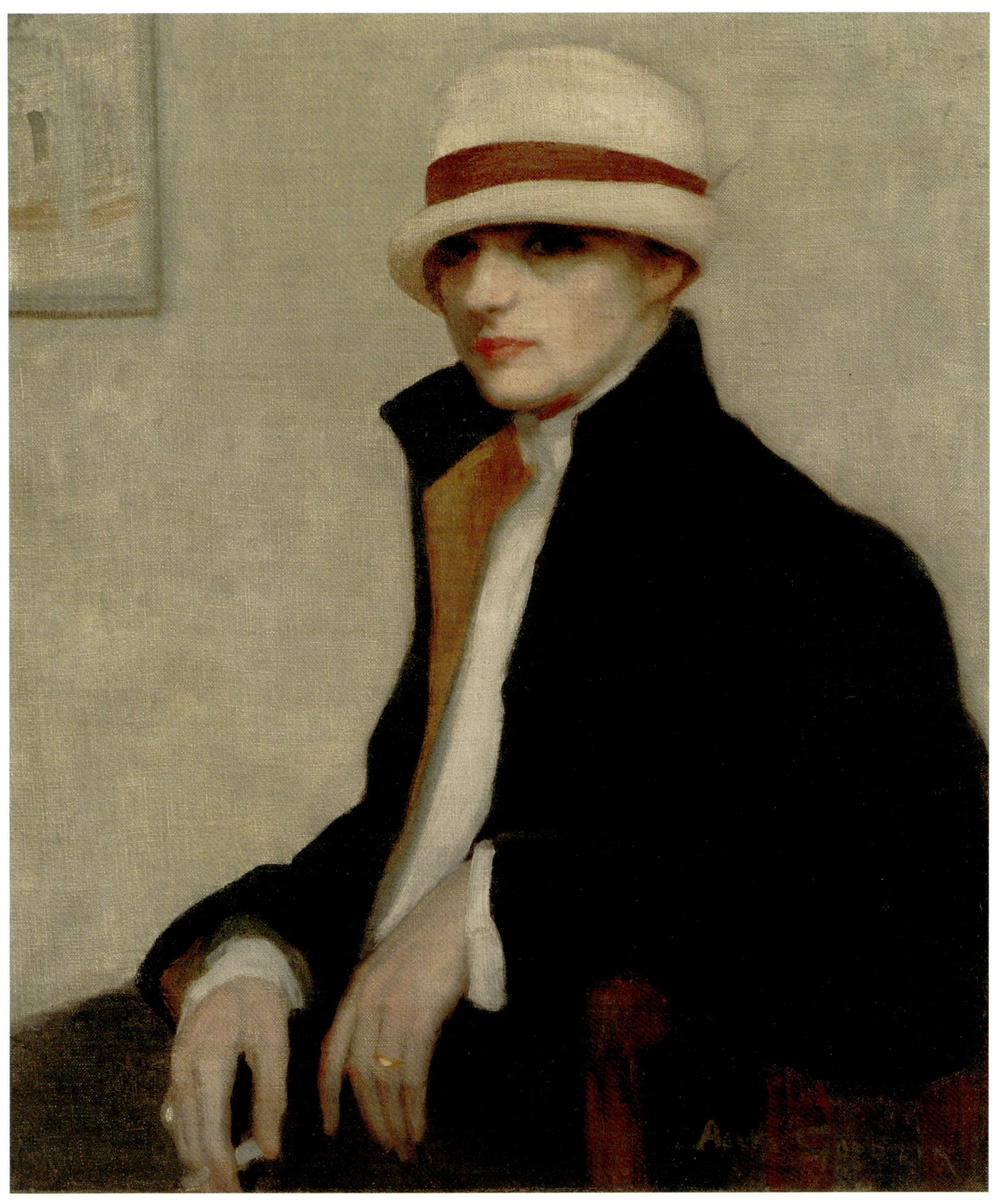

27 Stella Bowen (1893–1947)

Mary Widney 1927

painted in Paris, France
oil on wood panel, 46 x 37.5 cm
National Gallery of Australia, Canberra, purchased 2004

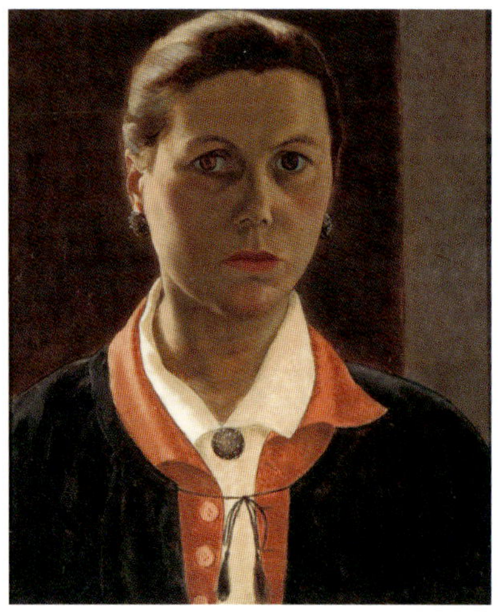

Stella Bowen
Self- portrait c 1929
oil on plywood, 45 x 36.8 cm
Art Gallery of South Australia, Adelaide,
gift of Suzanne Brookman, the artist's niece, 1999

'Stella was the most courageous, vital and harmonious personality that I have known ... she had so much to live for and such a genius for living.'[44] The Australian expatriate artist Stella Bowen was a remarkable woman with a passion for both art and life. She sought her own form of visual expression in her portraits and believed that 'this gift of creating life at a touch is the most enviable gift that a painter can have'.[45]

Bowen studied art in Adelaide, before travelling to London in 1914 to further her training and to pursue her dreams of becoming an artist. In London, the American poet Ezra Pound befriended her and introduced her to many avant-garde writers and artists, some of whose portraits she painted. In 1917 she met the novelist Ford Madox Ford, a man almost twenty years older than she, and they began a nine-year relationship. Bowen gave birth to their only daughter Julie in 1920, and in 1922 they moved to Paris where they mixed with leading literary figures of the day.

Among their friends were Mary and Bill Widney, wealthy Americans living in Paris, with whom Bowen and Ford often played bridge. Portrait commissions were an important source of income for Bowen and it is likely that Mary or her husband commissioned the portrait with this in mind. The Widneys owned two other paintings by Bowen, *Ford playing solitaire* 1927 (AGSA) and *Ford's chair* c 1928 (private collection).

Bowen depicted Mary Widney from two viewpoints, a three-quarter profile and from behind, using the device of a reflected mirror image of the back of the sitter. The two views do not, however, present alternative aspects of Widney's appearance; rather they suggest a public and private persona, with the back view alluding to the existence of a separate and hidden self. There is an austere quality to this work; the palette is limited to sombre browns and black. Widney's appearance is solemn and tranquil, her hair is neatly tied back and a mysterious smile plays at the corner of her mouth. The fur collar of her coat frames her face. Her blue eyes do not meet the viewer but look towards her right, as if Widney's attention was directed elsewhere or she was absorbed in thought.

Anne Gray

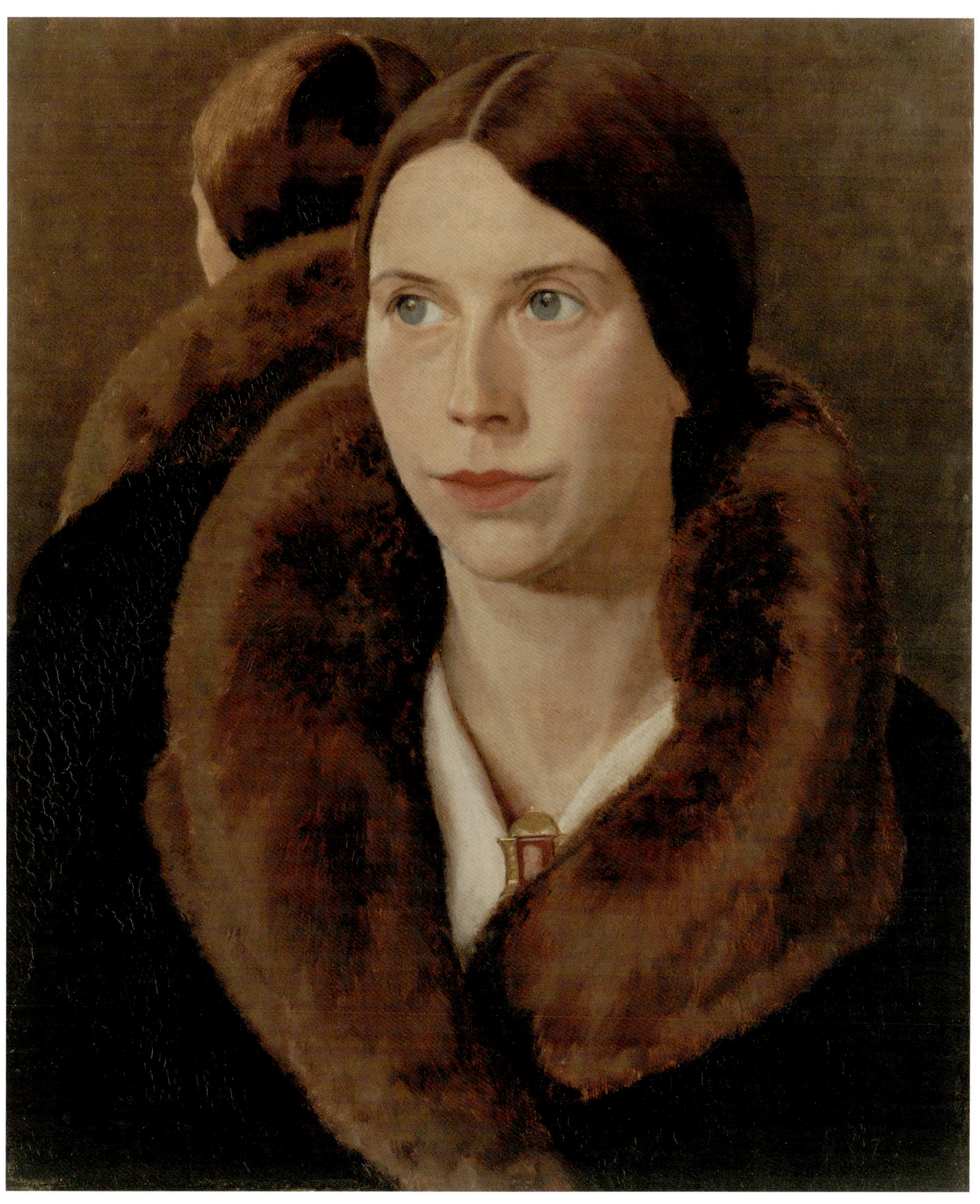

28 **Grace Crowley** (1890–1979)

Portrait study 1928

painted in Paris, France

oil on composition board, 79.2 x 59.8 cm

National Gallery of Australia, Canberra, bequest of Grace Crowley 1979

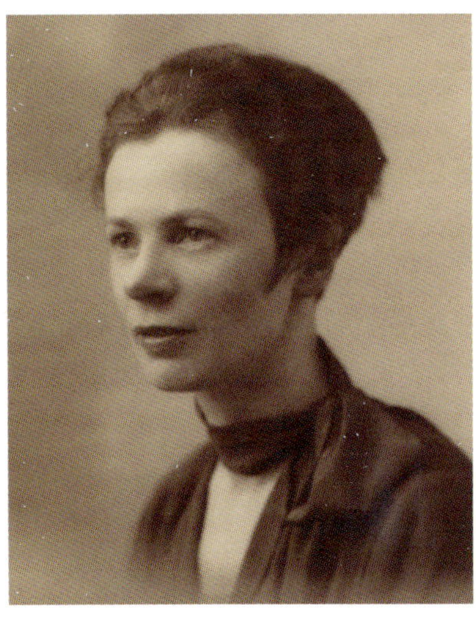

Grace Crowley, c 1927

Research Library, Art Gallery of New South Wales, Sydney

A convert to Modernism after several month's study with the charismatic cubist painter Andre Lhote, Grace Crowley noted that it was the first time she had heard about dynamic symmetry and the *section d'or*—that it was necessary to make a PLAN for a painting ...'

Crowley's *Portrait study* shows how well she had absorbed Lhote's teaching. The placement of the figure, the position of her hands and the angle of her shoulders all conform to an underlying geometric scaffolding based upon the proportions of the golden mean (*section d'or*). Crowley did not record who the sitter for this work was. However, it is possible that the subject was Lucie Beynis, a professional model in Paris, whom Crowley used on at least one other occasion for her *Portrait of Lucie Beynis* 1929 (AGNSW), a work which was first exhibited simply as *Portrait*. They share the same dark colouring, heavy-lidded eyes, full lips and long nose, and both have a similar stylish, languid look. Like many modernists, portraiture was an important genre for Crowley yet even when painting people who were close to her, such as her cousin in *Miss Gwen Ridley* 1930 (AGSA), Crowley's principal interest always lay in pictorial construction, in solving the problems of painting, rather than in depicting individual identity.

In the pose of the sitter and Crowley's use of the round-backed chair, *Portrait study* also makes conscious reference to *Madame Devaucay de Nittis* 1807 (Musée Conde, Chantilly) by nineteenth century neo-classical artist Jean-Auguste Dominique Ingres. Lhote encouraged his students to analyse the composition of the old masters, and Crowley's high regard for Ingres is borne out by a postcard of *Madame Devaucay de Nittis* which she kept with her throughout her life.

On her reluctant return to Australia in 1930 after four years in Paris, Crowley became a champion of Modernism and an influential teacher, introducing cubist principles and eventually pushing her own work towards total abstraction.

Elena Taylor

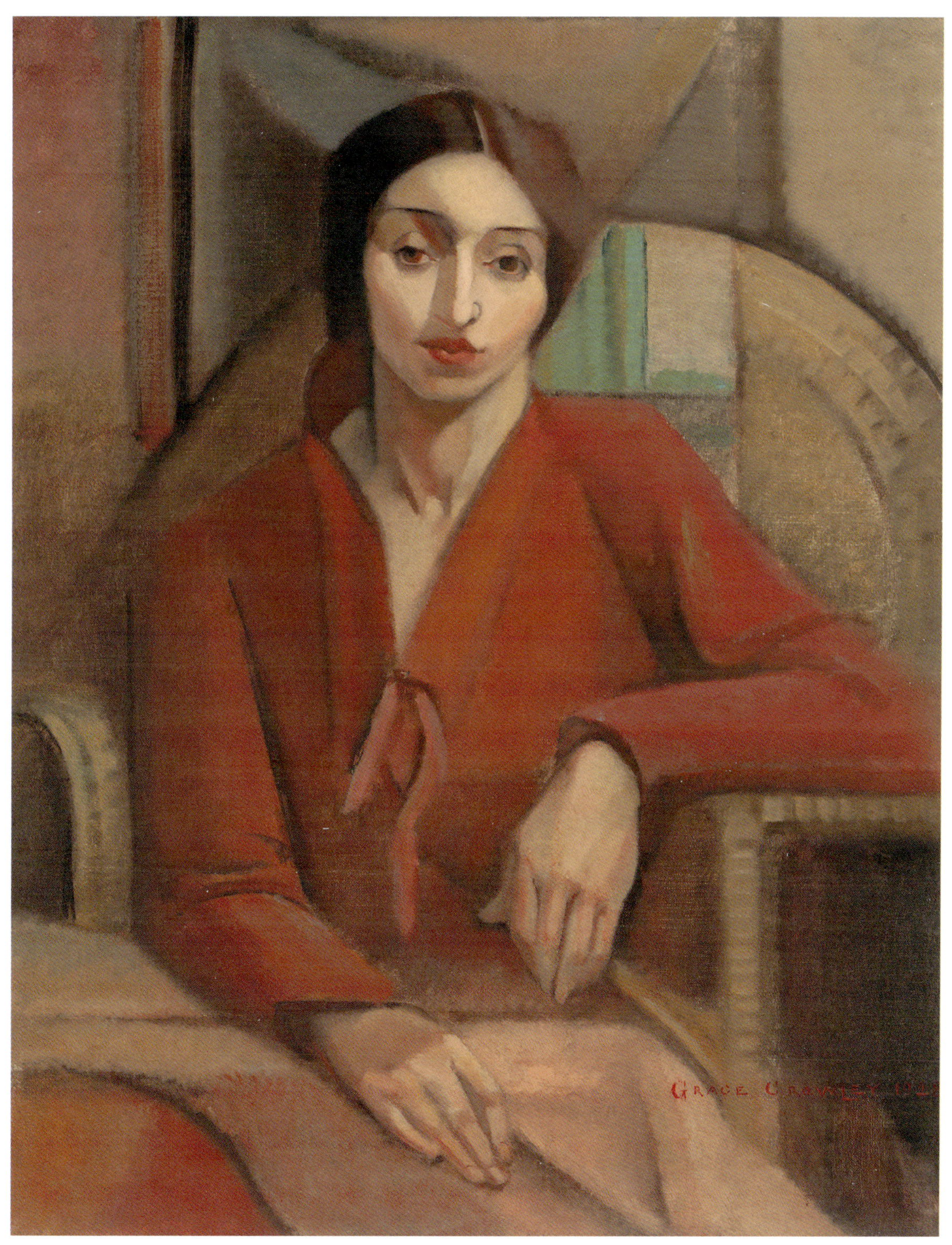
GRACE CROWLEY

29 **Napier Waller** (1893–1972)

Christian Waller with Baldur, Undine and Siren at Fairy Hills 1932

painted in Melbourne, Victoria
oil and tempera on canvas mounted on composition board, 121.5 x 205.5 cm
National Gallery of Australia, Canberra, purchased 1984

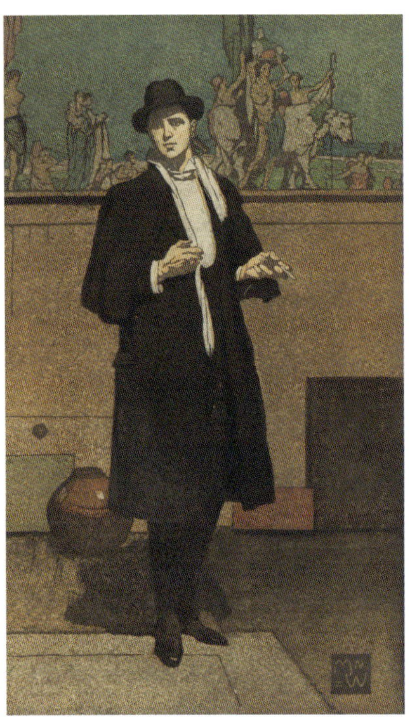

Napier Waller
The man in black 1925
linocut on paper, 30.7 x 17.6 cm
National Galley of Australia, Canberra, purchased 1975

In 1932 Napier Waller painted this portrait of his artist wife, Christian (1894–1954) seated on the ground, in the company of her Airedale terriers. It was a time when Napier was becoming a man of the world, while Christian was retreating into an esoteric religion.

The frieze-like precision of this painting and its cool, crisp colours underscore the formality of their marriage. Christian sits on the grass in front of their Arts and Crafts style home, situated on the banks of the Darebin Creek at Fairy Hills, a picturesque enclave in suburban Melbourne. She is dressed in white and looks directly at the viewer with an expression of quiet resignation. The dogs' wavy hair matches her own, and one lies at her feet with its head resting dolefully on the ground. The other two dogs, however, are lively and alert, seeming to want Christian to join them at play. The painting, almost of mural proportions, was the centrepiece of their dining room, hanging over the massive fireplace; it was also visible from the minstrels' gallery.

The early 1920s and 1930s were years of professional acclaim for both husband and wife. Serving in France from the end of 1916, Waller was wounded in action in 1917 and lost his right arm. Despite this, he became a successful mural and mosaic artist and printmaker. In his linocut self-portrait *The man in black*, he posed himself in front of his commissioned mural for the State Library of Victoria. In 1929–30 Napier and Christian travelled together to England and Europe to study stained-glass design and production—Christian also seeking out William Butler Yeats, a leading Irish devotee of the Golden Dawn movement. During the 1920s Christian Waller became a notable book illustrator, and also produced woodcuts and linocuts. In 1932 she published her book on theosophical ideas *The great breath*, containing a series of linocuts that received an enthusiastic response.

Appropriately, for an artist steeped in symbolism, Waller used the decorative form of branches of elongated leaves of the willow tree (long associated with sadness and isolation) to frame the elements of his composition.

Roger Butler

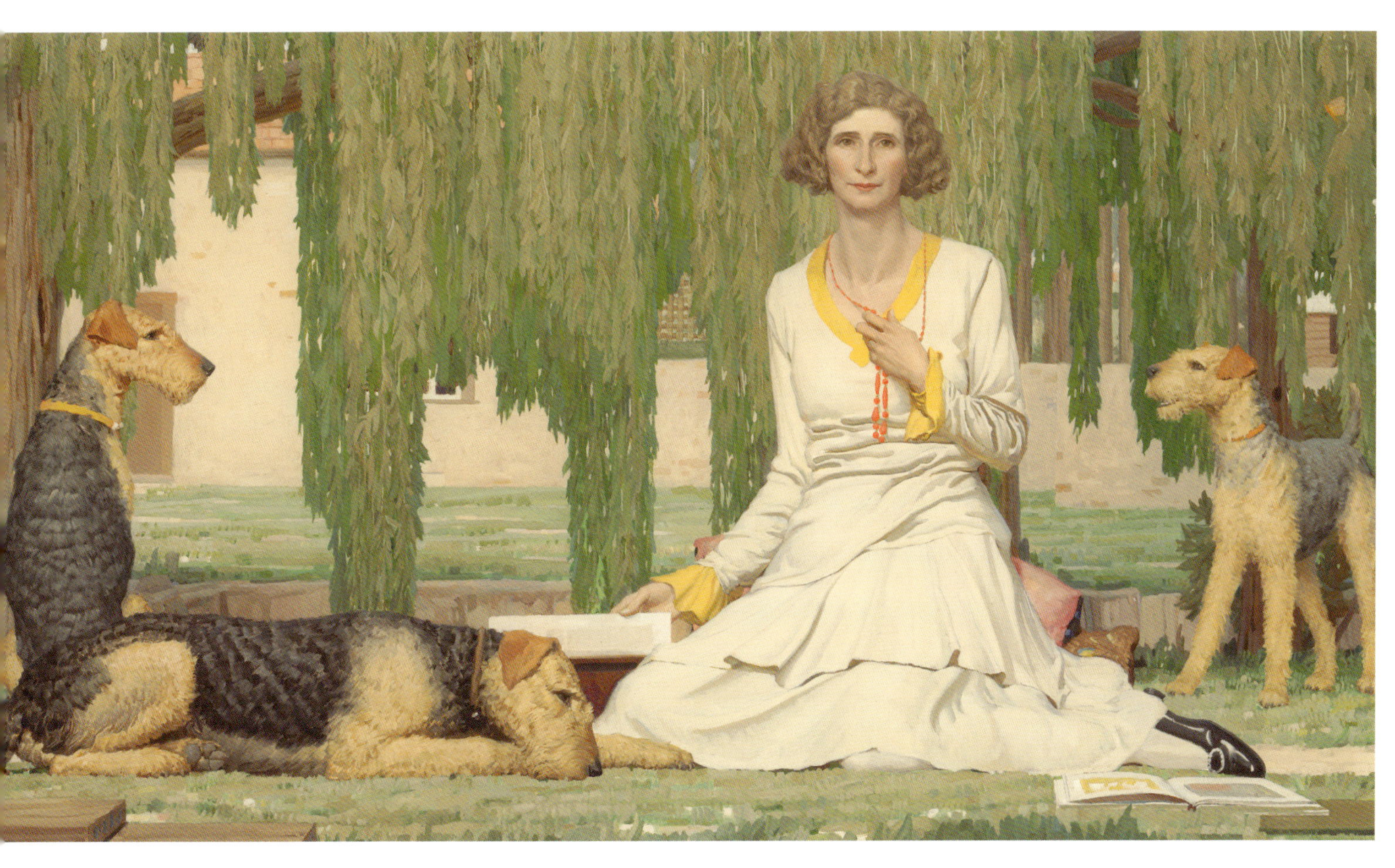

30 **Nora Heysen** (1911–2003)

London breakfast 1935

painted in London, England
oil on canvas, 47 x 53.5 cm
National Gallery of Australia, Canberra, purchased 1996

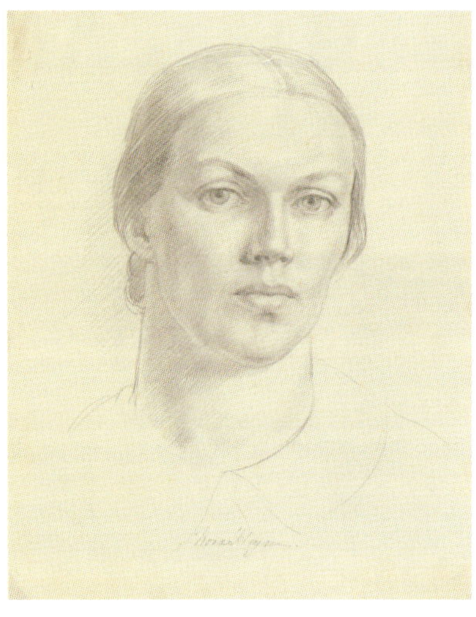

Nora Heysen
Self-portrait c 1935
pencil on paper, 36.4 x 28.4 cm
National Gallery of Australia, Canberra, purchased 2000

Nora Heysen always wanted to draw or paint.[46] In *London breakfast* she depicted her friend Evie (Everton) Stokes wearing a blue dressing-gown, against a yellow-cream background, with the strong yellow-ochres of a cut pumpkin. There are white flowers in a blue vase on the breakfast table, and there is a blue and white plate on the bookshelf behind. Heysen was concerned with arranging forms and colours—opposing blues and yellows, keeping the colours as pure as possible.[47]

Heysen painted the portrait in the studio-flat in Duke Street, Kensington that she shared with Evie at this time, where they took turns in posing for each other, half a day each. But Evie did not strictly pose for this picture, rather Heysen depicted her immersed in everyday life: Evie reading a book, enjoying a pot of tea and a simple meal of bread and jam, with her slipper casually balanced on her foot. Despite the casual nature of this work, we would be deceived if we thought that the elements on the table—as well as the parallel horizontals and verticals of the chair, table and bookshelf—had not been meticulously arranged for the picture.

In composition Heysen adopted some of the features of Whistler's famous portrait of his mother; but instead of Whistler's subdued palette, Heysen used bold contrasting colours, and in place of the master's spare composition, Heysen filled the space with practical objects. The portrait is also a homage to Vermeer, whose reproduced works hung in Heysen's family home. As in so many of Vermeer's paintings, Heysen's subject is dressed in blue and engaged in a tranquil occupation, a pearly light comes into a domestic scene from a hidden window on the left, and there is a careful placement of objects in a clearly defined architectural space. Heysen even emulated Vermeer's use of dark wood for the frame of her painting.

Adelaide-born Nora Heysen was one of eight children of the Australian landscape painter Hans Heysen. She studied at the School of Fine Arts in Adelaide under F Millward Grey from 1926 to 1930. And at the time she painted this portrait, Nora Heysen was studying in London at the London Central School under Bernard Meninski. It was a period of remarkable development in her work—and just three years before she became the first woman to be awarded the Archibald Prize.

Anne Gray

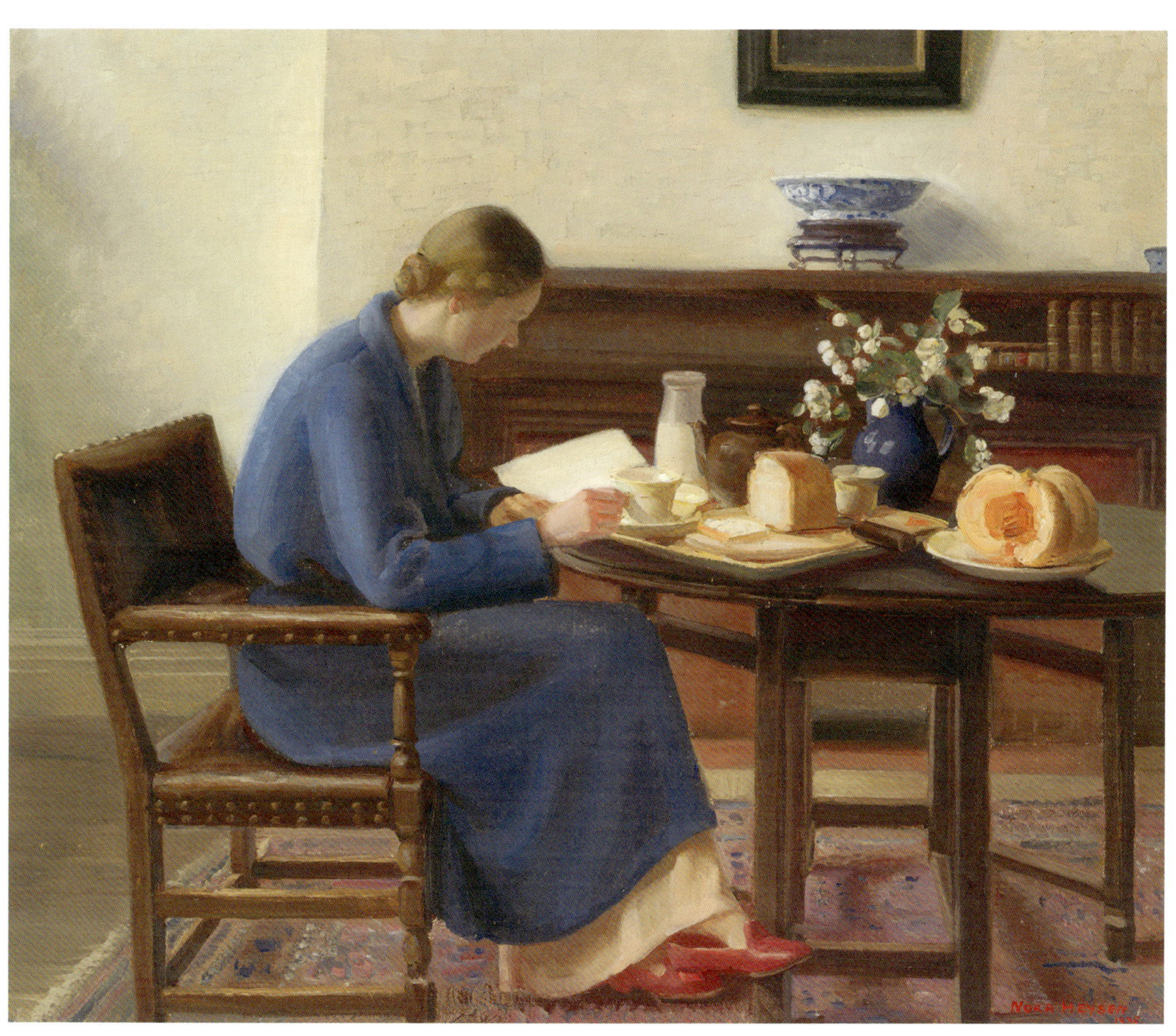

31 **Eric Wilson** (1911–1946)

Domestic interior 1935

painted in Sydney, New South Wales
oil on canvas on plywood, 43.3 cm (diameter)
National Gallery of Australia, Canberra, purchased 1983

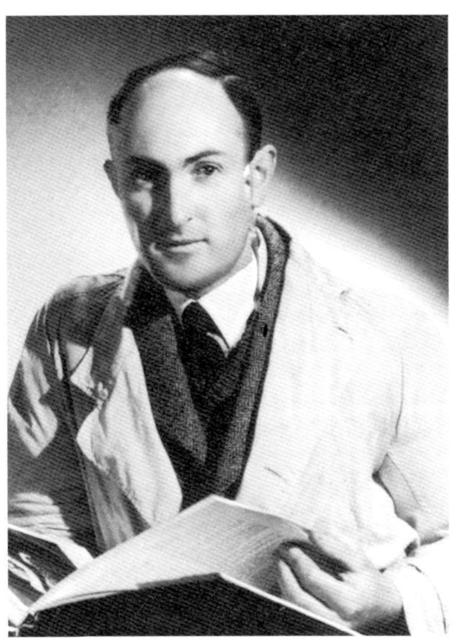

Eric Wilson, 1942
Jean Appleton collection

A scholarship winning tour-de-force, Eric Wilson's *Domestic interior* employs the unusual tondo, or circular, format to great effect as a metaphor for the intimate family circle. Wilson's mother is placed at the centre of the work, contentedly absorbed in her mending. To her right a young girl, an open book on her knees, is eating an apple. Is this perhaps the apple of knowledge that is being tasted? A tabby cat, ears pricked and watching intently, completes the group. *Domestic interior* is above all an image of domestic harmony, presided over by the figure of his mother, its calm mood reinforced by the clarity and emphatic geometric structuring of the composition.

It is almost certain that when painting *Domestic interior* Wilson had in mind Arthur Murch's tondo *The idle hour* 1933 (AGNSW), an intimate picture of a mother and two children. While students of Julian Ashton's Sydney Art School often felt that in the teaching there was not enough emphasis on composition, in *Domestic interior* Wilson orchestrates a virtuoso arrangement of interlocking figures tightly contained within the circular frame. This circular form is repeated throughout the work, in the curve of the cat's back, the round table and in the mother's hat that is contrasted with the rectangular painting on the wall behind. A shaft of brilliant light falls diagonally across the scene, intersecting the forms into a complex play of lights and shadows, creating a highly patterned and decorative effect.

The son of a saddler, Wilson was born in Sydney in 1911. Around 1928 Wilson enrolled in evening classes at Julian Ashton's while continuing to work part-time. Hardworking and ambitious, Wilson set his sights upon winning the NSW Travelling Scholarship. He entered four times before finally being successful in 1937 with a group of works including *Domestic interior*, *The artist's mother* 1937 [32] and *Self-portrait as bather* 1935 (NGA). On award of the scholarship Wilson travelled to London to study—where, at the Westminster School and at the London Academy under Amedée Ozenfant he experimented with Cubism and abstraction.

Elena Taylor

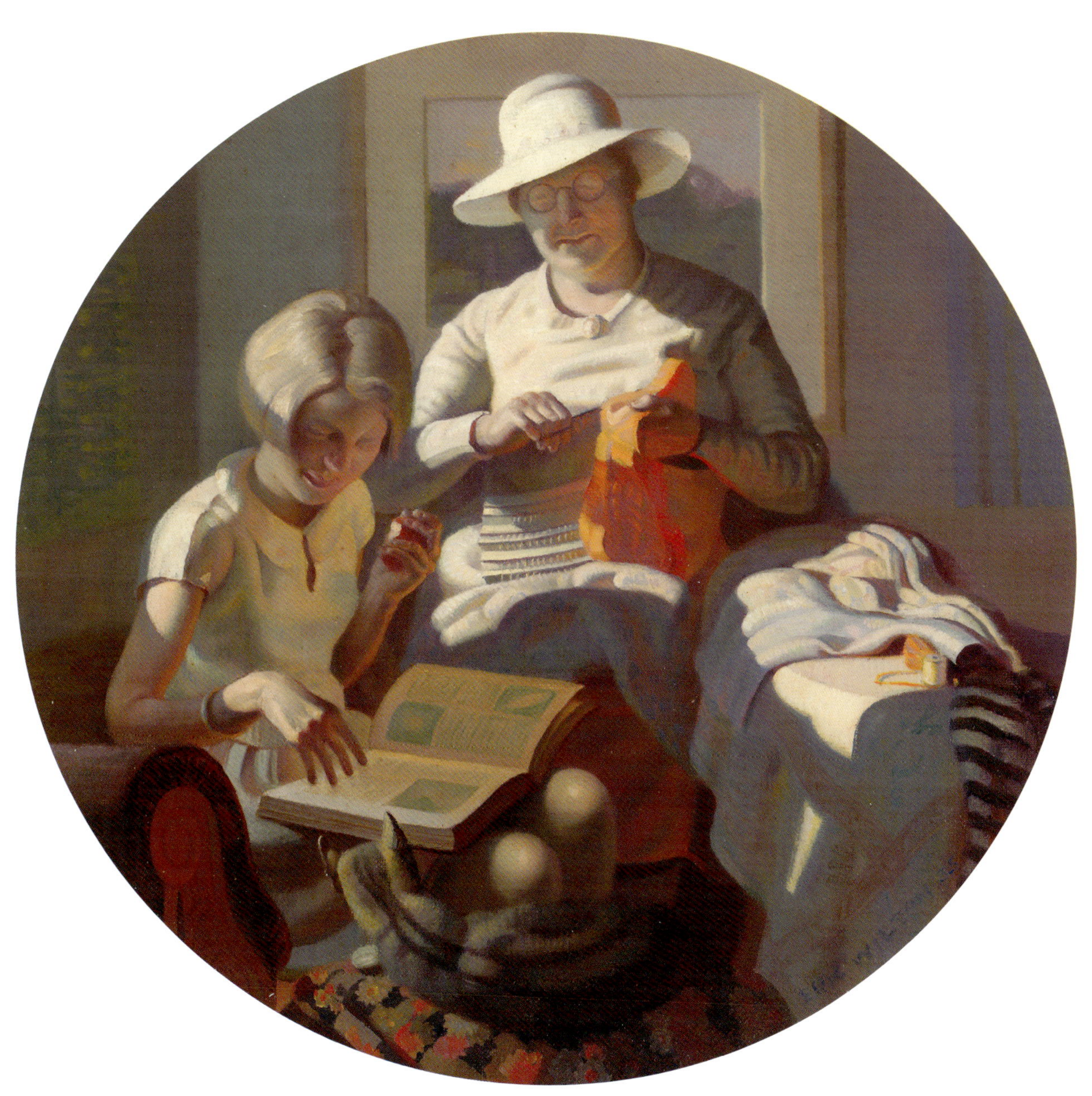

32 **Eric Wilson** (1911–1946)

The artist's mother 1937

painted in Sydney, New South Wales
oil on canvas, 95 x 71.6 cm
National Gallery of Australia, Canberra, purchased 1975

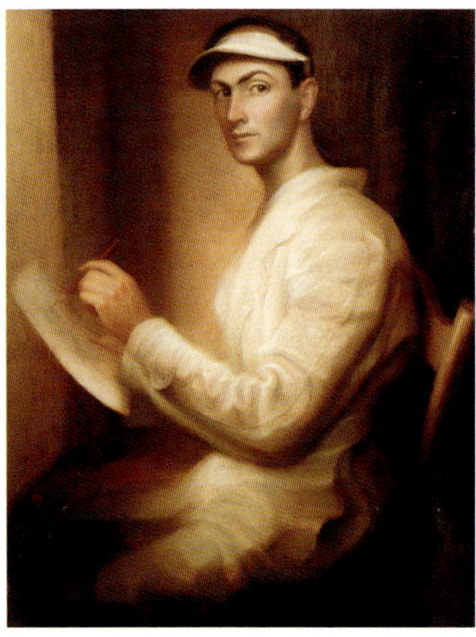

Eric Wilson
Self-portrait 1945
oil on canvas, 91.5 x 71.1 cm
Art Gallery of New South Wales, Sydney, gift of Miss Jean Appleton 1959

Skilfully composed of contrasts of light and dark, punctuated by three brilliant red highlights, *The artist's mother* is a sober, unadorned image, somewhat as we suspect the sitter's personality to be. She looks out at her son, a little warily, sitting stiffly, conscious of being observed. Dressed in her Sunday best with silk blouse and fur-trimmed coat, she is an unremarkable middle-aged woman, a respectable and upright member of the community and most probably, like her son, a devout Seventh Day Adventist. With hat on and gloves and umbrella in hand she appears as if ready to go out but delayed by her son's request to pose for him. It is this quality, beyond the meticulous realism with which it is painted, which gives the work its particular photographic quality, of a moment captured rather than the many sittings which would have gone into painting this portrait.

Wilson gives us few clues as to the subject, the wedding band and poppy hinting at the intersection between personal and national narratives. More telling is the way in which Wilson has composed the portrait so that his mother's form takes up almost the entire canvas. Placed centrally against a neutral background there is nothing in the picture except her, and it is easy to speculate that in his life Wilson accorded his mother the same central importance.

Madeline Wilson (née Hawkes) was born in Wagga Wagga in 1880 and married in 1908. She was supportive of her son's ambition to become an artist and, while mothers can make convenient models, it is also likely indicative of their closeness that Wilson painted his mother several times. She is the central figure in *Domestic Interior*, and the subject of his Archibald Prize entries in 1942, *The artist's mother* c 1942 (NRAG) and in 1944, *The painter's mother* c 1944 (NGV). Madeline Wilson died in 1950, surviving her son by four years.

Elena Taylor

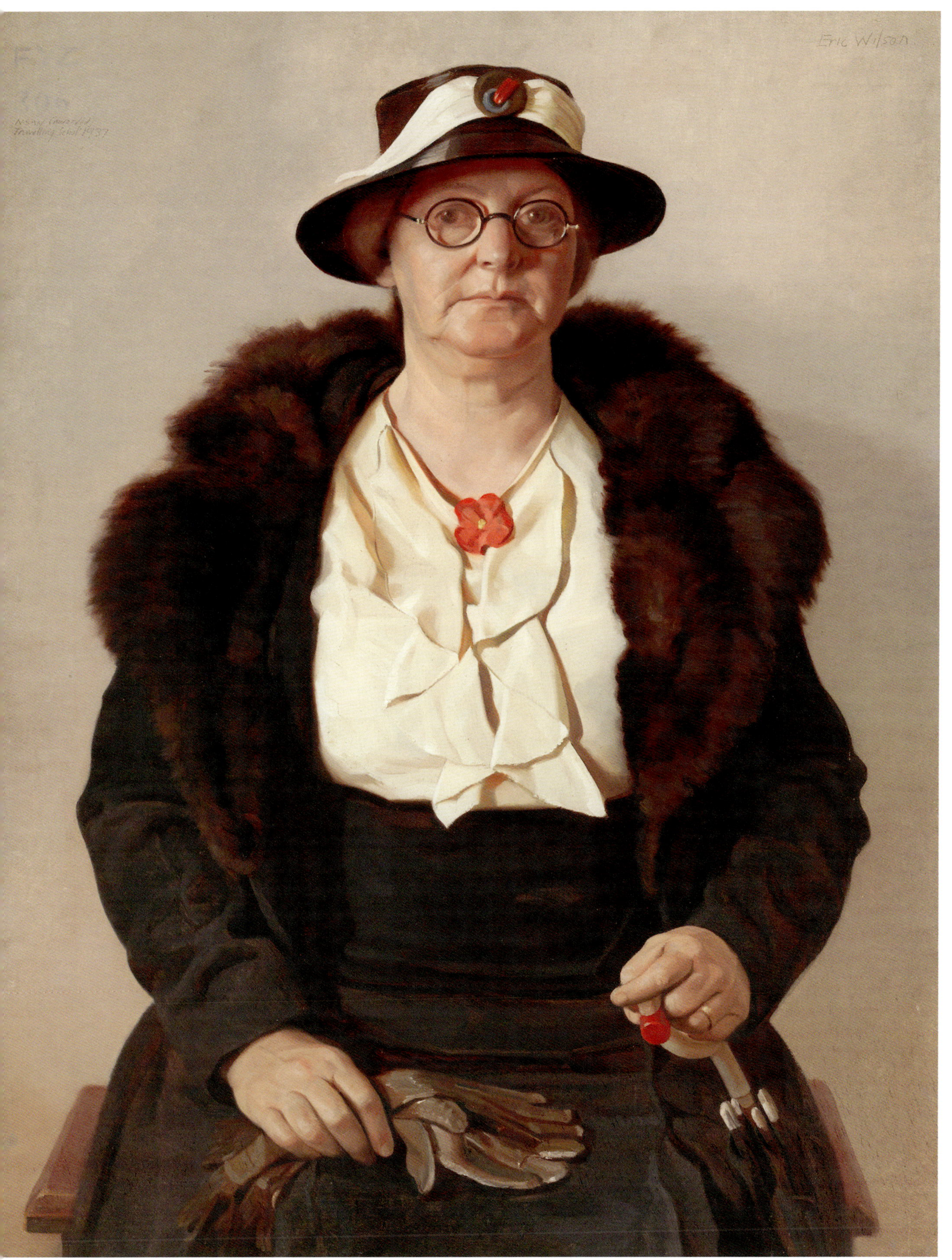
Eric Wilson

33 Albert Tucker (1914–1999)

Self-portrait 1937

painted in Melbourne, Victoria
oil on paperboard mounted on composition board, 56.4 x 42.8 cm
National Gallery of Australia, Canberra, purchased 1983

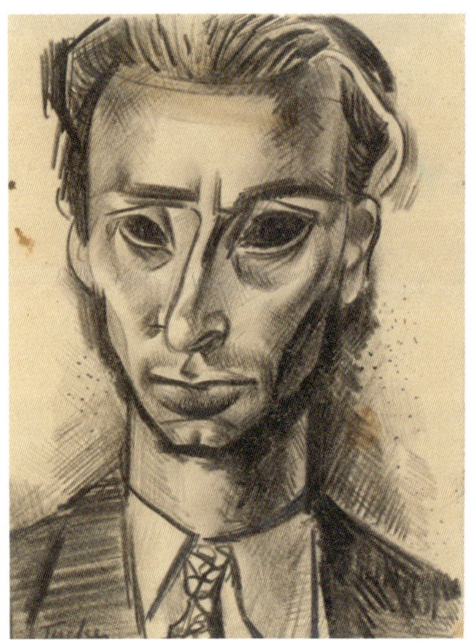

Albert Tucker
Self-portrait 1939
pencil on paper, 17.5 x 12.6 cm
National Gallery of Australia, Canberra, gift of Mrs Barbara Tucker 1979

I didn't fit into the middle class because I was too poor, and I couldn't function with the working class because I was conditioned to different values and aspirations. [48]

Born in Melbourne in 1914, Tucker's formative years were shaped by the Great Depression as he was caught between his mother's middle class pretensions and the reality of poverty. He had been keen to study at the National Gallery of Victoria School but was unable to afford full-time study. Instead he had his beginnings in commercial art and life-drawing classes at the Victorian Artists' Society.

Self-portrait 1937, painted by Tucker when he was 23 years old, is a work of contrasts and contradictions. On first sight the intense young man seems confident as he is portrayed with strong colours and a wide stare. He is tidily though not expensively dressed. His green tie sits neatly and is set against the pink shirt and red scarf that is casually tossed over his shoulder. This conservative image is finished with the white highlight of a folded handkerchief in his breast pocket. All this, together with his carefully combed hair, indicates an urbane man of his time—and yet Tucker subverts the effect by painting himself unshaven.

While not as obvious as in later portraits, the centre of this self-portrait is directed around the curve of the artist's nose, broken while at school, and the lift of his mouth and left eyebrow. The features seem mobile. Tucker does not provide a background in which to place himself; instead he focuses more closely on his face, directing our gaze and making the painting all the more penetrating.

On closer inspection though, the confidence that is first assumed is belied by the fact that Tucker looks up through exaggeratedly large eyes, while his head tilts slightly downwards. We realise that the artist is not quite as self-assured as he first appears.

This early work stands apart from the direction that Tucker was soon to follow. He describes 1937 as his turning-point year. The portrait captures him on the brink of what was to become a long and successful career.

Dominique Nagy

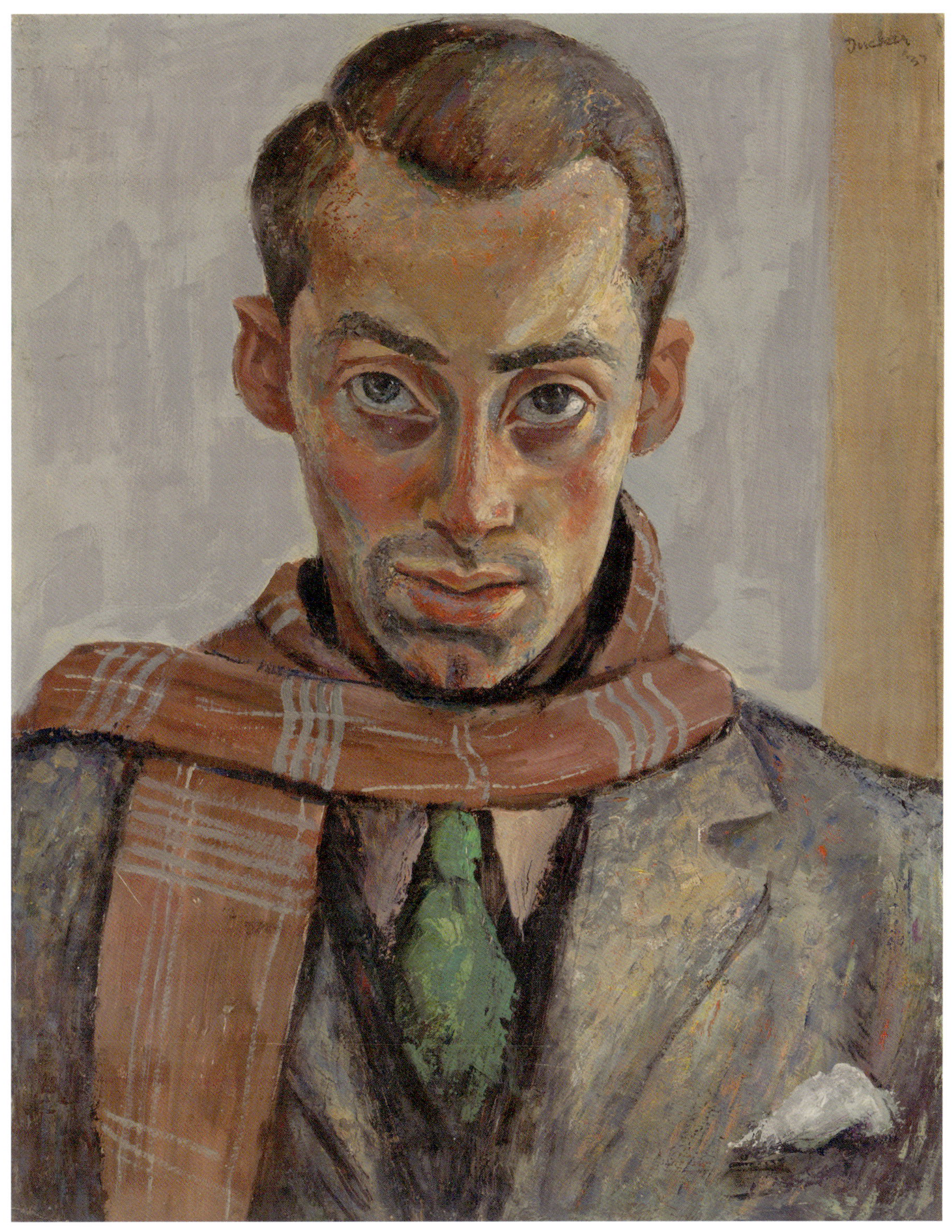

34 **Arthur Boyd** (1920–1999)

Mary Boyd 1937

painted at Open Country, in Murrumbeena, Victoria
oil on canvas on hardboard, 50.6 x 59.4 cm
National Gallery of Australia, Canberra, The Arthur Boyd gift 1975

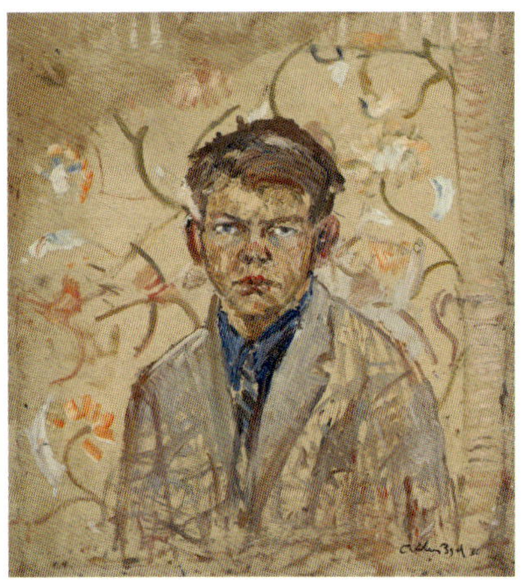

Arthur Boyd
Self-portrait in a blue shirt 1936
oil on canvas mounted on composition board, 68.4 x 59.4 cm
National Gallery of Australia, Canberra, The Arthur Boyd gift, 1975

Arthur Boyd is one of Australia's most celebrated artists and is best known for his paintings of the Australian landscape, biblical scenes and the Bride series (*Love, marriage and death of a half-caste* 1953–56). He was born in 1920 to the potters and painters Merric and Doris Boyd, and learnt to pot and paint from a young age on the large family property at Murrumbeena, Victoria.

Boyd frequently painted family and friends as a way of trialling new ideas, materials and techniques of painting. *Mary Boyd* is Boyd's earliest portrait of his youngest sibling (born 1926), and was painted when he was 17 years old. In this portrait Boyd depicted an 11-year-old Mary at an unconventional, yet very relaxed angle, alluding to the familiarity between the painter and his sitter. Boyd positioned the face and torso of his sister across the lower left of the canvas, almost as though she was about to slide off its edge. Behind the figure he used striking bright yellow hues with intersecting blue diagonal lines. These lines mirror Mary's position and bring to mind the curves and patterning of a family settee.

Boyd's brushstrokes are energetic and expressive. From a young age he experimented with his application of paint, sometimes squeezing directly from the tube—thanks to supplies from an uncle's paint factory and his grandfather's encouragement. This experimentation is evident in the thick and vigorously applied paint of Mary's red hair; a tangled, wild and unruly mass that exudes the liveliness and innocence of her age. Boyd appears to have curbed his energy in the portrayal of Mary's face. Her blue eyes are luminous and energised yet stare distractedly outside the painting's frame, as though lost in thought.

Mary Boyd married artist John Perceval in 1944, Arthur Boyd's wartime acquaintance. The pair raised four children, three of whom were later to become painters. The couple separated in the early 1970s and in 1977 Mary married Sidney Nolan. Lady Nolan still lives on an estate in Britain that she and Nolan ran as a centre for communal art activities.

Miriam Kelly

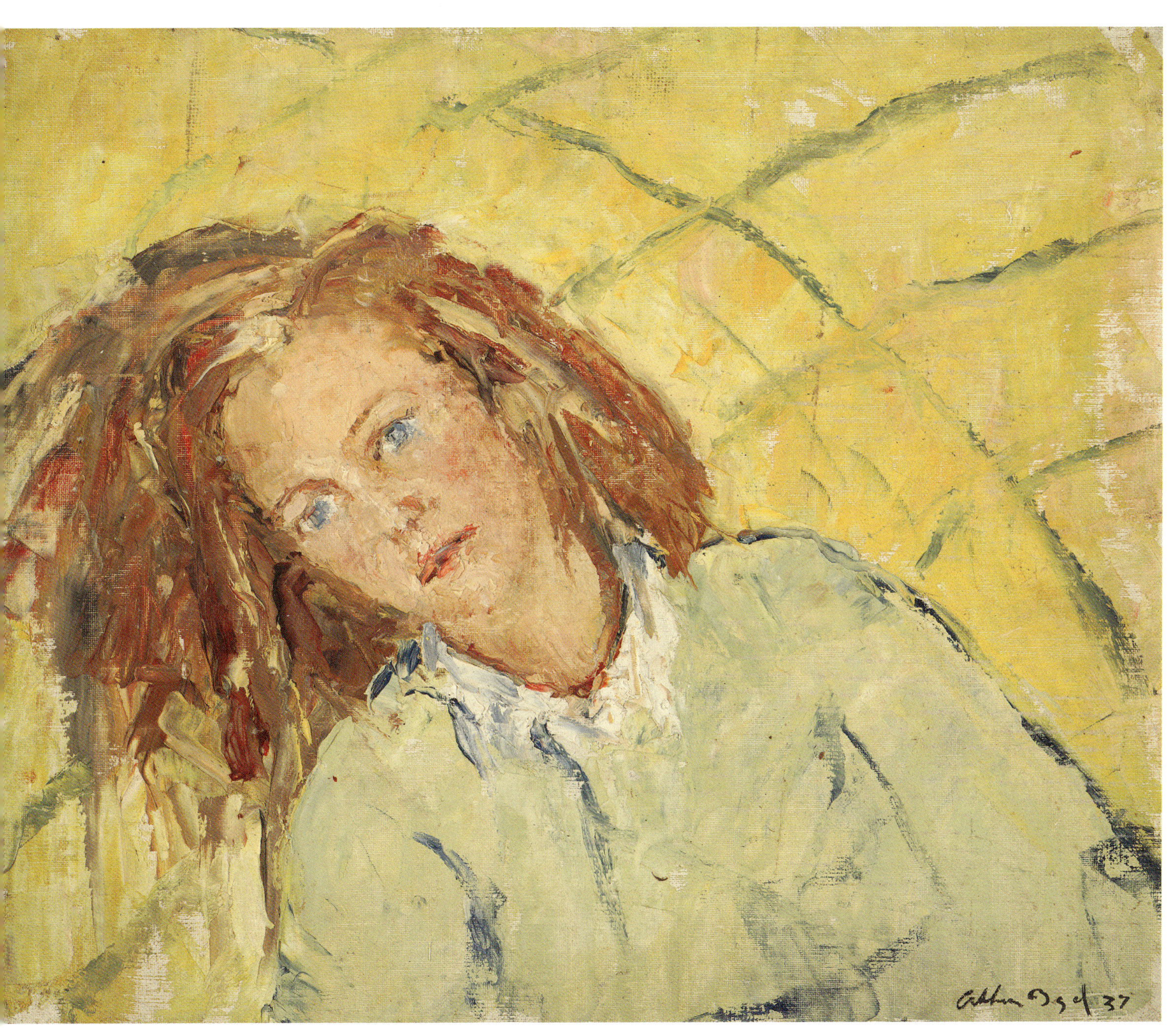

35 **Herbert Badham** (1899–1961)

Self-portrait c 1937

painted in Sydney, New South Wales
oil on paper on cardboard, 35 x 24.7 cm
National Gallery of Australia, Canberra, purchased 2009

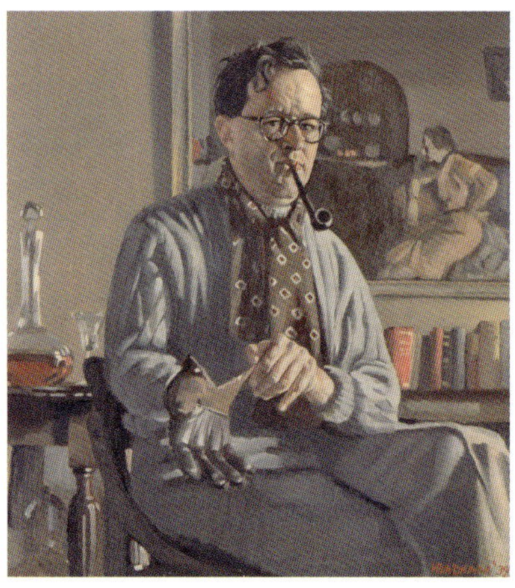

Herbert Badham
Self-portrait with glove 1939
oil on canvas, 33.4 x 29.7 cm
National Portrait Gallery, Canberra

Herbert Badham is known for his distinctive images of everyday life in Sydney during the forty years from the 1920s until the 1960s, including a number of striking self-portraits.

Badham's *Self-portrait* was the cover illustration for the catalogue accompanying his first retrospective exhibition at Sydney's Macquarie Galleries in 1979. The artist looks out from the painting, his face at a slight angle, with a concentrated expression and a penetrating gaze through his bold, dark-rimmed glasses. The gesture of the hand putting pressure on his mouth suggests an intense curiosity about the self and about self-portraiture. As an introspective, deeply personal observation, *Self-portrait* transcends conventional desires to please either the sitter or the audience. Instead, Badham invites us to stop, look and think about the way we see ourselves and to question the extent to which the tangible, physical body is a true reflection of the self.

Beyond the impact created by his hand gesture, we become aware of the artist's highly stylised painting of his face and clothes, and the intricacy of the composition. Badham's colours are muted and his paint has generally been applied with even, exact strokes. While his features are crisp, the blocky details of his surroundings suggest a blurring of focus and create an unusual sense of perspective. The intensity of his foreground image contrasts with the calmer world of the middle ground, where a woman sits in a dimly lit interior, absorbed in her activities and oblivious to Badham. Behind her and on top of a dark shelf, we glimpse another Badham painting. Badham's use of light and his distinctive compositions are theatrical. This feeling for theatre is reminiscent of the work of one Badham's teachers, George W Lambert.

Badham was born in Sydney in 1899. He studied at the Julian Ashton School in the 1920s and 1930s, alongside a generation of painters that included William Dobell, Grace Crowley and Douglas Dundas. Badham was head of the intermediate art department at the National Art School (variously known as East Sydney Technical College) from 1938 to 1961. In 1949 Badham published the populist historical survey, *Study of Australian art*, and in 1954 the pictorial survey of Australian painting in *A gallery of Australian art*. Badham died in Sydney in 1961.

Miriam Kelly

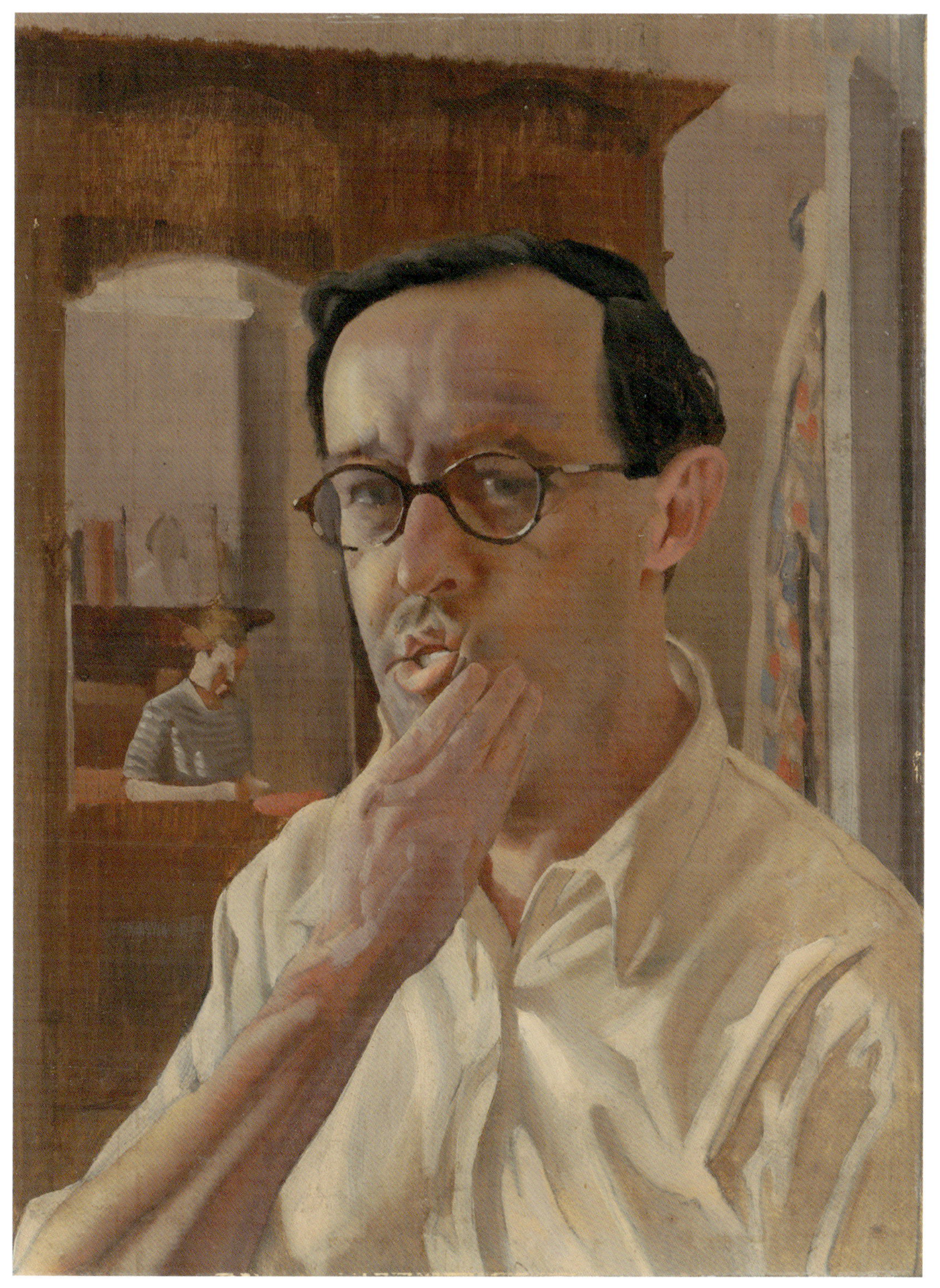

36 **Elise Blumann** (1897–1990)

Charles, morning on the Swan 1939

painted in Perth, Western Australia

oil and crayon on canvas, 101.8 x 76.8 cm

National Gallery of Australia, Canberra, purchased 1978

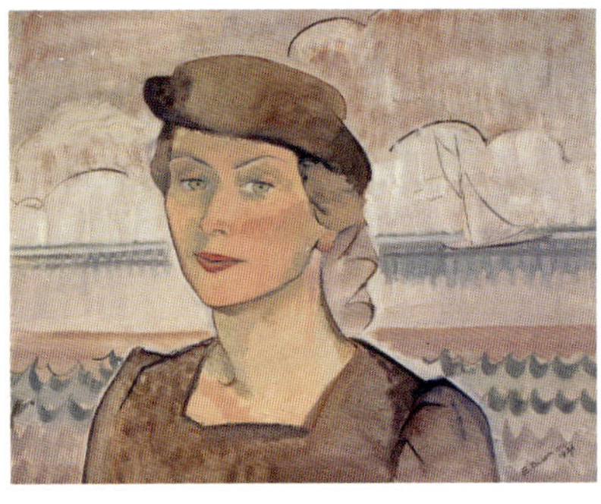

Elise Blumann
Self-portrait 1937
oil on board, 52.5 x 62.5 cm
Cruthers Collection of Women's Art at the University of Western Australia, Perth

Charles … with strong legs and thin arms … everything in nature interests you … you always try to understand: you won't let go until you find a solution … Charles, thinker and dreamer, you constantly lively spirit.[49]

So Elise Blumann wrote of her son Charles in 1931, when he was aged seven and she and her family were living in Germany.

In 1938 Blumann migrated to Western Australia as a refugee from Nazi Germany with her husband, Dr Arnold Blumann, and their two sons. Soon after their arrival she depicted Charles, at the age of fifteen, in *Charles, morning on the Swan*. The location was the foreshore of the Swan River near her home in Crawley, a suburb of Perth.

The image is dominated by the vertical figure of the young man, completely self-absorbed. He is centrally placed, his feet almost touching the bottom of the image and his head near the top. He looks down at the ground, which suggests he was a thinker and dreamer, as his mother had described him eight years earlier. He is posed as if moving forward, but neither walking nor standing, balanced in a moment of stillness. Behind him, the landscape stretches out in horizontal bands, with a blue-violet sky, green-blue river and an ochre shore. The upper body is in the sky, the lower in front of the river.

Blumann painted the work using clearly visible, broad rhythmic brushstrokes, a network of hatch marks. She employed a rhythmical line to describe the contours of the body. The painting is modern in its flat, patterned surface, and with the figure pushed to the foreground plane. But it also shows Blumann's respect for traditional art and the poses of classical sculptures of Apollo in which the figure stands poised between movement and repose.

Blumann noted that Charles was interested in observing nature and in this painting she expressed the dynamism of nature. She melded the boy into his surroundings through the overall patterned surface of paint. She contrasted the bold outlines of the boy's figure with the repeated curves that suggest the rippling motion of the water. She wrote in her notes: 'The sensuous awareness of beauty and harmony which enters into the constitution of all living plants and bodies … is the formal foundation of all works of art.'[50]

Anne Gray

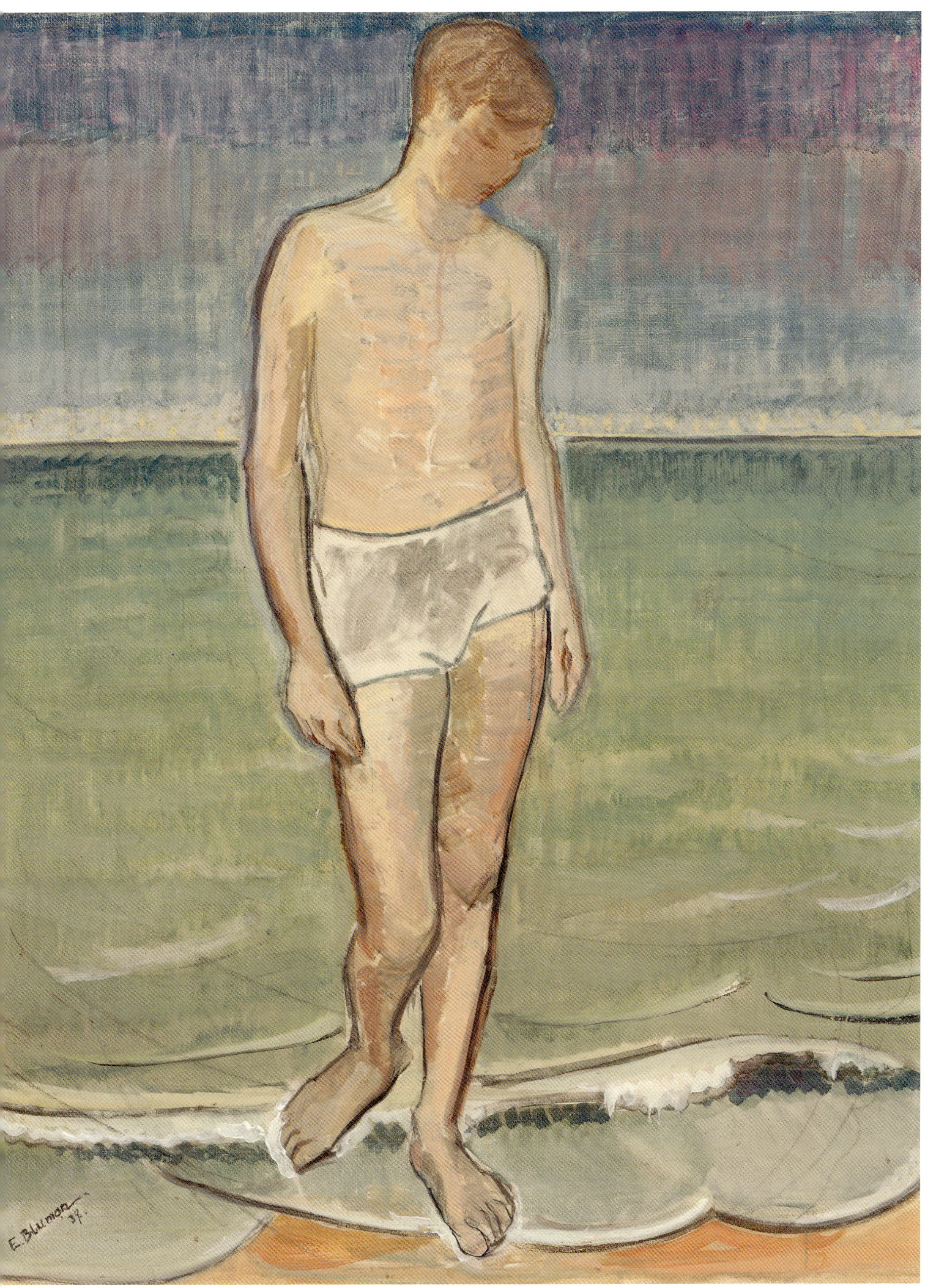

37 **Sali Herman** (1898–1993)

The artist's wife (Paulette) 1940

painted in Sydney, New South Wales
oil on canvas mounted on composition board,
73.6 x 52 cm
National Gallery of Australia, Canberra, gift of the artist 1969

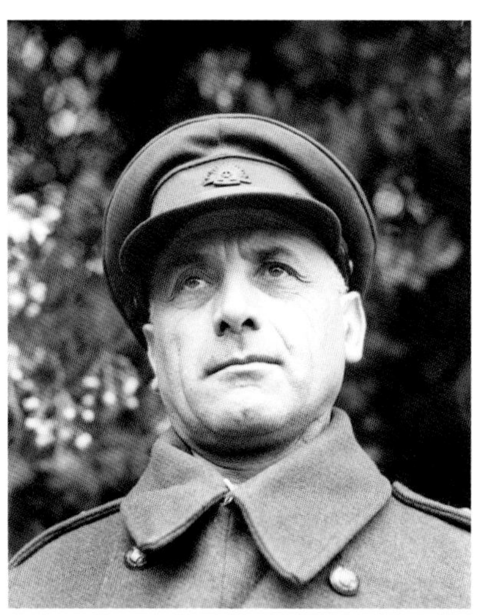

Sali Herman, 1945
Australian War Memorial, Canberra, purchased 1979

Sali Herman was born in Zurich in 1898. Primarily known for his urban subjects, Herman travelled extensively in Australia and around the world painting landscapes, still lifes and portraits both as a civilian and during his time as an official war artist in the Australian Army.

French-born Paulette Briand married Herman in 1929. They migrated to Australia in 1937 along with his two children from a previous marriage, leaving Europe as part of an exodus in response to the rise of Nazism. These European émigrés settled in many corners of the world, not always receiving a warm welcome in their adopted homes. The Hermans initially settled in Melbourne, later moving to Sydney to escape what they (and many other migrants) felt to be a stultifying parochialism. Russell Drysdale, Herman's fellow student at Melbourne's George Bell School, followed shortly thereafter. Drysdale told Herman that if he wanted to paint Australia he would need to have been born here—an attitude that the migrant family no doubt encountered on a regular basis.

Whilst at first glance her large blue eyes and relaxed hands give an impression of self-assurance, Paulette is withdrawn, with arms crossed, a slumped posture and a touch of anxiety about the mouth. In other contemporary portraits by Herman the subjects appear at ease in their surroundings, occupying the picture plane with confidence. An exception to this is *The artist's mother* 1944–54 (AGNSW) in which the sitter, who also migrated to Australia, seems similarly uncomfortable.

The artist's wife (Paulette) is a portrait of contrasts. On the one hand, with her steady gaze, black hat and 'going out' clothes, Herman has created a portrait of a strong and capable woman who faced life with courage, raised children and attained the fluency and poise she needed to take up a teaching post in her new home. Yet in her subtle discomfort the painting also encapsulates the migrant experience of being part of, but never quite at one with, a new culture.

Bronwyn Campbell

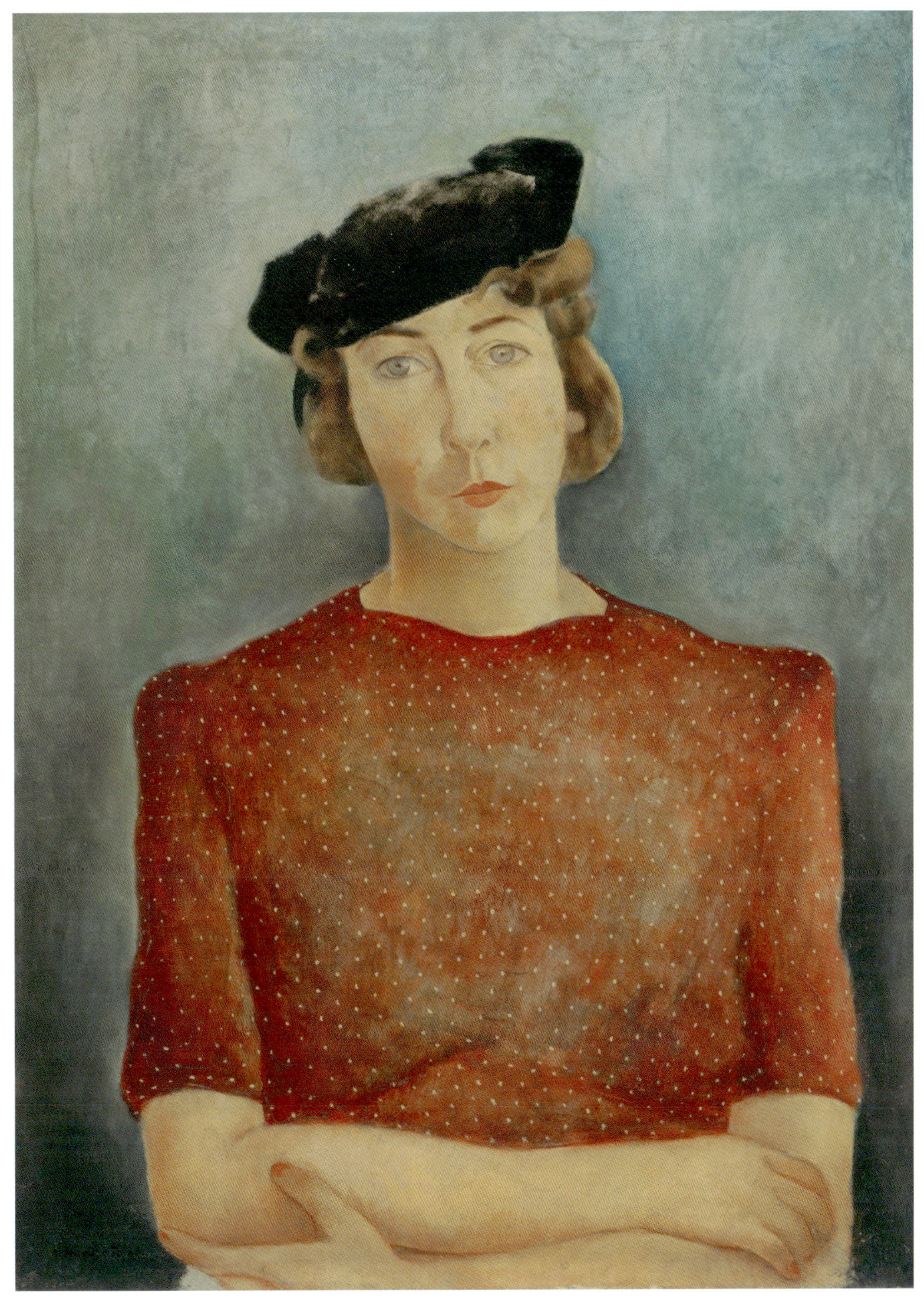

38 Albert Tucker (1914–1999)

Self-portrait 1941

painted in Melbourne, Victoria
oil on paper board, 45 x 32.6 cm
National Gallery of Australia, Canberra, purchased 1982

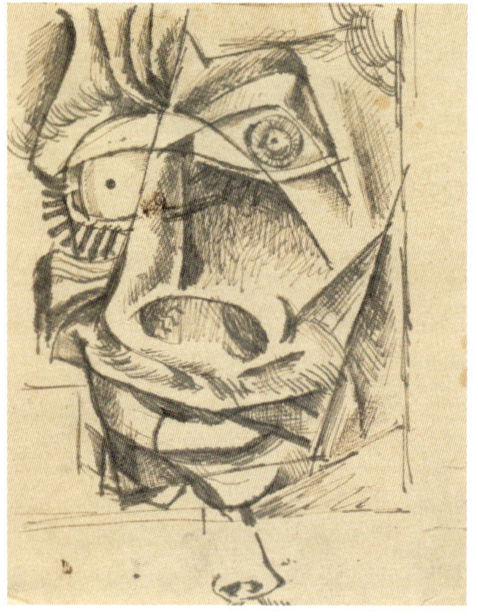

Albert Tucker
Study for painting 'Self-portrait' 1941
pen and ink on paper, 16.2 x 11.5 cm
National Gallery of Australia, Canberra, purchased 1979

Albert Tucker's 1941 *Self-portrait* is a highly personalised image, which, but for the title, is barely recognisable as a portrait.

International styles of art such as Cubism, Surrealism and German Expressionism appear as points of inspiration for Tucker's response to the prevailing 'blue and gold' landscape tradition and the horrors of the Second World War. As an artist he aligned himself with Modernism and was one of a radical group of young men who contributed to the journal *Angry Penguins*. For a short period in the late 1930s and early 1940s, Tucker defined himself as a Social Realist, finding much in common with German Expressionists such as Otto Dix and Max Beckmann. Looking back, he explained:

> The whole world, and all the people I knew, seemed to be seething with ideas and energies and experiences; and my own mind was a seething mess … the highly emotional, overwrought expressionist paintings suited my state at the time.[51]

The structure of the artist's face in this self-portrait is made from a series of close-up, interlocking planes. The manifestly uncomfortable presence is accentuated by strident colour and coarse, irregular brushstrokes. Three eyes like targets stare wide-eyed in fear or anger at some unseen terror on either side of a huge nose, its one cavernous nostril placed at the centre of the composition. The breakdown of a fixed viewpoint, the palette of blood reds, acid greens and yellows—and the stark contrast between light and shadow—create the synergy of Tucker's heightened sensibility at the time.

A pen and ink drawing from 1941, also bearing the title of self-portrait, shows something of Tucker's preparation for this painting. In the drawing the edge of the face is distinct from the background while the planes of the nose, cheek and chin are cross-hatched in keeping with cubist explorations of form and space. Some of Tucker's physical characteristics, such as his prominent chin, strong nose and brow furrowed in concentration are evident in the drawing but its delicacy and finesse are abandoned in the painting.

The expressive intensity of Tucker's 1941 *Self-portrait* suggests a psychological rather than a physical state. In its brutality Albert Tucker conveys the 'seething mess' he recalled so vividly forty years later—a unique reminder of individual turmoil when Europe was once again being ravaged by war.

Adriane Boag

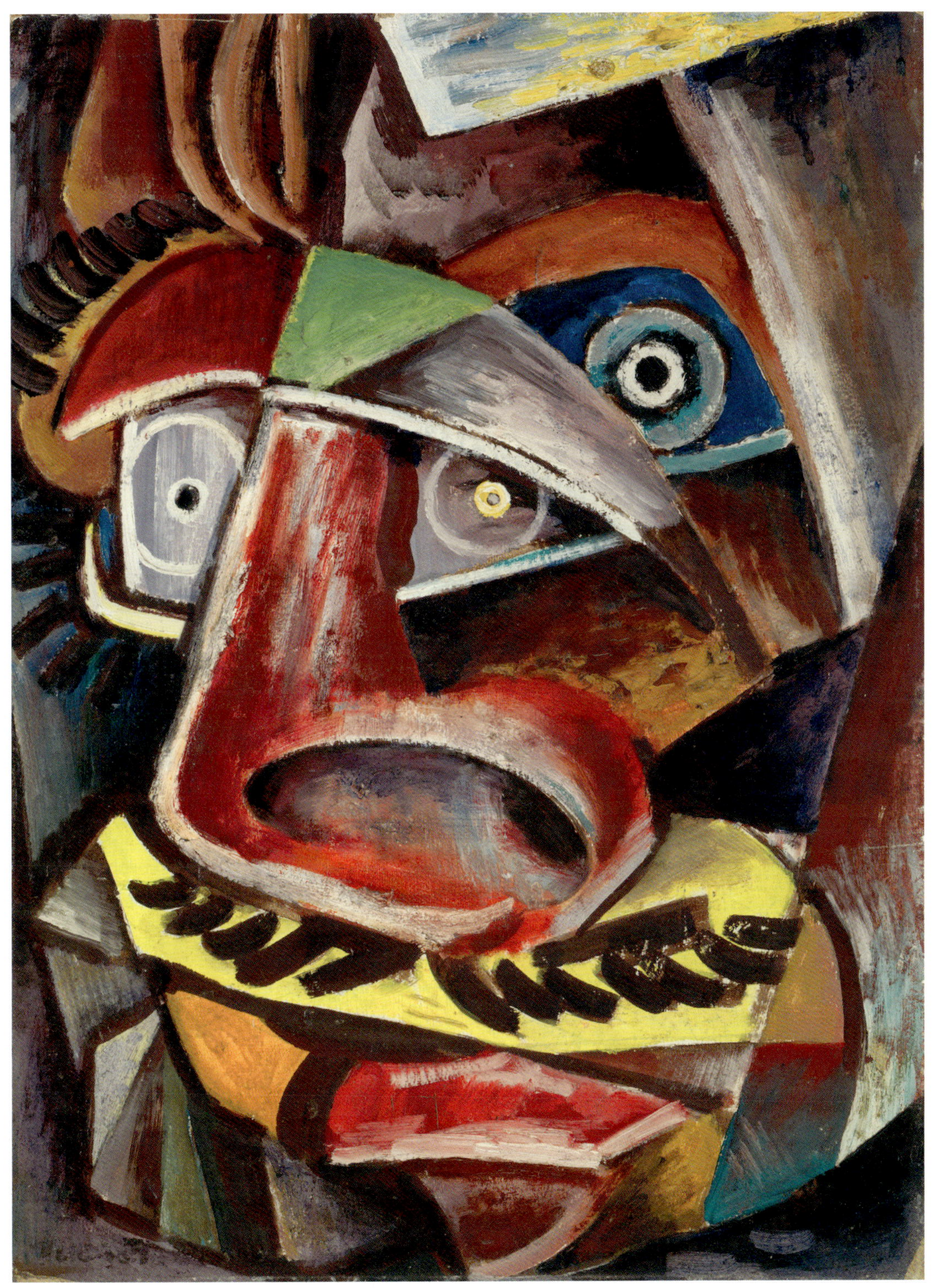

39 **Sidney Nolan** (1917–1992)

Head of soldier 1942

painted at Heide, in Bulleen, Melbourne, Victoria
enamel on cardboard, 75.8 x 63.3 cm
National Gallery of Australia, Canberra, purchased 1976

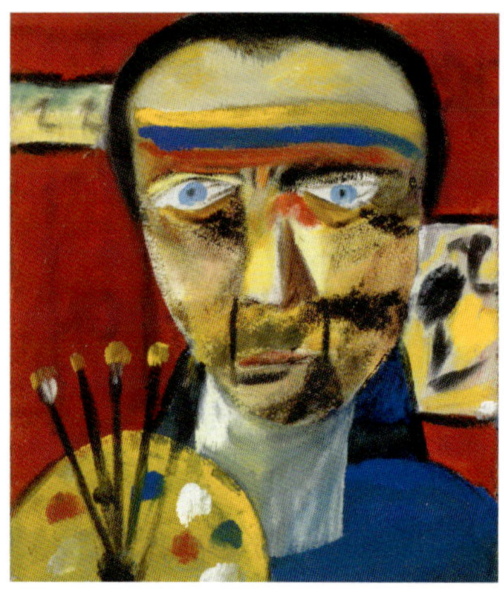

Sidney Nolan
Self-portrait 1943
ripolin enamel on hessian sacking on hardboard, 61 x 52 cm
Art Gallery of New South Wales, Sydney, purchased with funds provided by the Art Gallery Society of New South Wales 1997

In 1945, Sidney Nolan's *Head of soldier* featured on the front cover of psychiatrist Reginald Ellery's publication *Psychiatric aspects of modern warfare*. In different ways Nolan and Ellery both dealt with what Ellery described in his introduction as lunacy and war; two subjects that 'have more in common than their names suggest'.[52]

Nolan was passionately against Australian involvement in the Second World War and despite trying everything to avoid active duty was enlisted into the army in 1942. Stationed in the Wimmera, the vast flat plains of western Victoria, his unit was responsible for guarding emergency food rations for one million people in the event of invasion. *Head of soldier* was painted during a short period of leave while visiting his friends and supporters Sunday and John Reed in their home at Heide, where Nolan would later complete his famous Ned Kelly series of 1946–47 (NGA).

The model for *Head of soldier* was his commanding officer Captain Bilby. Nolan admitted in 1978 that this portrait was neither flattering nor accurate. By depicting Bilby stripped of glory, rank or other identification, Nolan suggests that this is the representation of a type and not a portrait. It is a powerfully expressive interpretation of a shell-shocked victim and exposes (as Ellery had done) the lunacy of war. The painting also lays bare Nolan's strong personal reaction to war as an unwilling recruit.

In 1943 Nolan wrote to the first Director of the Australian War Memorial, inviting him to his exhibition and including a copy of the invitation that featured a black and white reproduction of *Head of soldier*. In the letter, Nolan expressed his view that he could more usefully serve the Australian Army as a war artist. John Treloar visited the exhibition but declined Nolan's application, being somewhat unenthusiastic about the artist's bold, penetrating works. Shortly after, in 1944, faced with the possibility of front-line service, Nolan absented himself from the army without approved leave.

Sidney Nolan has become one of Australia's most celebrated artists. He began formal training twice at the National Gallery of Victoria School of Art but preferred to educate himself in a range of mediums and innovative approaches to artistic practice. He was very widely read and enthusiastic about the cause of modern art. In 1981 Nolan was knighted for his significant contribution to Australian art, and was awarded the Order of Merit in 1983.

Miriam Kelly

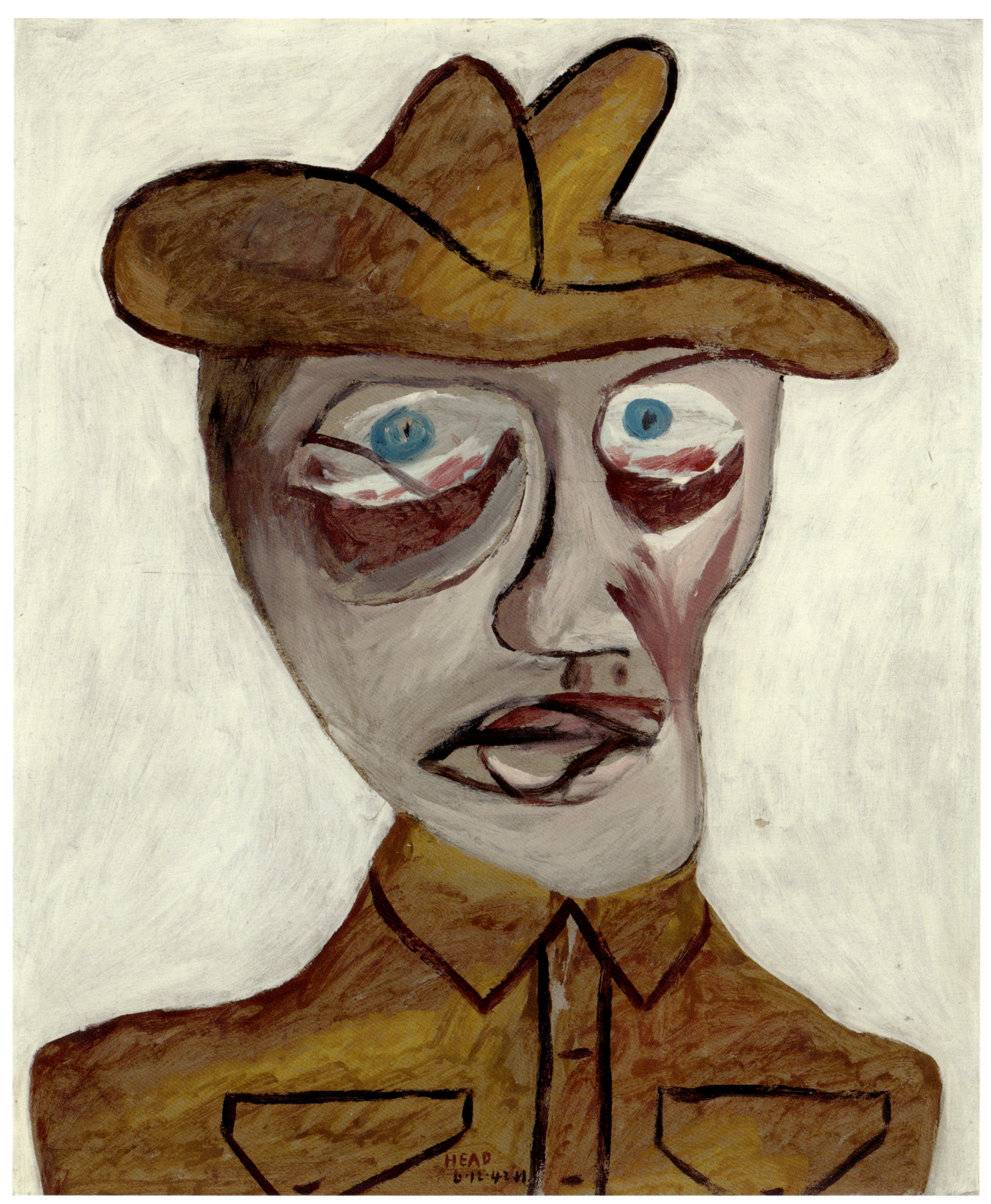
HEAD

40 **John Perceval** (1923–2000)

Boy with cat 2 1943

painted in Melbourne, Victoria
oil on composition board, 50.9 x 43.8 cm
National Gallery of Australia, Canberra, purchased 1970

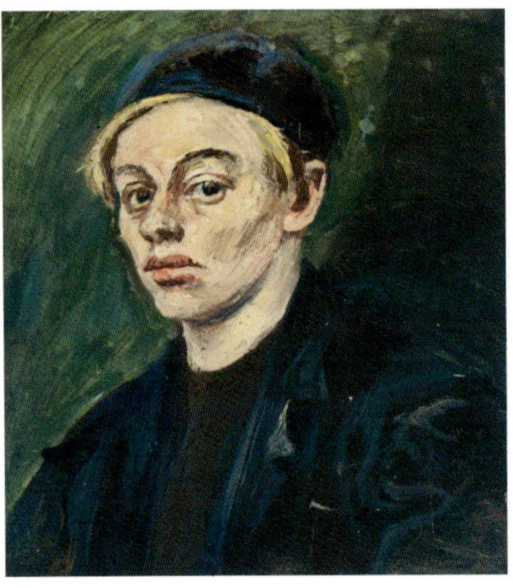

John Perceval
Self-portrait 1946
oil on composition board,
64.2 x 56.5 cm
National Gallery of Australia, Canberra
purchased 1977

Give me a child until he is seven and I will give you the man.[53]

Portraits of children often create a nostalgic aura around the idea of childhood, casting these formative years in a rosy glow. Idyllic portraits of children, posed in comfortable rooms or playing in gardens, accompanied by tame, loyal family pets, abound in the history of art. John Perceval turns this romantic notion on its head with his terrifying image *Boy with cat 2*. Here the boy is locked in a wretched embrace with a wild cat. With sharp claws bared, extended tail bristling and demonic red eyes, the feline creature looks up at the boy who has his eyes shut tight; his face contorted in pain. Gradually, as we contemplate this image, we realise that the cat is inseparable from the boy—a projection of his own tortured state of mind.

Perceval created astonishing expressive images in the 1940s. Like his friends Arthur Boyd, Sidney Nolan, Joy Hester and Albert Tucker, he was concerned about the fate of humanity during the war years, and was able to express anxieties in personal and universal ways. The emotive tenor of *Boy with cat 2* recalls the German Expressionists, while the shallow stage set echoes the surrealist artist, Giorgio de Chirico.

Personal childhood memories also play a part. When Perceval was only eighteen months old, his parents' marriage broke up and his mother departed the family home. A sense of early abandonment along with memories of his father's violent outbursts informed his emotional and artistic landscapes. For instance, Perceval was traumatised by his father's insistence that his small son and daughter decapitate chickens on the farm for the family meal. The difficulty of coordination for a child 'holding a live neck in the left hand while landing an axe with the right' was a chilling memory.[54] In *Boy with cat 2* the creature rising up epitomises a desperate struggle for physical and emotional survival. Perceval's affliction with polio as a teenager cast another long shadow.

Later in life Perceval battled with alcoholism and psychological disturbance that may partly be related to his early experiences. The intense power of *Boy with cat 2* was undoubtedly informed by a depth of feeling that both points to Perceval's own circumstances and transcends them. He reminds us that childhood is often fraught with difficulty; fodder for great art but often far from the proverbial bed of roses.

Deborah Hart

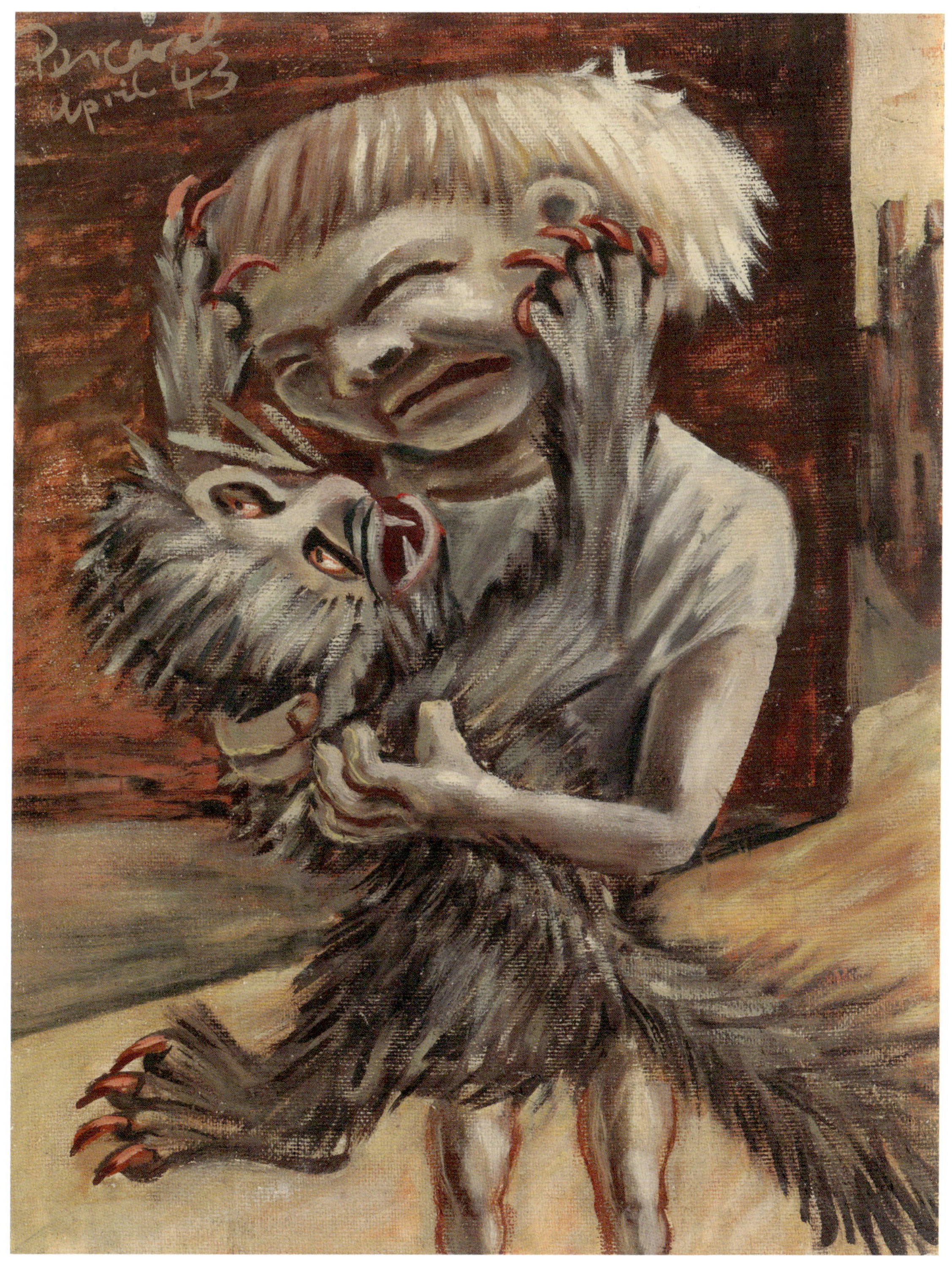
Percival
April 43

41 **Arthur Boyd** (1920–1999)

The brown room 1943

painted at Open Country, in Murrumbeena, Victoria
oil on cotton gauze on cardboard, 63.1 x 75.2 cm
National Gallery of Australia, Canberra, The Arthur Boyd Gift 1975

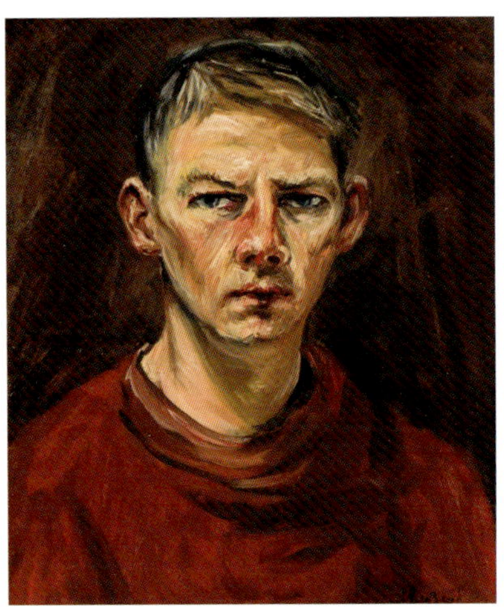

Arthur Boyd
Self-portrait 1945–46
oil on canvas on composition board, 89 x 78.5 cm
private collection, on long-term loan to the National Portrait Gallery, Canberra

Arthur Boyd was raised in a house that was built by his father on Open Country, a small orchard property at Murrumbeena on the outskirts of Melbourne. The 'brown room' was the central room in the house—the living space where the family spent most of their time and where artists and intellectuals gathered for discussion, entertainment and inspiration.

In the painting, the brown room has bare floorboards and is sparsely furnished, its shabbiness reflecting the poverty experienced by the family during the years of the Depression. Seated on a sofa is the artist's father Merric Boyd, his silver hair aglow with the light that pours from the window behind him. On the floor in front of him and at the centre of the painting, Merric's nephew Laurence Beck plays with Peter, the family dog. To the left is Arthur's brother David, seated and playing the piano. In spite of the realism engendered by the balanced, domestic composition, the subjects' massive heads, claw-like hands and unnatural eyes—hollow and blank or huge and staring—are grotesque distortions. To many viewers the image would appear oppressive; the harsh vibrancy of Boyd's style belies the fondness the artist felt for the subjects.

The brown room not only harks back to Arthur Boyd's earliest work when he enlisted family members and local dogs as subjects but also anticipates his later series, when the same subjects were drafted into symbolic roles in his religious and mythological paintings. As in these works, where Boyd avoids 'event' moments in a narrative, *The brown room* evokes the home and the family as a whole, rather than simply the individuals shown.[55] Other members of the family are drawn into the painting through the props in the room. For instance, the piano was a gift from Hatton Beck, the husband of Arthur's older sister Lucy—and Laurence was their child. Arthur's uncle made the chair and through the window is a glimpse of the neighbouring home of his beloved grandparents. *The brown room* is more than a group portrait; more than the depiction of a room. It is part of the artist's complex layering of his art and life.

Bronwyn Campbell

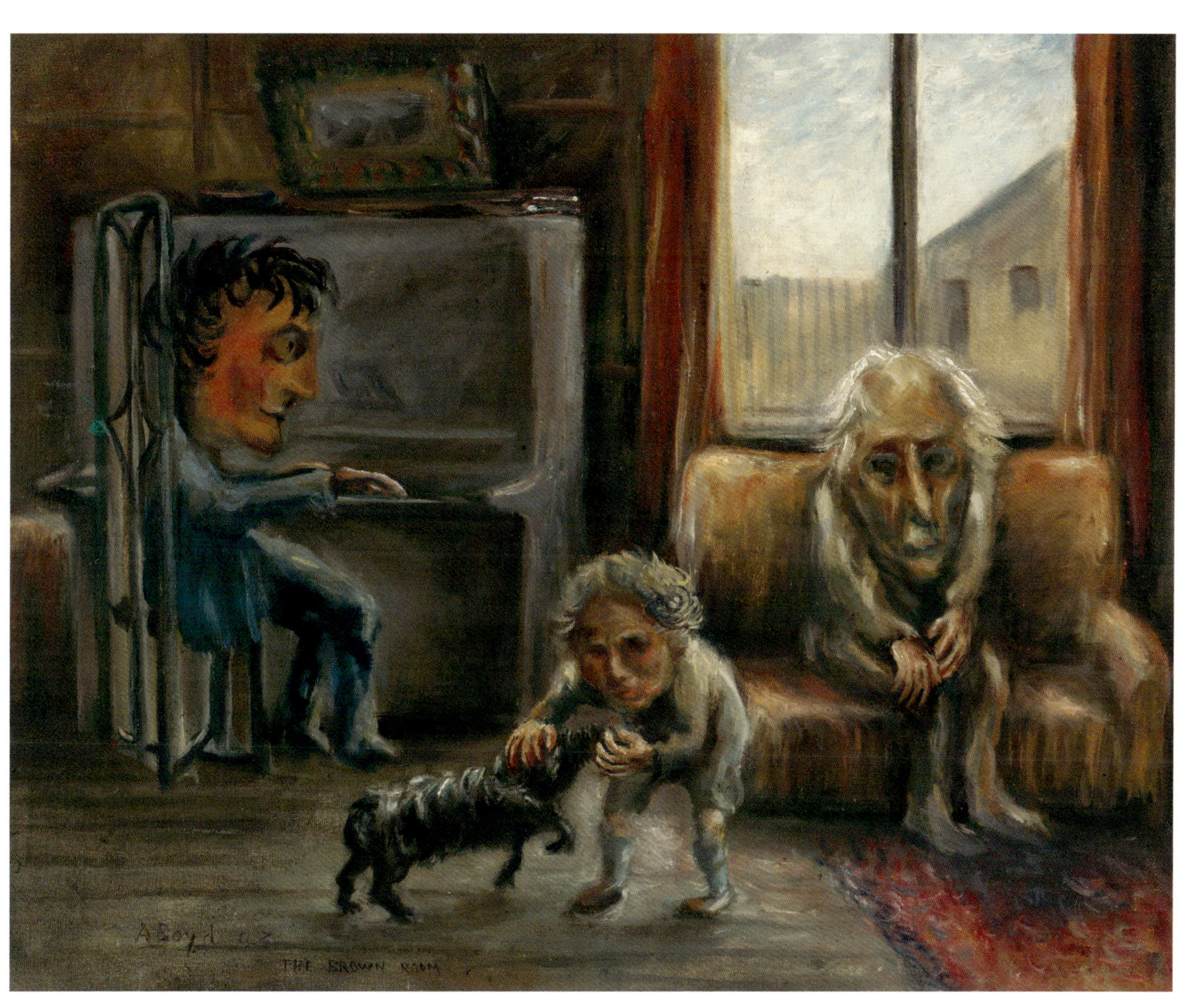
A Boyd
THE BROWN ROOM

42 **Roy de Maistre** (1894–1968)

Self-portrait c 1945

painted in London, England
oil on canvas, 71 x 56 cm
National Gallery of Australia, Canberra, purchased 1975

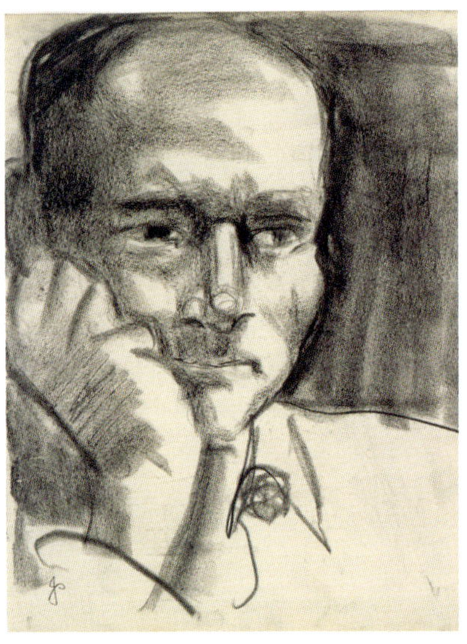

Jean Shepeard
Roi de Mestre (Roy de Maistre) c 1930
pastel on paper, 27.7 x 21.2 cm
National Portrait Gallery, Canberra

Self-portrait c 1945, with its strong interlacing lines, illustrates the influence of Cubism on Roy de Maistre's work. Set in the intimate environment of his studio, we see only a reflection of the artist's head and shoulders above a roaring, well-stoked fire, a shelf packed with books and a glimpse of stairs leading upwards. The artist's world appears private and contained.

The surface pattern of the painting is similarly contained; constructed and arranged with a reduced palette and active but irregular shapes. The artist however appears comfortable, the hand gesture perhaps suggesting a moment captured mid-sentence in a lively discussion.

In London, de Maistre established a wide circle of friends including critics, poets, politicians and musicians. Patrick White and Francis Bacon became close friends. On their meeting in the summer of 1935, White reflected that de Maistre 'was a snob, and an artist of integrity, a Modern who affected Edwardian manners, a homosexual of extreme discretion, and a melancholy man of great charm'.[56]

Self-portrait embodies this discretion: de Maistre frames his reflection as he does his life, inviting the viewer's gaze on his own terms and at a distance. The fire, too, has clear boundaries and yet indicates a passionate creative spirit. The artist fuels the fire and fire fuels the artist; the triangular black hood connects with his collar and shirt and the artist's hand almost catches the tips of the flames.

Roy de Maistre was a pioneer in Australian Post-Impressionism and Cubism. When he died, on his request, his notes and letters were destroyed and only his paintings and the memories of family and friends remain as an insight into the man and the artist.[57]

De Maistre studied at the Royal Art Society of NSW and Julian Ashton's Art School. Interested in the relationship between painting, music and colour, he first exhibited with Roland Wakelin and Grace Cossington Smith in Sydney in 1916 and again with Wakelin in 1919, showing some of the first abstract paintings seen in Australia.[58] During the 1920s he travelled to England and France, leaving Australia permanently for London in 1929.

Georgia Connolly

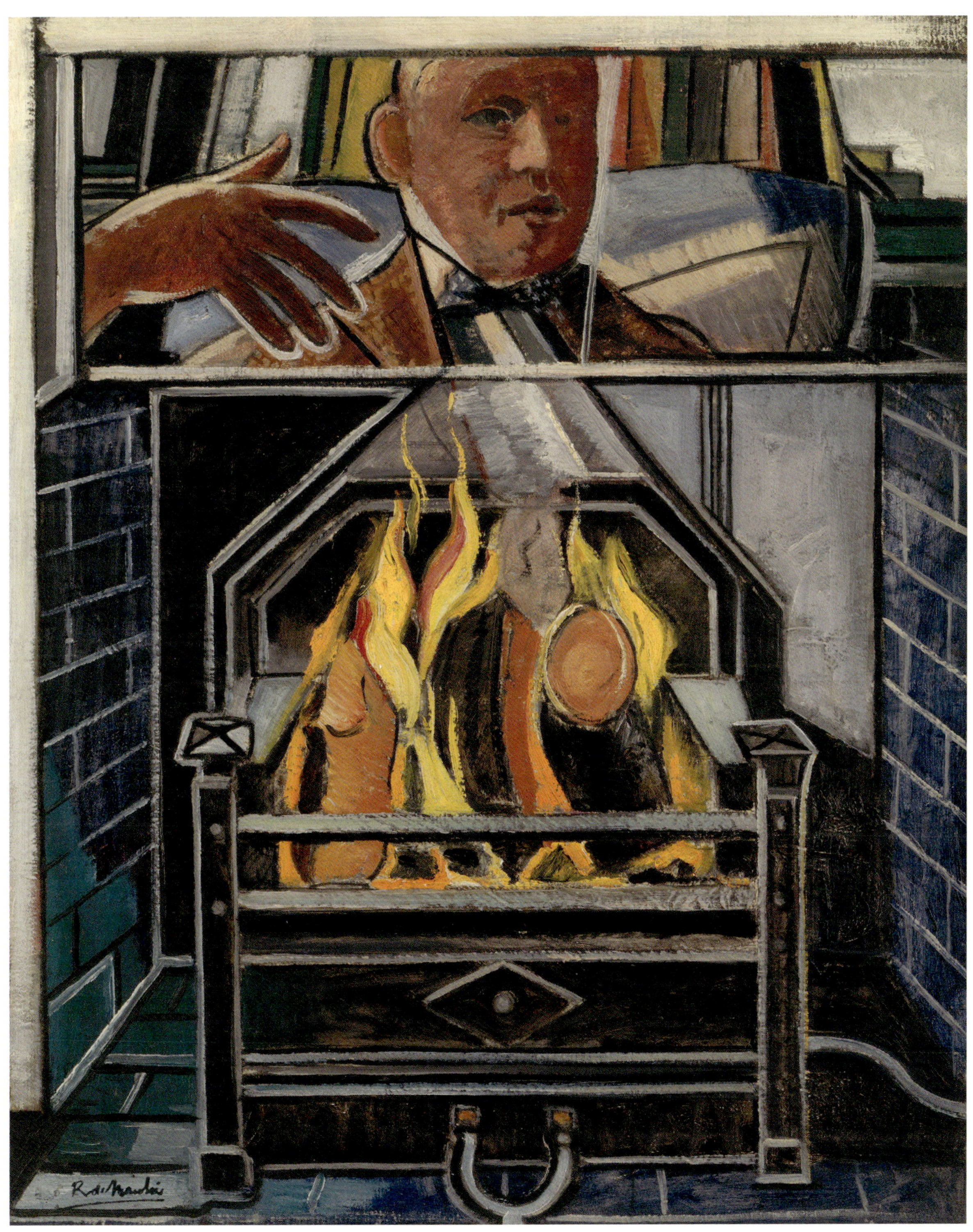

43 **Sidney Nolan** (1917–1992)

Ned Kelly 1946

painted in Melbourne, Victoria
enamel on composition board, 74.5 x 61.5 cm
National Gallery of Australia, Canberra, purchased 1970

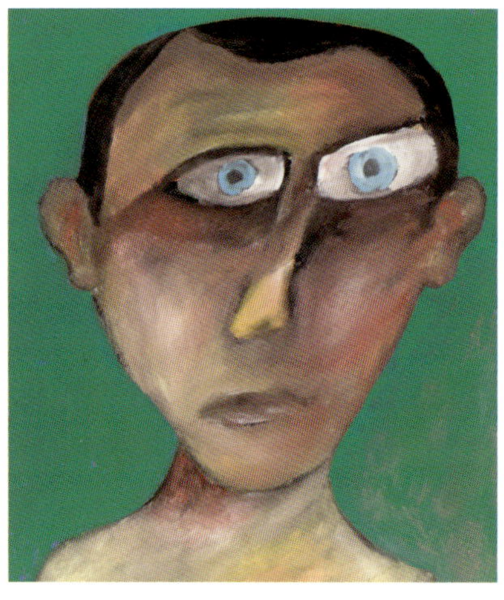

Sidney Nolan
S.N. 1947
synthetic polymer paint on composition board, 74 x 61.5 cm
Art Gallery of South Australia, Adelaide, gift of Sidney & Cynthia Nolan 1974

Sidney Nolan was one of the most important Australian painters of the twentieth century. His iconic Ned Kelly series of 1946–47 (NGA) depicts key moments in the story of bushranger and folk-hero Ned Kelly (Edward Kelly 1855–1880) and is one of the most recognisable series of works in the history of Australian art.

Ned Kelly 1946 resembles a photograph of the bushranger at eighteen years of age, preserved on Kelly's Beechworth goal record (Public Record Office of Victoria, Melbourne). If this photograph were Nolan's inspiration, he would have been just eleven years older than Kelly when it was taken, in 1873. Nolan became obsessed with Kelly and would continue to depict him in drawings and paintings until the year of his own death in 1992.[59]

Unlike many of Nolan's other paintings of Kelly, here he shows the young man unmasked, without his black-box armour. The facial features of Nolan's subject are blurred and indistinct, like an endlessly repeated tale that loses its finer points. Nolan simplified Kelly's face into a series of marks: horizontal slashes for eyes and strong eyebrows, a vertical stroke of a nose, and an impassive horizontal slit for a mouth. Kelly's eyes fix on the viewer, like the eyes in a painted portrait from a haunted house.

Ned Kelly became an outlaw following an altercation at his mother's home that led to a local constable claiming that he was shot in the wrist. From then on, Kelly and his gang took to the bush. While in hiding, they shot and killed three policemen who were in pursuit of them near Stringybark Creek. Dressed in crude suits of armour the Kelly gang staged their last stand in the town of Glenrowan. Police laid siege to the hotel where they were holed up, shooting several hostages, and eventually setting fire to the building. Ned was the only one of his gang of four to survive and was captured after being shot several times. He was convicted of murder and hanged at the Melbourne gaol on 11 November 1880.

Melanie Beggs-Murray

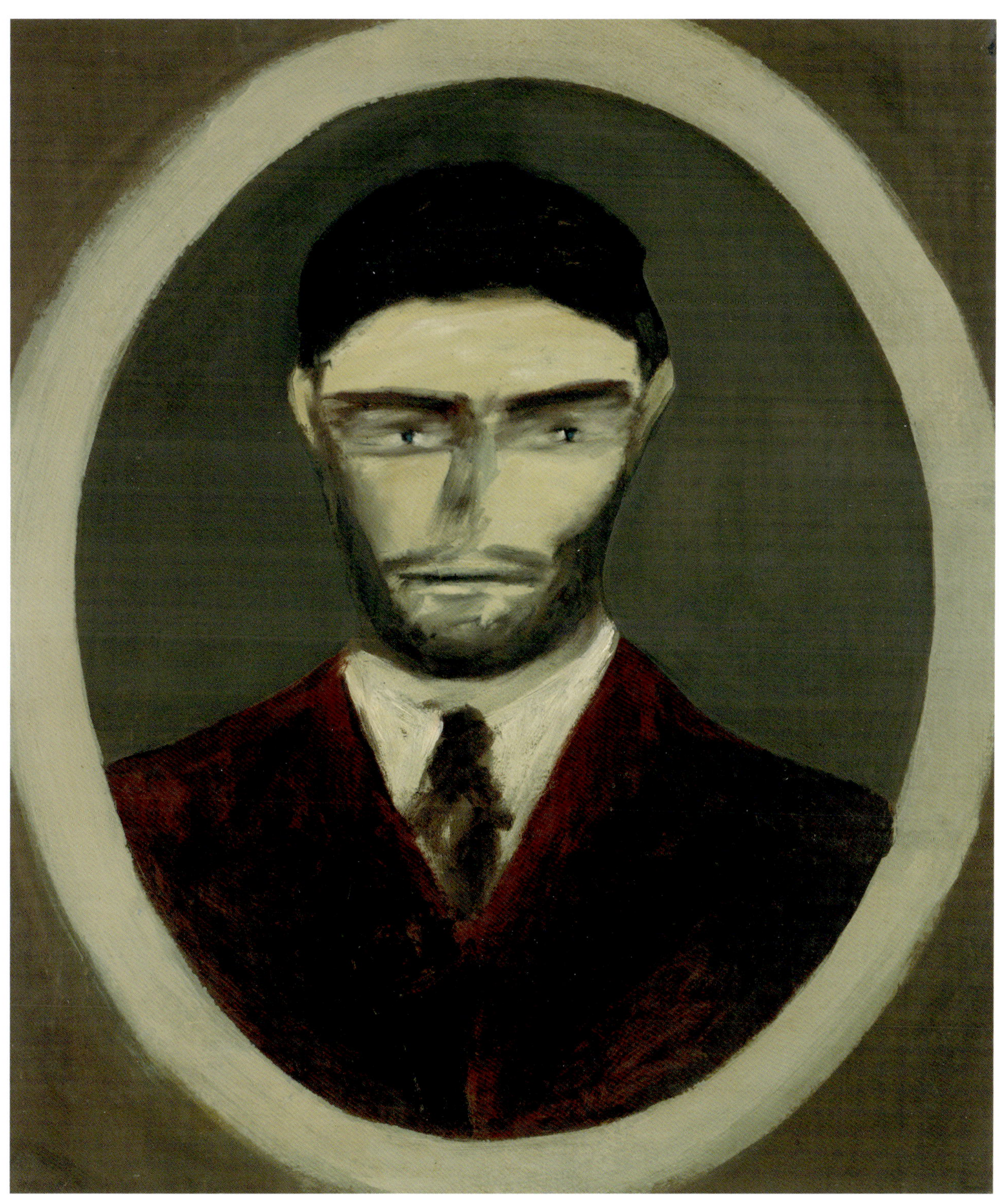

44 Albert Tucker (1914–1999)

Sydney Fox 1946

oil on cotton gauze on cardboard, 63.8 x 76 cm

National Gallery of Australia, Canberra, purchased 1981

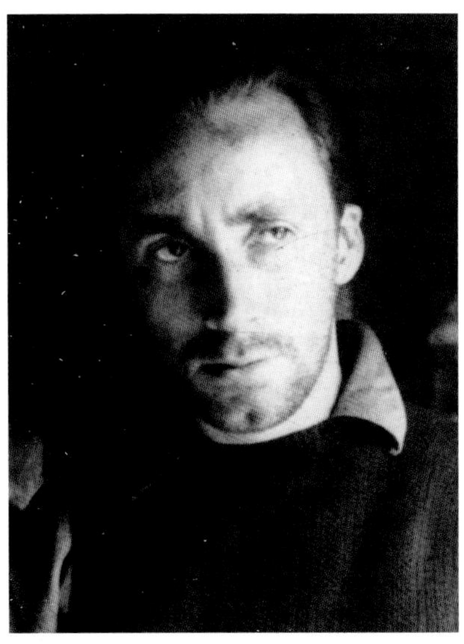

Albert Tucker
Self-portrait, 26 Little Collins Street, Melbourne 1940
National Library of Australia, Canberra

What manner of man gazes from the hooded, deeply shadowed, inset eyes and face illuminated by a single, concentrated light-source just outside the frame? There is something not quite 'right' about him despite the schoolboy neatness of his appearance. There is a weakness in him that pulls you back from embracing and identifying with the man. The sharply lit almost jagged white collar around his neck lends a further sense of disquiet. After taking this in, what remains for the viewer is an almost mesmeric flicker between the staring eye and shadowed drooping eye—back and forth, back and forth.

Tucker's deliberate and expert paintwork is rich and expressive. His exploration of the subject is forensic, controlled and relentless; the facial features finely sculpted.

There is fascination in the artist's method, though he studies from a distance, projecting himself into the mind and circumstance of Sydney Fox. Nothing in the work distracts the viewer from the subject—the space is shallow, the background plain, the palette tonal and subdued, the light strong and dramatic.

Intent and intense, Albert Tucker in the 1940s was an artist confronted by the psychology of madness and the moral outrage of war. He spent six months in the military (1941–42) and said of his commanding officer:

> He was probably the only military commander who had a respect for artists … He also knew that he was sending off these batches of troops in many cases to be killed … Again this curious omnipotent finger … put me in a position in the hospital where I was able to be a witness to the effects of war on people.[60]

At the Heidelberg Military Hospital, Tucker observed men in psychiatric wards struggling with the brutality and human carnage that accompanies war—fractured minds seared with images that made no sense and allowed no peace. Tucker's experience feeds into portraits like *Sydney Fox*, each a 'social-psychological landscape' to be investigated.

What manner of man was Sydney Fox? A psychopath who at the age of thirty-one was the last man hanged in Maidstone Prison in Kent, for murdering his mother.

Belinda Cotton

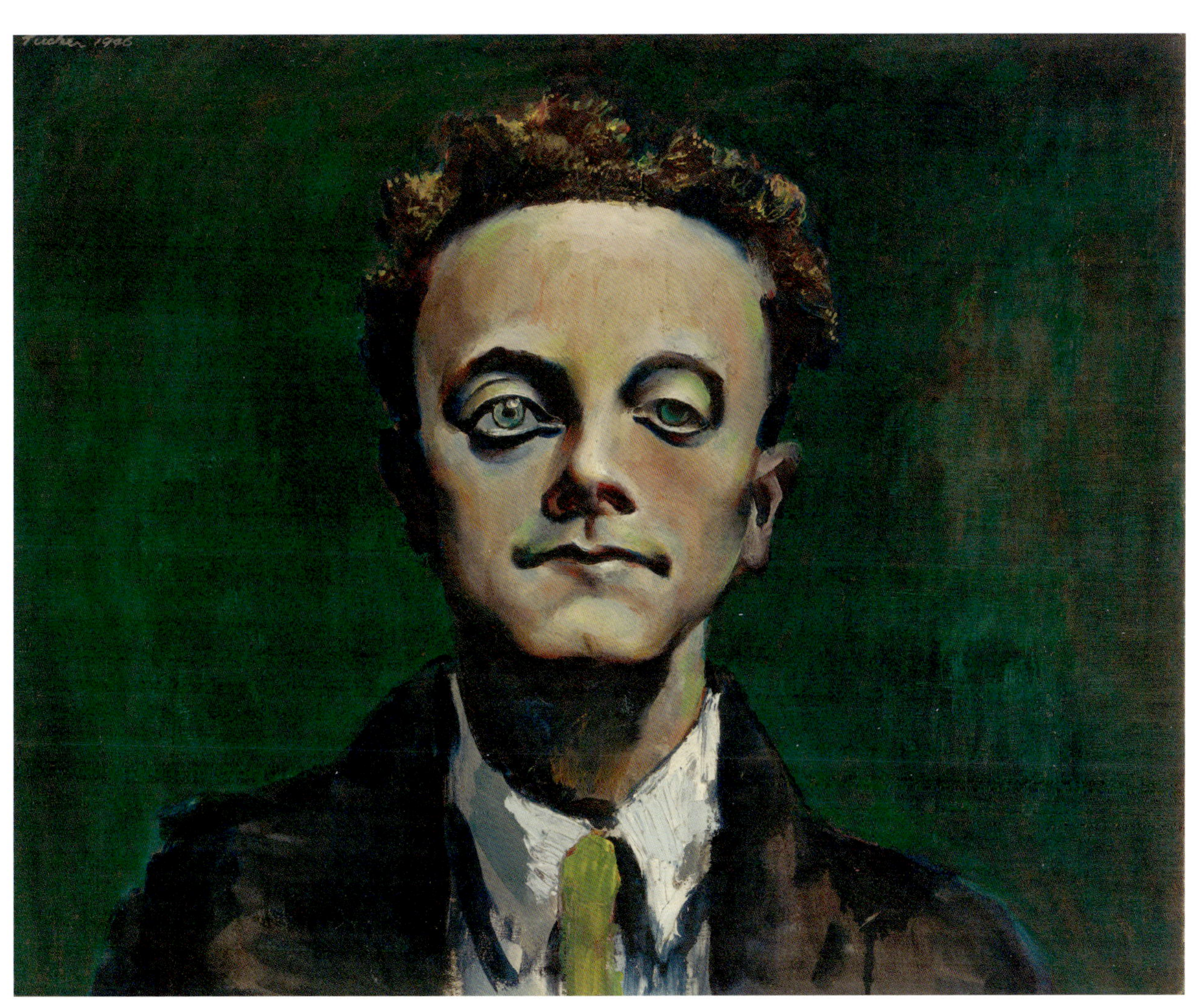

45 Albert Tucker (1914–1999)

Man's head 1946

painted in Melbourne, Victoria
oil on cotton gauze on cardboard, 63.4 x 76 cm
National Gallery of Australia, Canberra, purchased 1981

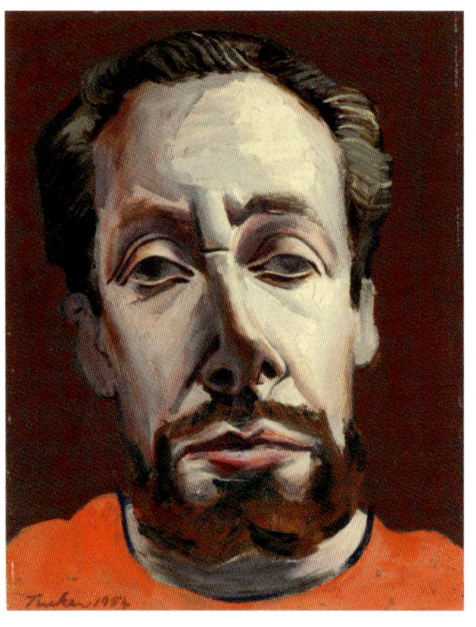

Albert Tucker
Self-portrait 1954
oil on paperboard, 51.1 x 38.6 cm
National Gallery of Australia, Canberra, purchased 1981

Melbourne-based Albert Tucker painted many works focusing on the anxieties and fears of individuals. In his *Images of modern evil* 1943–47 (NGA) he depicted the sordid behaviour of servicemen on leave and prostitutes in Melbourne during the Second World War. These established him as a maker of highly expressive images of modern life.

Tucker painted *Man's head* during the period he was working on his *Images of modern evil*, and in it he conveyed a similar distaste for the darker side of humanity. He based the portrait on a photograph published in a newspaper of a man who had been charged in court with kicking a small dog to death. The man did not know that Tucker had painted his portrait. Tucker said that he painted it because he was 'fascinated with the utterly dissolute face of this man' and thought he had a 'look about him, a collapsed kind of face, a kind of moral disintegration'.[61]

This portrait is the artist's interpretation of what the man looked like. Indeed Tucker later found the newspaper photograph and thought his portrait was really nothing like the man's face, that he had 'extracted the corrupt disintegrating element in it'.[62] Tucker exaggerated distinctive features to suggest the man's character and mood: the asymmetric head, the furrowed brow, dark hollow staring eyes, crooked nose and swollen lips make the man appear zombie-like. The unkempt shirt collar on the man's short neck makes him appear dissolute. The yellowish-blue tinge to the skin, the dark shadow over the left (sinister) side of his face and the flashes of red in his hair, set against the green-blue background, add to this impression of moral disintegration. What is more, Tucker applied the paint thickly, and used the agitated brushstrokes to assist in evoking the physical presence of a brutal man.

In painting this portrait Tucker realised that it was not the actual individual that fascinated him; rather he was interested in depicting what he thought to be a type, a symbol. Tucker saw in this man a 'kind of refracting prism for the human condition', 'a social-psychological landscape'.[63]

Anne Gray

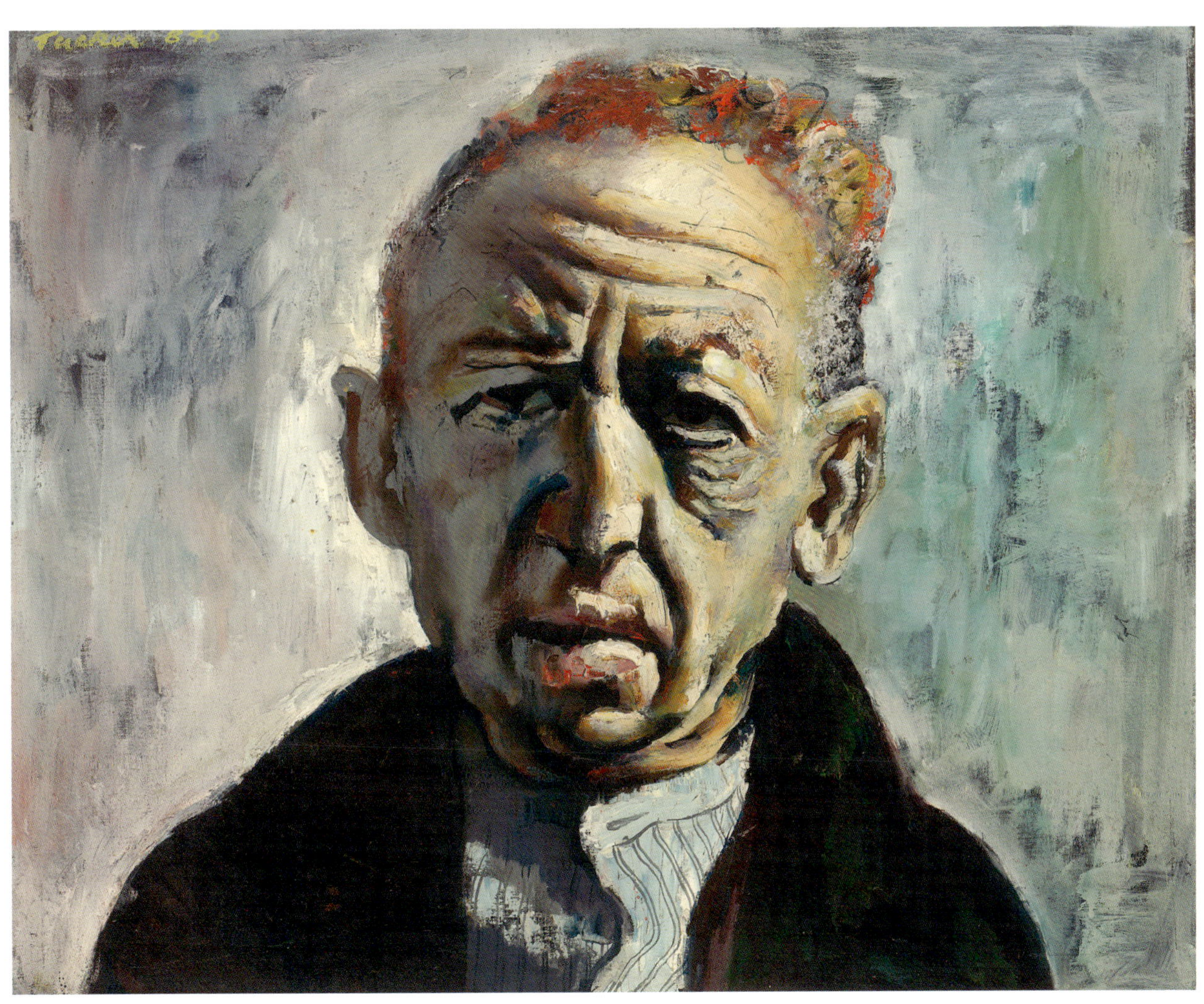

46 **Russell Drysdale** (1912–1981)

Margaret Olley 1948

painted in Sydney, New South Wales
oil on canvas, 61.6 x 51.2 cm

National Gallery of Australia, Canberra, gift of American Friends of the National Gallery of Australia, Inc, New York, NY, USA, made possible with the generous support of Mr and Mrs Benno Schmidt of New York and Esperance, Western Australia, 1987

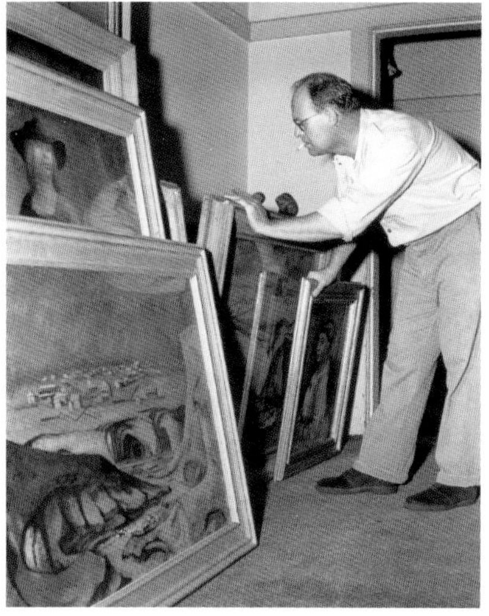

Max Dupain
Russell Drysdale c 1948
National Portrait Gallery, Canberra

Russell Drysdale's portrait of Margaret Olley captures her as a confident and impish young woman. Drysdale, with an already distinctive approach, renders Olley in layered earthy tones. The portrait has a rustic quality seen in Drysdale's outback figures in the landscape from the late 1940s to early 1950s. Yet, unlike the anonymous subjects of these works, Olley's big dark eyes, petite rounded face and loosely, but stylishly pulled-back hair are instantly recognisable.

In the year this portrait was painted, Drysdale also opened Margaret Olley's first, very successful solo exhibition. In 1948, she also sat for William Dobell, whose portrait of her went on to win the 1949 Archibald Prize. Unlike Dobell's portrait, Drysdale's *Margaret Olley* received little coverage in the press and escaped the controversy of the day surrounding the question of likeness.

Margaret Olley is well known in Australian art. Born in Lismore in 1923, she trained as a painter in Brisbane and Sydney and later studied in Paris. Here she encountered the influential work of artists such as Matisse and Bonnard. She developed an approach to colour and composition, and a passion for still life that continued throughout her career. In 1995 she said: '[I]t's not fashionable these days to celebrate life. But I suppose that's what I do. There's no terrible message in it! I have an absolute obsession to paint. I go to bed and can't wait to wake up and be painting again.'[64]

Painter, philanthropist and subject of a number of portraits, Olley's generosity, warm personality and colourful approach to life have endeared her to the Australian public and colleagues alike. In 1990, she established the Margaret Hannah Olley Art Trust, which has funded many important acquisitions by public arts institutions in Australia. For her services to the arts, Olley was honoured with the Office of the Order of Australia (AO) in 1991 and the Companion of the Order of Australia (AC) in 2006.

Russell Drysdale created an original and sophisticated visual language with strong, melancholic and rich red images of inland New South Wales and Queensland. Drysdale's vision was of a countryside drought-stricken and eroded, with abandoned towns and eerie derelict buildings. These images influenced the development of postwar art in Australia, and the impression of Australia and its art internationally.

Miriam Kelly

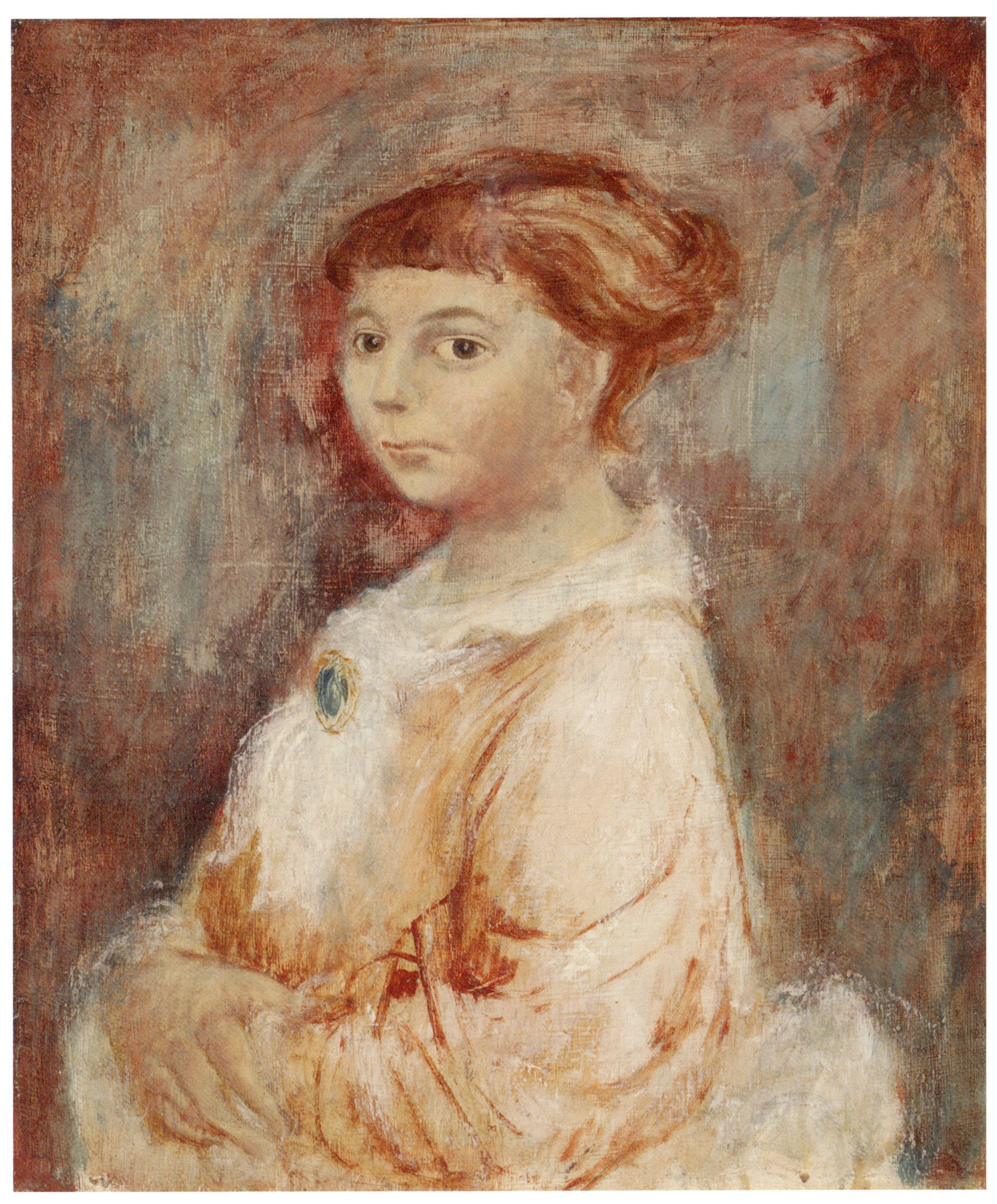

47 Sidney Nolan (1917–1992)

Daisy Bates at Ooldea 1950

painted in Sydney, New South Wales
enamel and oil on composition board, 90.2 x 109.3 cm
National Gallery of Australia, Canberra, gift of American Friends of the National Gallery of Australia, Inc, New York, NY, USA, made possible with the generous support of Mr and Mrs Benno Schmidt of New York and Esperance, Western Australia 1987

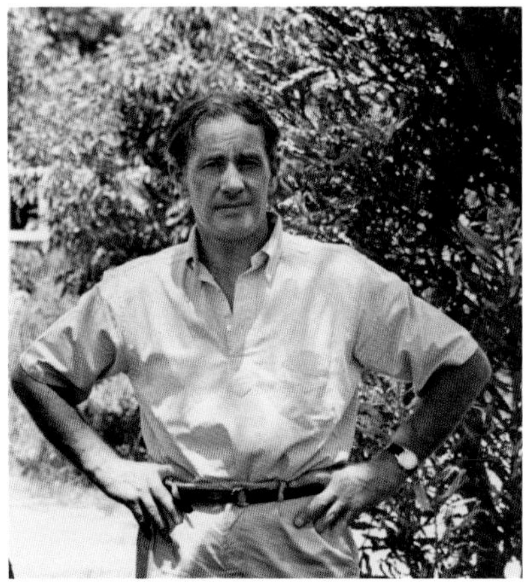

David Moore
Sidney Nolan, Western Australia 1962
National Portrait Gallery, Canberra

It is only in myth that the truth about any country can be found.[65]

In June 1949 Sidney Nolan travelled with his wife Cynthia and daughter Jinx to Central Australia. This trip would have a profound impact on Nolan's paintings and would provide the opportunity and impetus for him to celebrate Daisy May Bates, a well-known Australian icon at the time.

Daisy Bates was born in Ireland in 1863 and migrated to Australia in 1884. An eccentric character, she created her own mythologies, linking herself to the aristocracy and marrying at least two men bigamously, one of whom, Breaker Morant, would loom large in the Australian consciousness. Daisy Bates, however, was most notable for her work with Aborigines, which saw her moving to Western and South Australia, eventually setting up camp at Ooldea in 1918.

For sixteen years Bates lived in Ooldea on the edge of the Nullarbor Plain, an isolated area even though the railway was inching through the desert. In her late seventies, Bates was still leading a peripatetic life. However, by 1949 she had moved to Adelaide and was living in a nursing home; she died in 1951 at the age of 88.

Painted in Sydney in 1950, Nolan's placement of Bates at the centre of an arid, dominating landscape with its big sky is also a portrait of determination. Appearing almost as an apparition, the figure of Bates stands erect, though her diminutive size emphasises an indomitable spirit. Bates's daintily shod feet are not firmly grounded in the land, an indication that she is not of the land.

Nolan does not need to identify a subject's features to convey the sense of his portrait; here Bates's face is obscured and unrecognisable. It is instead her long Edwardian skirt, crisp white shirt, white gloves, parasol and veil that signify something of Daisy Bates's character; her strict resolve to adhere to an outdated and impractical costume for her chosen way of life.

Nolan's work cements the image of Daisy Bates in the Australian psyche and, while immortalising her, he continues to explore the idea of Europeans as fragile aliens in the Australian landscape. It is Nolan's portrait of the continent.

Dominique Nagy

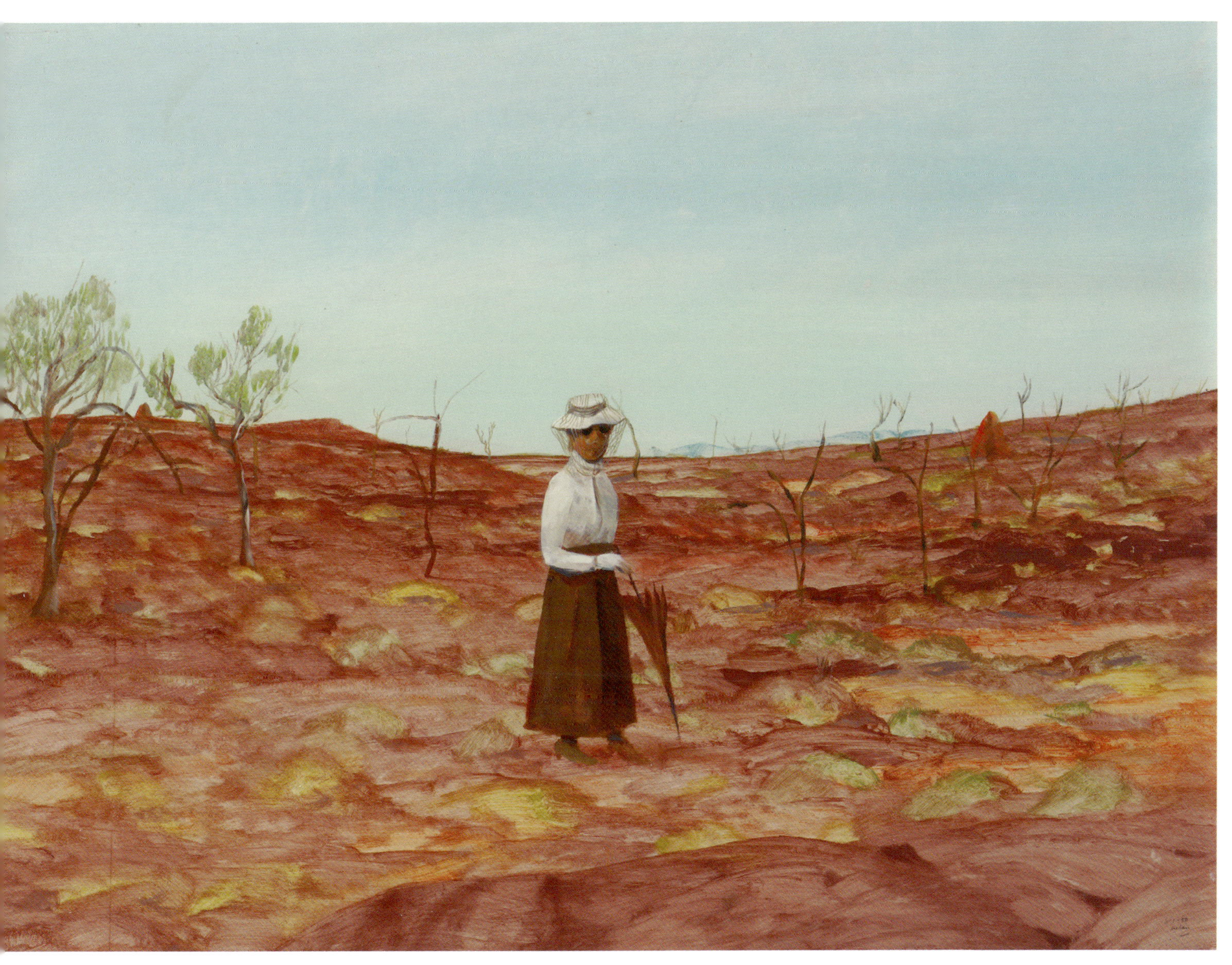

48 **Dušan Marek** (1926–1993)

My wife c 1952

painted in Sydney, New South Wales
oil on plywood, 36 x 29 cm
National Gallery of Australia, Canberra, gift of James Agapitos OAM and Ray Wilson OAM 2007

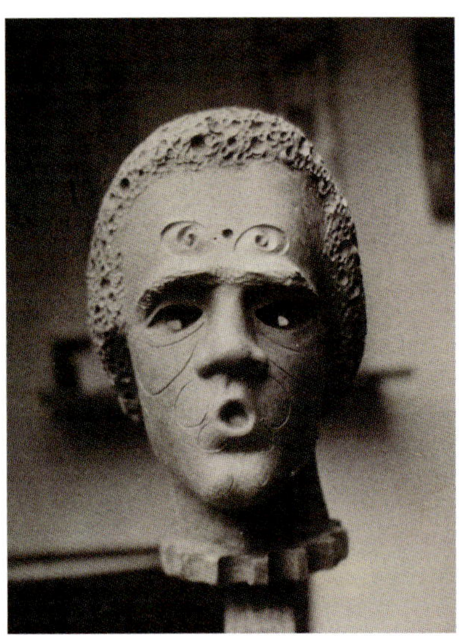

Voitre Marek
Dušan 1946
clay, 30 x 20 x 20 cm
private collection

Dušan Marek and his brother immigrated to Australia in 1948 to escape the impending Russian takeover of Czechoslovakia. They took the long journey by sea on the *SS Charlton Sovereign*, with over one thousand other eastern European refugees. On board, Dušan Marek met a beautiful young woman named Helena Jakubova, originally from Prague. Dušan had joined Helena in reciting poetry into the sea spray on the bow of the ship; from that moment on they became inseparable companions.[66] On their arrival in Australia, the pair settled in Adelaide, which had been described to them as 'the City of Churches' and which they hoped would be reminiscent of Prague. They married in Adelaide in January 1951, shortly before departing for Tasmania and later moving to Sydney.

My wife c 1952 is a striking portrait. While the woman depicted is unmistakably the attractive, fair-haired Helena Marek, she has undergone a Picasso-esque transfiguration of form. Her head floats atop thin black lines, reminiscent of her shoulders and torso, and her delicate features and luscious locks are smooth cubist blocks of bold flattened colour. Marek appears to have portrayed the movement of his wife's face from profile to front views, capturing multiple luscious red lips but just a single, spectacular eye. This striking compositional choice might reflect the nature of the Mareks' relationship. Helena was wife, lover, mother, critic, manager and muse. She told researcher Cheri Donaldson that when she commented on the small mouths and large eye, her husband retorted, 'you appeared to see everything but say little'.[67] Yet, just as she was everything to him, he was everything to her; *My wife* holds a very special place in the heart of Helena Marek.[68]

This mirage of transfigured beauty alludes to Marek's philosophy of making art, which, like his general approach to life, was governed by his desire to convey a world beyond the physical; to reveal what is seen in the mind's eye and held in the subconscious.

Marek's Surrealism was deeply rooted in spirituality. In Adelaide, he had initially found supportive like-minded artists in Ivor Francis and Douglas Roberts—South Australian artists who had been at the fore of surrealist practice in the late 1930s to early 1940s. However, Marek's works received criticism from the wider public, other artistic circles and the press. Regardless, Marek persevered with a wholehearted commitment to Surrealism throughout his life and career.

Miriam Kelly

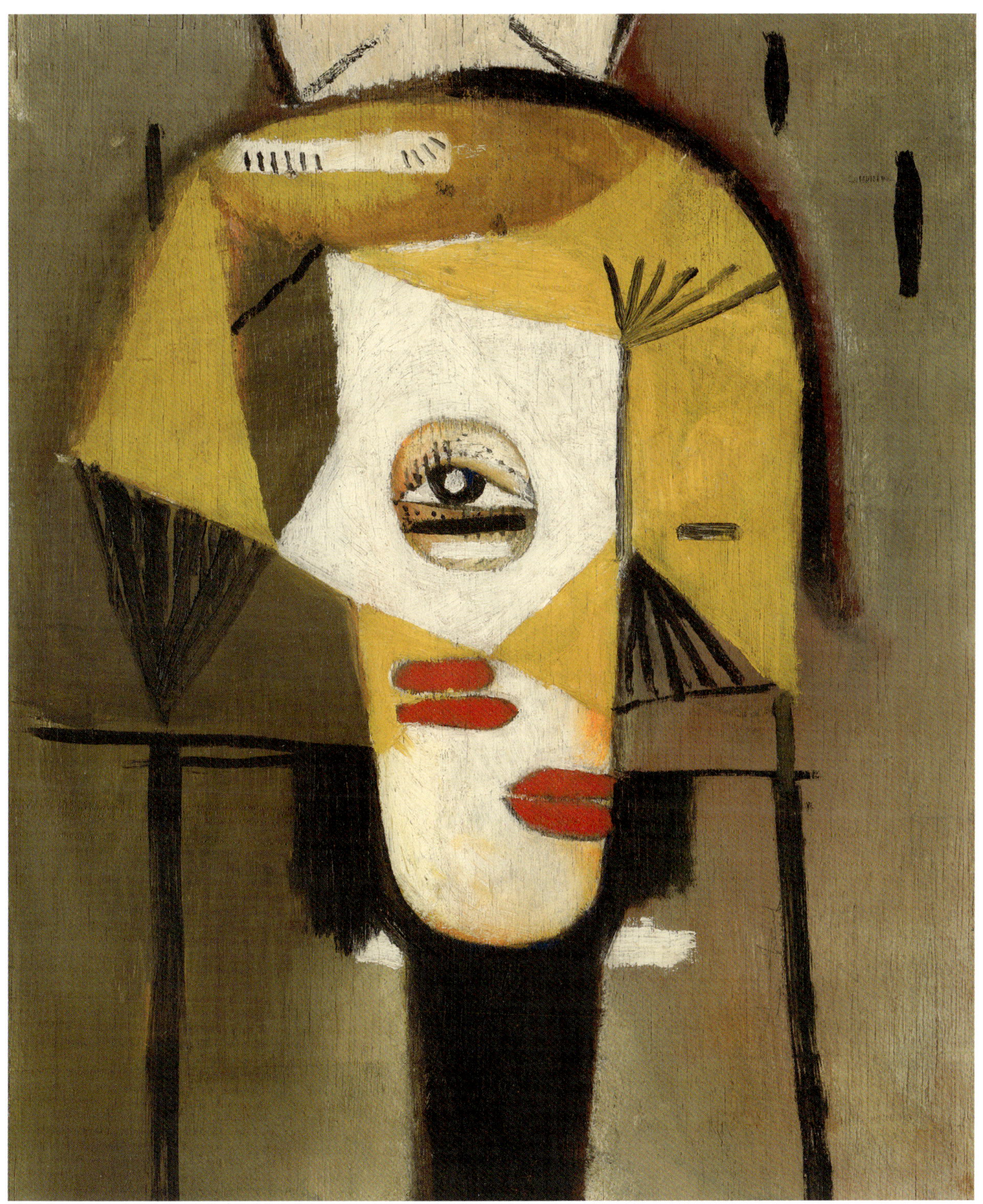

49 **Laurence Hope** (b 1927)

Self-portrait with mumps 1953

painted in Melbourne, Victoria
oil on cotton gauze on board, 60 x 64.8 cm
National Gallery of Australia, Canberra, purchased 1990

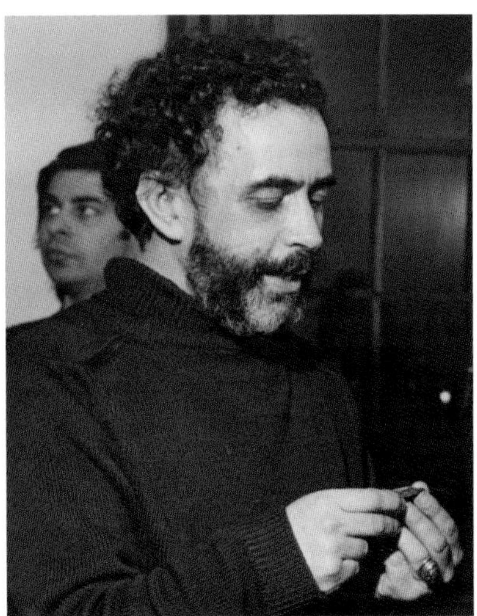

Laurence Hope, 1971
National Library of Australia, Canberra

Fever, lassitude, headaches and swollen glands are painfully evoked in Laurence Hope's *Portrait of the artist with mumps*. In this painting, Hope depicts himself stubbled and puffy, enduring the hot and cold sweats in an over-sized coat, staring longingly out a window as he waits for the day of return to good health.

Laurence Hope was born in Sydney to parents who encouraged his interest in art and literature. In the early 1940s he enrolled at the National Art School (also known as East Sydney Technical College) to study art, but soon chafed under the institution's traditional approach. In 1945 he left for Queensland, the home state of his parents. It was in Brisbane, then a culturally conservative town still under wartime restrictions, that Hope really embarked on his artistic career. Making friends with the writers of the Barjai group, he also became a founding member of the Miya Studio, a group of young artists whose insistence on freedom of expression was considered avant-garde.[69]

After some success with exhibitions, Hope travelled around Australia before settling in Melbourne, where he was to remain for more than a decade. There he forged strong friendships with many of Australia's leading artists and was involved in the establishment of the Contemporary Art Society. It was there that he painted his portrait with mumps while staying with his 'adopted family', the cosmopolitan Georges and Mirka Mora. It is Georges's coat that he wears in the painting, and the Mora's son Philippe who looks on as if he shares the malaise.

Having refined his practice in Melbourne, in 1963 Hope moved to London, where he was to remain, though travelling extensively through Europe, North Africa, Mexico and Cambodia. While neither a prolific artist, nor a frequent exhibitor, he has been consistent in focusing on the figure and, in particular, the fragile psyche. His paintings and drawings, often set within the urban environment and darkly evoking the loves, intimacies, isolation and solitude of its inhabitants, are characteristically ambivalent, romantic and melancholy.

Portrait of the artist with mumps, a strong expression of Hope's unwavering quest for an emotional connection with the viewer, was the cover image for the publication *The art of Laurence Hope*, which accompanied his 2002 retrospective in Australia.

Simon Elliott

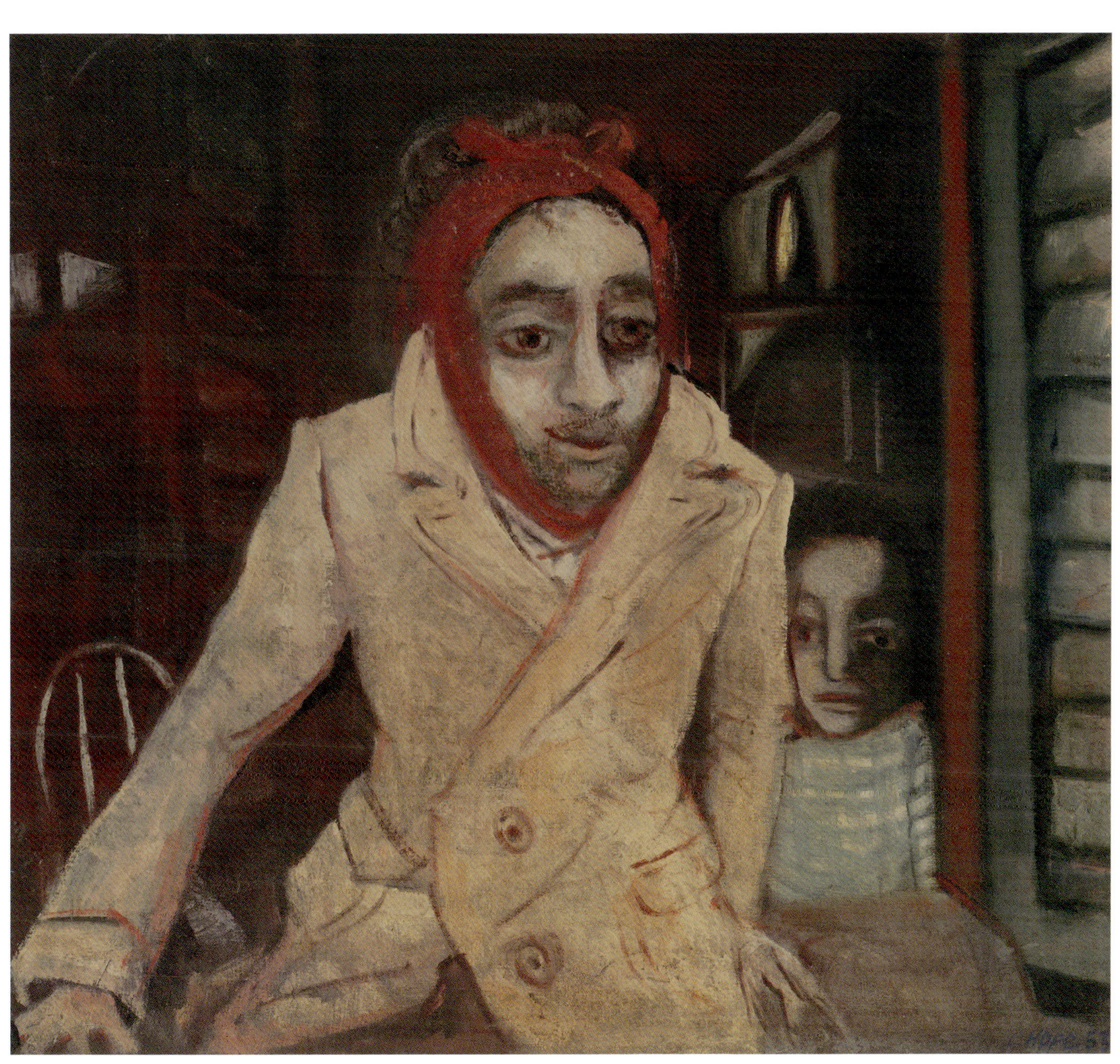

50 **John Brack** (1920–1999)
The baby drinking 1955

painted in Melbourne, Victoria
oil on canvas, 38.4 x 36.2 cm
National Gallery of Australia, Canberra, purchased 1993

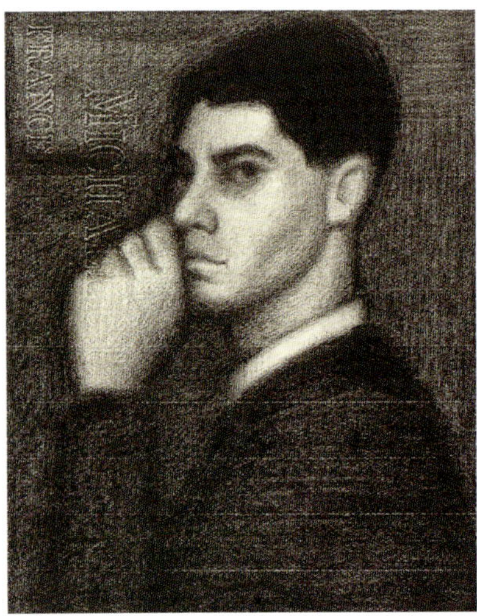

John Brack
Self-portrait 1949
pastel, 32.3 x 25.1 cm
National Portrait Gallery, Canberra, purchased 2010

You know with a newborn baby that it has a future and it comes from the past . . . John saw it as the next chance.[70]

John Brack's *The baby drinking* conveys a state of being. Although his young daughter Charlotte provided the starting point for the painting, he wanted to go beyond a straightforward likeness to convey an understanding of the human condition of childhood.

The idea of integrating the particular and the general was not uncommon in Brack's oeuvre. He understood that to bring a deeper perspective to bear upon human nature, it was important to observe people closely. This observation involved capturing particular psychological traits and, at times, the essence of the activities his subjects were engaged in: a conversation, a ballroom dance, the act of drinking.

The brilliance of this compact painting is the way Brack reveals the child's total absorption. The eye that conveys a steady gaze is a vital element here—completely at one with the 'guzzling' of the milk. The baby is drinking from a cup, not a bottle, and there is a keen sense both of being fed and the act of feeding. Helen Brack recalls that the easiest way to feed the child was to stand up. 'It is like feeding a lamb.'[71]

John Brack was a master of composition and intricate balance in his paintings. Each part of the whole is always carefully considered and it is no coincidence that the mother's firm hold on the cup is echoed by the child's small hand curled around the chair's arm. The fulsome curves of the baby's shoulders and face, the circular base of the cup and the soft tresses of hair contrast with the angular edges of adult body and chair. Tones of dark and light bring vitality to the whole while the warm and bright whites impart a feeling of milkiness and purity.

Brack's baby drinking has taken the first steps in life's journey yet we still have a sense of her newness; of the miracle and strangeness of a new life intimately observed. The future lies ahead, filled with possibility. In the act of drinking the baby is in the moment, untroubled by complexity. With considerable insight, Brack suggests the way young children encapsulate something that we have lost as adults and keep trying to regain—a meditative sense of simply 'being' in the world.

Deborah Hart

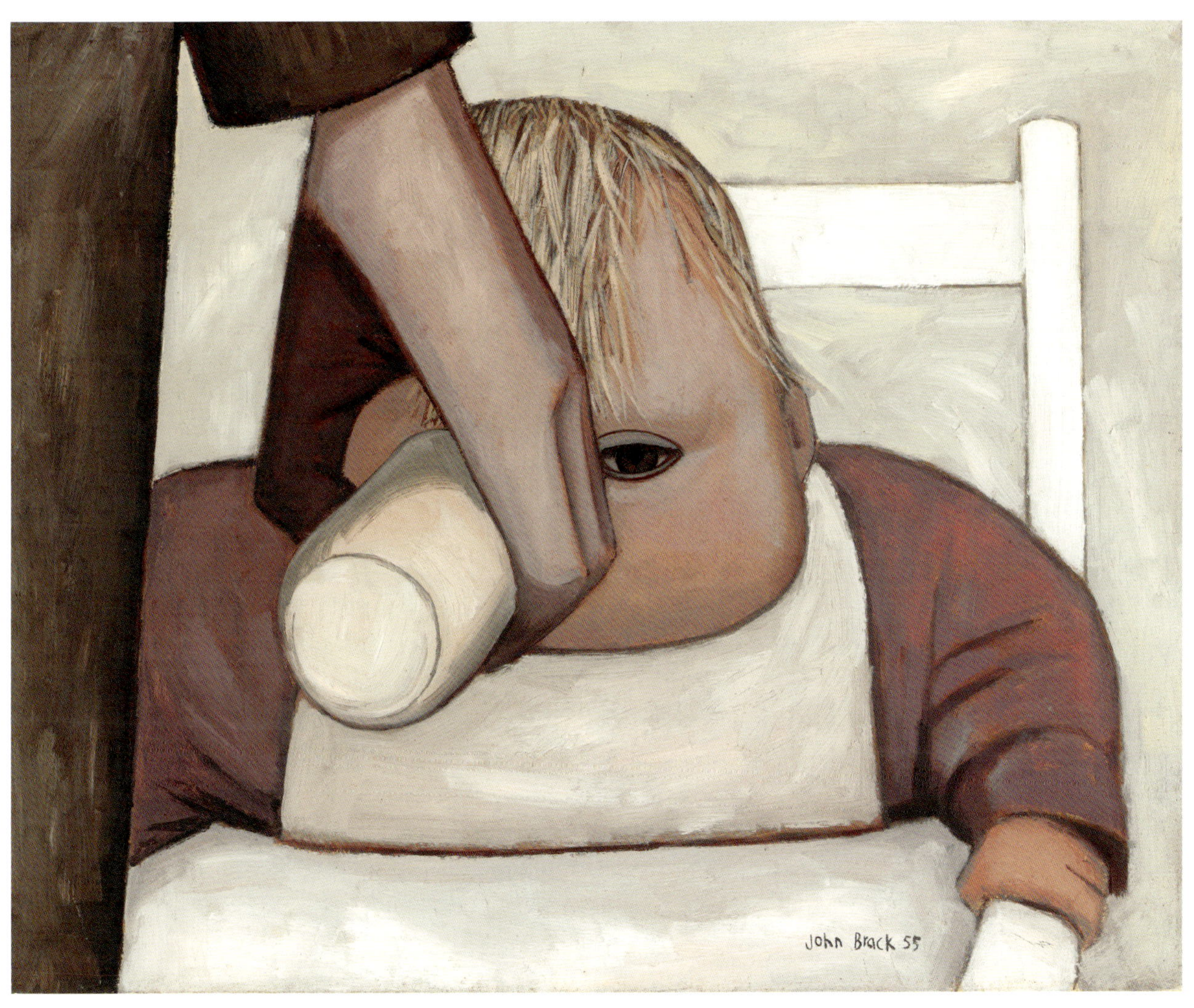
John Brack 55

51 William Dobell (1899–1970)

Sketch portrait of Dame Mary Gilmore c 1956

painted in Sydney, New South Wales
oil on composition board, 45.2 x 27.5 cm
National Gallery of Australia, Canberra, purchased 1962

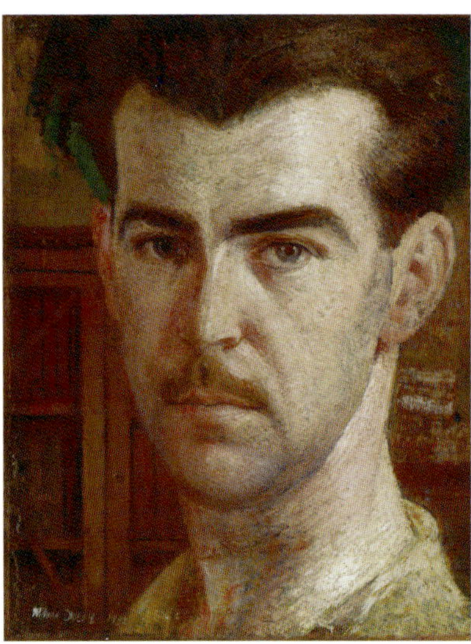

William Dobell
Self-portrait 1932
oil on wood panel, 35 x 27 cm
Art Gallery of New South Wales, Sydney
purchased with assistance from the Trustees of the Sir William Dobell Art Foundation 1985

Commissioned by the Australasian Book Society to commemorate Dame Mary Gilmore's ninetieth birthday with a portrait, William Dobell described his first impression as being 'struck by her dignity and the colour scheme'. [72] In this preparatory oil sketch the dignified lady is there but the colour scheme is temporarily muted, while Dobell concentrates on what he saw as essential to a portrait—the depiction of character. The composition is triangular, the neck attenuated, the filigreed lace at her collar in the final portrait indicated here by a thin, swirly flourish of white paint.

Dobell's working method underscored his commitment to retaining first impressions. At a sitting he would make a number of pencil sketches, then, back in the studio, create a few small painted studies such as this, without the sitter present. The artist said, 'I get the main design from my best study and then I put them away. But I never work with them in front of me, it constipates me.'[73]

William Dobell enrolled in evening classes at the Julian Ashton School, Sydney in his mid twenties, commencing full-time study at the Slade School, London in 1929. After a decade absorbing the work of great masters in Europe, Dobell returned to Sydney in 1939 and took up a teaching position at the National Art School (also known as East Sydney Technical College). It is the notoriety surrounding the artist's 1943 Archibald Prize win with a portrait of Joshua Smith, a work criticised (and challenged in the courts) as caricature, for which Dobell is best remembered. This controversy had a deep, some say inhibiting, effect on the artist, driving him into seclusion. The portrait of Dame Mary Gilmore is widely regarded as his comeback piece, demonstrating his recovery with the assuredness of an expert painter.

Dame Mary provided substantial material for the artist to work with. By the time of their meeting Gilmore was a prominent socialist poet and journalist, a champion of the workers and the oppressed. Her most notable foray, along with other socialist idealists, was the establishment of a communal settlement called New Australia in Paraguay in 1896. It was there she married William Gilmore in 1897. By 1902 the utopian experiment had failed and the Gilmores returned to Australia. Her first volume of poetry was published in 1910 and her reputation grew thereafter. Dame Mary Gilmore has become one of Australia's most widely read poets.

Katherine Russell

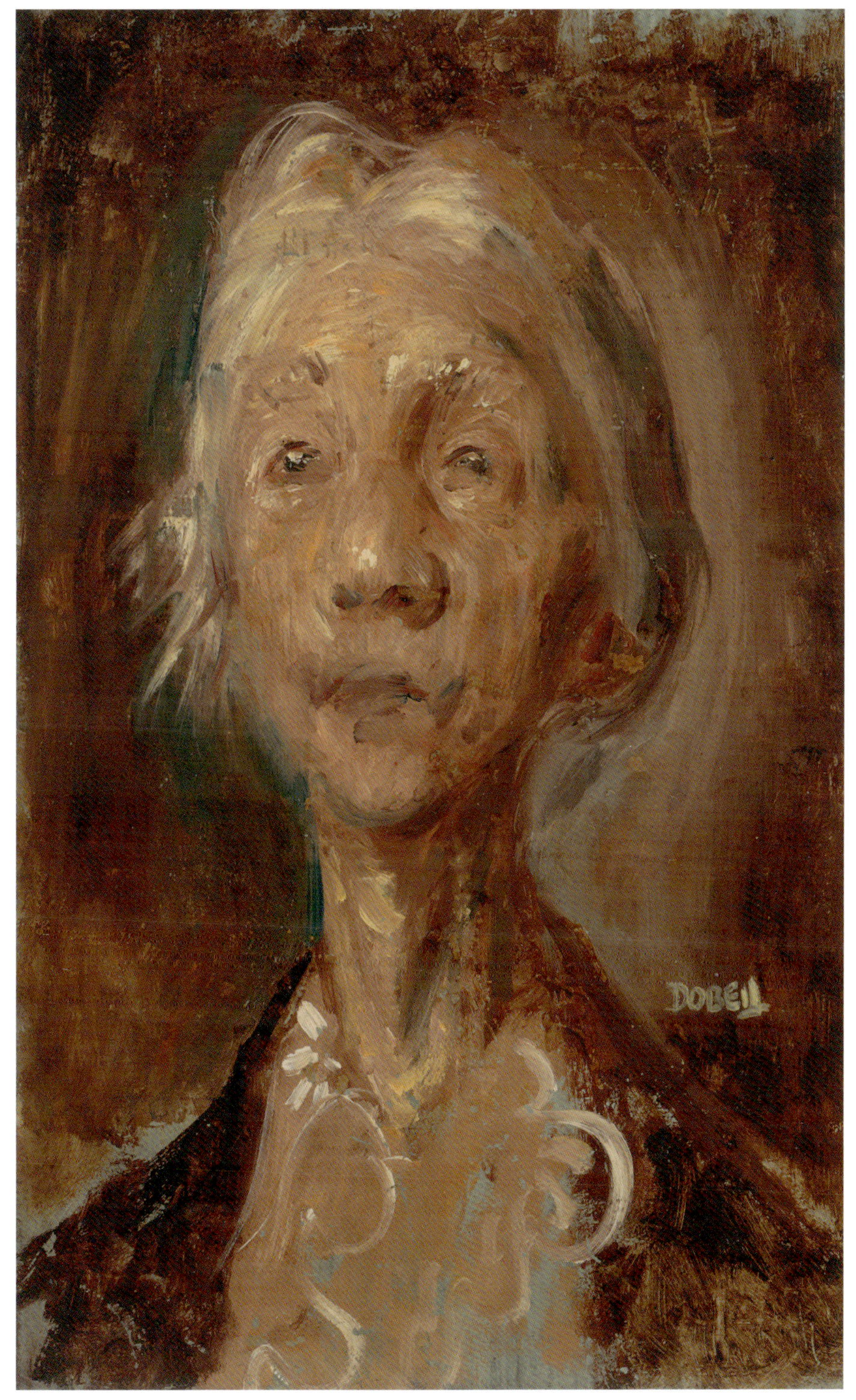
DOBELL

52 **William Dobell** (1899–1970)

Sketch portrait of Helena Rubinstein 1957

painted in Sydney, New South Wales
enamel on composition board, 15.1 x 14.2 cm
National Gallery of Australia, Canberra, purchased 1976

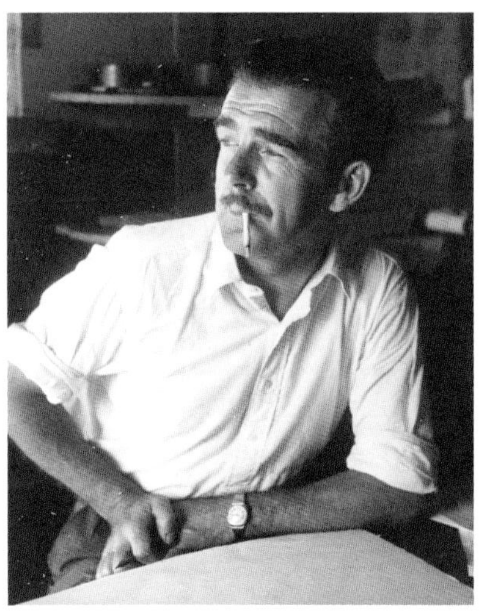

Max Dupain
William Dobell 1942
National Library of Australia, Canberra

William Dobell was drawn to people with an inherent sense of self. One such individual who came to fascinate him was Polish cosmetics magnate, Helena Rubinstein (1870–1965). Although Rubinstein only sat for Dobell twice, he made eight paintings of her in six years.

In this oil sketch for a major portrait which won the £1500 Australian Women's Weekly Portrait Prize in 1957 we see Rubinstein in profile, in a decidedly posed seated position, with right hand on hip and the left resting in her lap—all the better to show off the jewel-encrusted bracelet and ring. Her dress is a plain wrap-around garment, whereas in the final portrait both head and body are turned to the right and the dress fabric richly patterned.

Talking about Rubinstein, Dobell reveals a delightful ambiguity about his sitter—finding her at once enthralling yet pitiful. 'She was a very sad woman for all her millions. She still liked to show off her things as though she'd just been given them … For instance, every now and then she'd disappear and come out with another dress: "Would you like to paint me in this?"—all over her arm. And honestly, over the arms of such an old woman it looked like a scene in a gypsy fair.'[74]

Born Chaja Rubinstein in Kraków, Poland, Helena Rubinstein came to Australia in 1894, finding a ready market for the pots of face cream she brought in her luggage. Although not the first to discover the skin beautifying properties of lanolin (extracted from sheep's wool), she had an abundant supply where she lived in the Western Districts of Victoria. To disguise the pungency of 'sheep's grease' in her skin creams Rubinstein experimented with lavender, pine bark and waterlilies. Her products were so-called medical formulas and ointments, reputedly sourced from the Carpathian Mountains. Rubinstein went on to open salons all over the world, effectively forming the first multinational cosmetics company and, in the process, becoming one of the world's richest women.

James Gleeson says of Dobell's late portraits that 'the style took its cue from the subject'. He goes on to emphasise that, 'one only has to look at a few square inches of painted sleeve to know what sort of person is wearing it'[75]. In this dramatic sketch we sense the artist's struggle to reconcile in paint both the multi-millionaire businesswoman and the complex individual behind the mask.

Katherine Russell

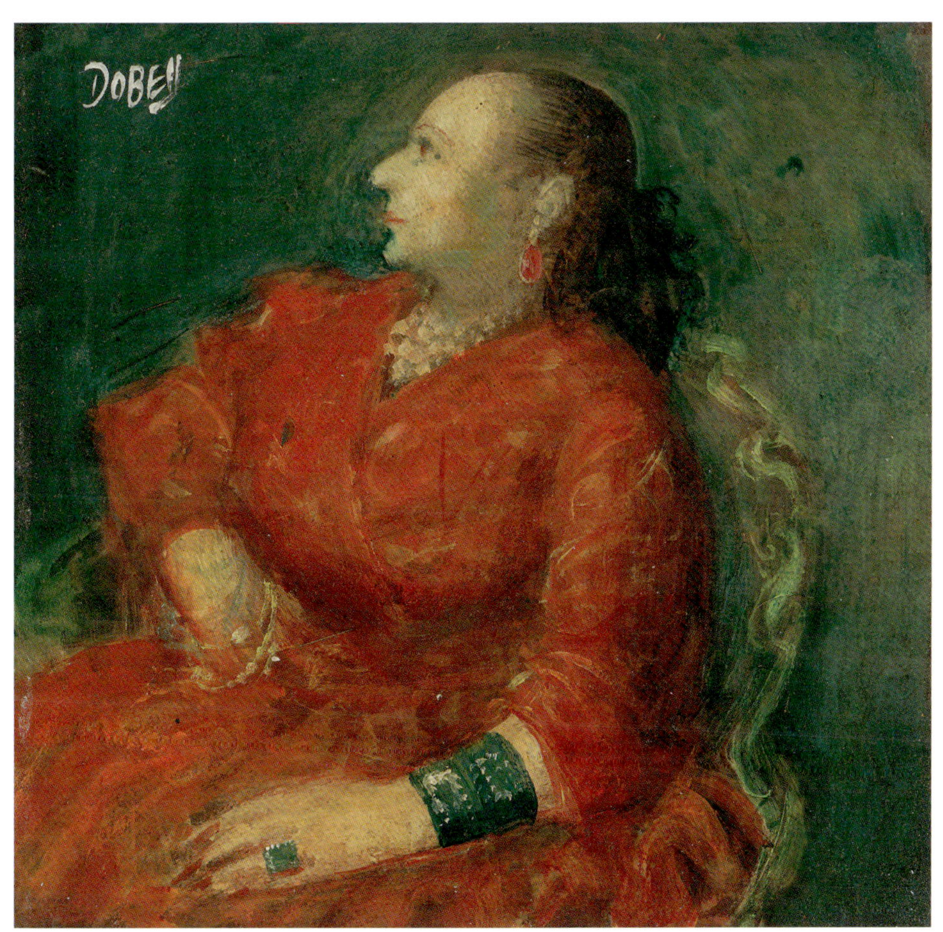
DOBELL

53 **John Brack** (1920–1999)

The girls at school 1959

painted in Melbourne, Victoria

oil on composition board, 77.4 x 57.7 cm

private collection, on long-term loan to the National Gallery of Australia, Canberra

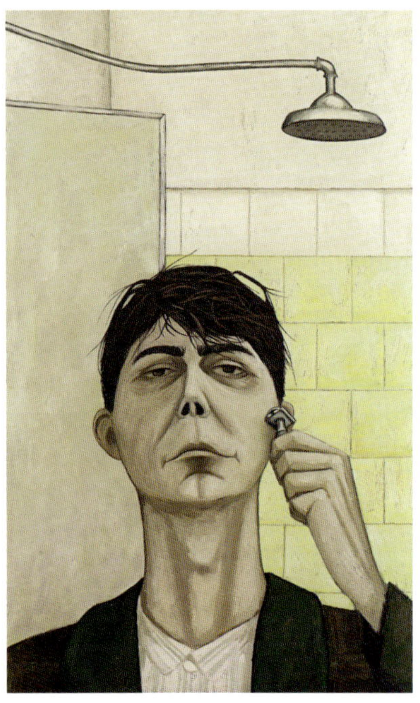

John Brack
Self-portrait 1955
oil on canvas, 81.5 x 48.3 cm
National Gallery of Victoria, Melbourne, purchased with the assistance of the National Gallery Women's Association, 2000

They have arrived at school and stand waiting. Now there is no movement, but a moment of pause. Though they stand for this moment, close together, they are already separated... [76]

It was 1959. The end of a decade. Parents contemplated their children's future. John Brack, now the father of four daughters, was well aware of the vulnerability of children and their inevitable transition from childhood innocence to the harsh reality of adolescence. *The girls at school* is an expression of this disquiet; in it he captures the essence of his three oldest daughters in the first phase of their transition to conformity.

Three girls cluster to the left of the picture, absorbed in a moment of seeming abandonment. Behind them looms the red brick school wall and to the right, the ominous shadow through which they must pass in order to learn of life. In deference to their fate, the two younger girls clench delicate posies of daisies in their baby-like hands: offerings of hope in an uncertain world.

Cocooned between her siblings, a shy, golden-haired girl gazes desolately at us, the mother-viewer. Her white and flesh-toned checked uniform forewarns of loss of individuality and purity defiled. The girl in front stares determinedly outside the picture plane. Shielded by her brown cardigan she is an image of order and stubborn resentment. Her satchel, a burden under her arm, is a reminder of the load of learning she will endure. Two tiny flesh-pink bows in her plaits flutter like fragile butterflies in metamorphosis.

The girl at the back has turned from us. She is self-contained and nearing adolescence. She embodies self-realisation and knows already of 'the transition from one state of being to another and... the pain of living'.[77] In her hair she wears a white bow of purity. Like the posies and white collars of her siblings, it is luminous amidst darker tones and with them forms a diagonal leading swiftly downwards and back up to the harsh angles of the red brick school walls and the shadowy unknown. The walls, with ordered meat-like striations, add further tension to this visual essay on the violation of innocence.

Brack's fourth daughter was too young and, perhaps, too carefree and effervescent to be included. But maybe she is there, in spirit, a fourth uniform button peeking out from behind the plait of her older sibling.

Anne McDonald

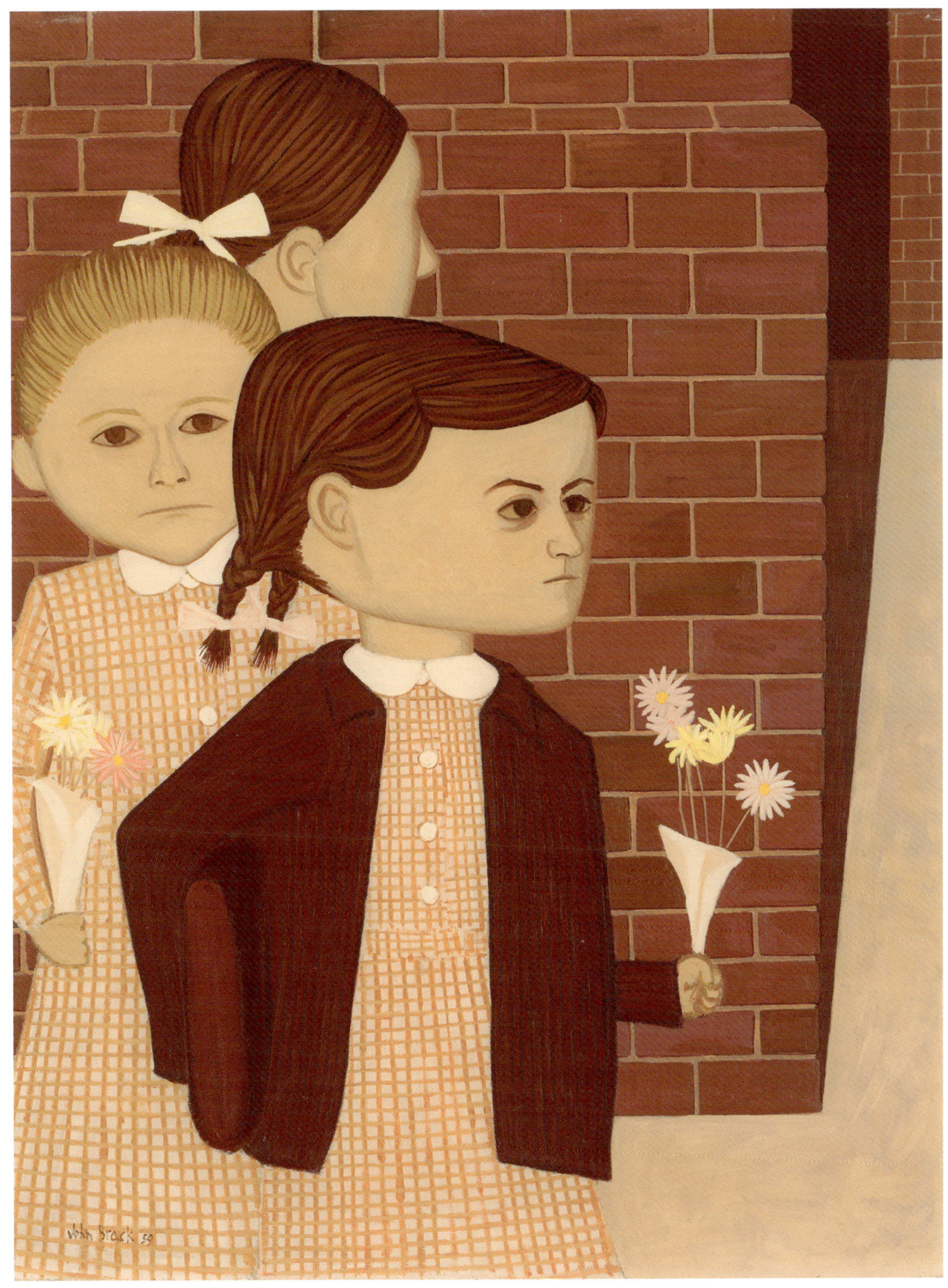
John Brack 59

54 **Ian Fairweather** (1891–1974)

Portrait of the artist 1962

painted on Bribie Island, Queensland
synthetic polymer paint and gouache on cardboard
mounted on composition board, 92.4 x 72.9 cm
National Gallery of Australia, Canberra, purchased 1976

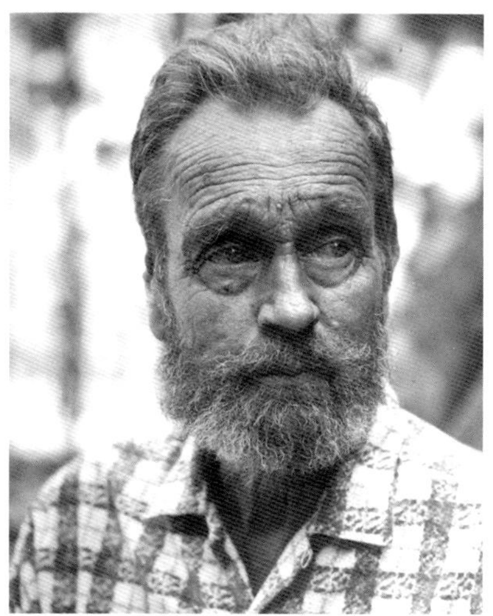

Geoff Hawkshaw
Fairweather at Bribie Island, Queensland 1966
National Library of Australia, Canberra

To me, painting is a personal thing. It gives me the same kind of satisfaction that religion, I imagine, gives to some people.[78]

Portrait of the artist was painted when Ian Fairweather was living in isolation in a makeshift hut on Bribie Island north of Brisbane. He had settled there in 1953 after years of travel and encounters with different cultures, particularly in Asia. His peripatetic life provided rich inspiration for his subsequent hermetic existence. Over time he had become a scholar of comparative religions as well as of Chinese literature, language and calligraphy. While Fairweather's linear approach is distinct from Chinese calligraphy, he understood from this discipline that art could be about process and interconnections; it could be ideographic and a performative act.[79]

In *Portrait of the artist* the surface is built up layer upon layer, dark over light and light over dark: the pink and white of the face and neck like a window in the dark surround. Over the pale ground Fairweather's dark emphatic line repeatedly circles the shape of the eyes as if to emphasise looking, while verticals and diagonals define his nose and scrubby beard.[80] The portrait appears honed by time, simultaneously expressive, fugitive and emblematic, a mirror to the nomad and the recluse. In 1962 one visitor recognised Fairweather from the 'far-looking expression of the blue eyes, in their cavernous sockets' and found that he had 'the physically durable look of a man who has never pampered himself.'[81]

When he completed *Portrait of the artist*, Fairweather was 71 years old. He was at the peak of his powers, having recently painted great works such as *Monastery* 1960 (NGA). His portrait is a touchstone on his journey as an artist; part of a bigger whole. It resembles the faces of the three wise men in another painting he had on the go in the studio, *Epiphany* 1962 (QAG).[82] Fairweather would not consciously have suggested this parallel. He understood the principles of renunciation and sublimation of the ego—the process of losing the self in order to find the self. In *Portrait of the artist*, his face is embedded in the painterly surface, at one with it in an almost alchemical way. Art was after all the substance of his life. It was his deepest reason for being, informing his heart and mind, his breath and energy—the ch'i—guiding, focusing and propelling him through the labyrinth of existence.

Deborah Hart

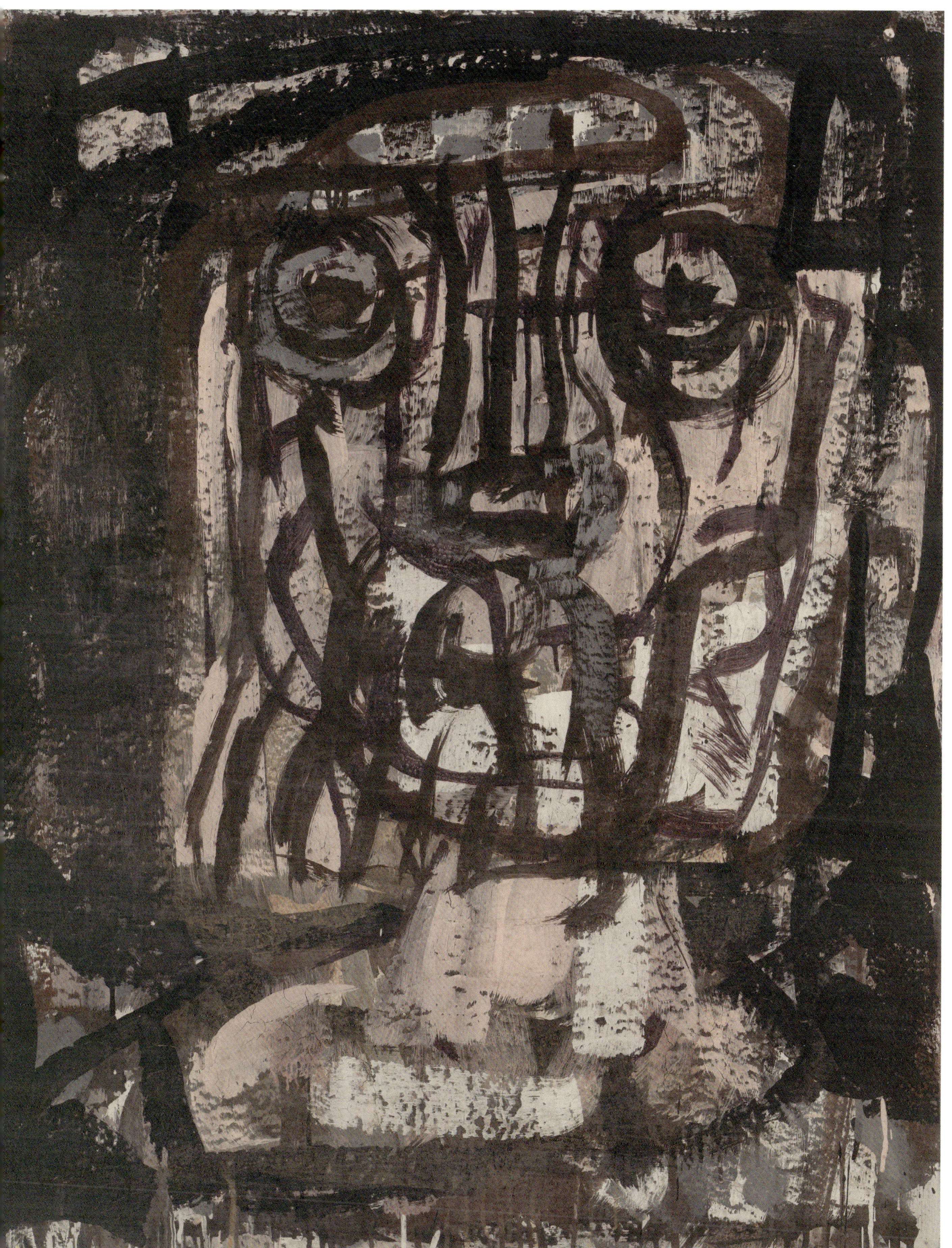

Notes

1 Family hearsay.

2 Roberts papers, ML A2481, SLNSW; quoted in Mary Eagle, *The oil paintings of Tom Roberts in the National Gallery of Australia*, National Gallery of Australia, Canberra, 1997, pp 51–4.

3 H McQueen, 'An Australian native', in A Gray, *Australian art in the National Gallery of Australia*, National Gallery of Australia, Canberra, 2002, p 82.

4 When *An Australian native* was purchased in 1979 from the women's club, the Melbourne-based Austral Salon, the subject was thought to be Lillie Williamson, Roberts's wife-to-be. But, as Mary Eagle has pointed out (above), Lillie had fair hair, a square jaw and wore glasses. Eagle also discusses a number of possible contenders.

5 Frederick McCubbin, in R H Croll, *Tom Roberts: Father of Australian landscape painting*, Robertson & Mullins, Melbourne, 1935, pp 172–3.

6 D H Souter, in Croll, as above, p 40.

7 Arthur Streeton, in R H Croll (ed), *Smike to Bulldog: letters from Sir Arthur Streeton to Tom Roberts*, Ure Smith, Sydney, 1946, p 68.

8 M Eagle, *The oil paintings of Tom Roberts* …, 1997, p 61.

9 'Letters from Tom Roberts to Frederick McCubbin', *La Trobe Library Journal*, vol 2, no 7, April 1971, 99. 64-76 (State Library of Victoria MS 8187; MS 8188).

10 A Gray, *The Edwardians: secrets and desires*, National Gallery of Australia, Canberra, 2004, pp 116, 212–13.

11 P Fullerton, *Hugh Ramsay, his life and work*, Hudson, Hawthorn, 1988, pp 72, 79.

12 P Fullerton, as above, p 60.

13 P Fullerton, *Hugh Ramsay 1877–1906*, National Gallery of Victoria, Melbourne, 1992, p 68.

14 M Eagle, *The oil paintings of E. Phillips Fox in the National Gallery of Australia*, National Gallery of Australia, Canberra, 1997, p 33.

15 M Eagle, as above, p 35.

16 R Zubans, *E. Phillips Fox: his life and art*, Melbourne University Press, Carlton, 1995, p 109.

17 E Wharton, *The reef* (1912), Scribner, New York, 1993, p 46.

18 Arnold Shore on Frederick McCubbin, *The Age,* Melbourne, 26 October 1957.

19 D Ghirlandaio (1449–1494), *Portrait of Giovanna Tornabuoni* (?), c 1485–88, tempera on walnut panel, 48 x 36 cm, Tokyo Fuji Art Museum, Japan; *Portrait of Giovanna Tornabuoni*, 1488, tempera on wood, 76 x 50 cm, Museo Thyssen-Bornemisza, Madrid, Spain.

20 M Eagle, *The oil paintings of Tom Roberts* …, citing Roberts to McCubbin, 14 November 1909, McCubbin papers, LTL 8525, SLV.

21 J Hetherington, 'Charles Wheeler: window in the city', *Forty profiles*, FW Cheshire, Melbourne, 1963, p 23.

22 J S MacDonald, 'Charles Wheeler, O.B.E., D.C.M.' *Australian painting desiderata*, Lothian, Melbourne, 1958, p 76.

23 J Hetherington, 1963, p 24.

24 'Clever boy artist: Australian's untaught work', *The Argus*, Melbourne, 3 March 1914, p 10.

25 M A Lee, 'Teague, Violet Helen Evangeline (1872–1951)', *Australian dictionary of biography*, vol 12, Melbourne University Press, Carlton, 1990, pp 189–190 .

26 George W Lambert, *Sketchbook: figure studies and horse studies* [1921–30], National Gallery of Victoria, Melbourne, p 31.

27 H Wilson, 'GW Lambert, ARA, painter', *Australian Quarterly*, Sydney, no 7, September 1930, p 93.

28 L Housman, 'The international exhibition of Fair Women', *Manchester Guardian*, 27 May 1910.

29 R Zubans, *E. Phillips Fox: his life and art*, 1995, p 64.

30 M Eagle, *The oil paintings of E Phillips Fox* …, 1997, p 63.

31 G Cossington Smith in conversation with Daniel Thomas, quoted in D Hart (ed), *Grace Cossington Smith*, National Gallery of Australia, Canberra, 2005, p 77.

32 Cossington Smith interviewed by Alan Roberts, quoted in *Grace Cossington Smith*, as above, p 12. Cossington Smith was also keen to point out that while Norah Simpson made a contribution, it was a myth that she introduced them to Post-Impressionism in 1914, because Dattilo-Rubbo had brought back reproductions from his European travels as early as 1906.

33 J Gleeson, quoted in *Grace Cossington Smith*, as above, p 80.

34 Grace Cossington Smith interviewed by Alan Roberts in *Grace Cossington Smith*, as above, p 11.

35 From a record of a conversation between Daniel Thomas and Meldrum's daughters, on the National Gallery of Australia artist's file, in which the daughters recalled their father's response at the time, NGA file 74/49/08.

36 George W Lambert, 26 August 1921, Lambert Family Papers, ML MS 97/10.

37 George W Lambert to Amy Lambert, 23 October 1921, Lambert Family Papers, ML MS 97/10.

38 MT Falkiner, correspondence with Director, National Gallery of Australia, 4 February 1983, NGA file 81/944.

39 Margaret Preston, quoted by C Moore in D Edwards, *Margaret Preston*, Art Gallery of NSW, Sydney, 2005, p 148.

40 Preston, as above. Through the 1920s the trustees commissioned 11 artists to paint self-portraits, including Arthur Streeton, Tom Roberts, Hans Heysen and Sydney Long.

41 R Butler, submission to the National Gallery of Australia's Council, 8 March 1988.

42 Email from Anna Gray to Deborah Hart, 28 October 2009.

43 See K Quinlan, *In a picture land over the sea: Agnes Goodsir 1864–1939*, Bendigo Art Gallery, Victoria, 1988, p 12.

44 Keith Hancock to Julie Lowe, 30 October 1947, quoted in L Wilkins, *Stella Bowen: art, love & war*, Australian War Memorial, Canberra, 2002, p 3.

45 S Bowen, *Drawn from life*, quoted in Wilkins, as above, p 4.

46 Interview with Nora Heysen, 25 August 1994, Oral History Collection, National Library of Australia.

47 Nora Heysen to her family, 6 February 1935, describing a related work, *Interior* 1935; quoted in J Hylton, *Nora Heysen: light and life*, Carrick Hill, Adelaide, 2009, p 22.

48 A Tucker quoted in J Mollison and N Bonham, *Albert Tucker*, Australian National Gallery, Canberra, 1982, pp 49–50.

49 C Polizzotto, *Approaching Elise*, Fremantle Arts Centre Press, Fremantle, 1988, pp 124, 126.

50 Elise Blumann, quoted in A Gray, 'Elise Blumann', *Art and Australia*, vol 16, no 4, June 1979, pp 369–71.

51 J Mollison and N Bonham, *Albert Tucker*, 1982, p 32.

52 R S Ellery, *Psychiatric aspects of modern warfare*, Reed & Harris, Melbourne, 1945, p 9.

53 Jesuit motto based on words passed on from Saint Francis Xavier (1506–1552).

54 T Allen, *John Perceval*, Melbourne University Press, Carlton, 1992, p 11.

55 J Mollison, 'Arthur Boyd', *Art and Australia*, vol 3, no 2, September 1965, p 118.

56 D Marr, *Patrick White: a life*, Random House Australia, Sydney, 1991, p 149.

57 H Johnson, *Roy de Maistre: the English years 1930–1968*, Craftsman House, Sydney, in association with G+B Arts International, 1995, p 9.

58 D Thomas, 'de Maistre, LeRoy Leveson Laurent Joseph (Roy) (1894–1968)', *Australian dictionary of biography*, vol 8, 1981, pp 277–8.

59 T G Rosenthal, 'Ned Kelly 1948–1992: a magnificent obsession', in *Unmasked: Sidney Nolan & Ned Kelly 1950–1990*, Heide Museum of Modern Art, Melbourne, 2006, p 18.

60 Interview with Albert Tucker by James Mollison, in *Albert Tucker: a retrospective*, National Gallery of Victoria, Melbourne, 1990, pp 9–10.

61 A Tucker, quoted in Mollison and Bonham, p 42.

62 Mollison and Bonham, as above.

63 Mollison and Bonham, as above.

64 Margaret Olley quoted in J Hawley, 'Queen of subjects', *Good weekend* magazine, *The Sydney Morning Herald*, 25 March 1995, p 36.

65 N Underhill (ed), *Nolan on Nolan: Sidney Nolan in his own words*, Viking Press, Melbourne, 2007, p 236.

66 C Donaldson, 'Deep and defiant: Dušan Marek; two European émigré artists in postwar (South) Australia', MA Art History thesis, University of Adelaide, 2007, p 32.

67 Correspondence with Cheri Donaldson, 26 March 2010.

68 Donaldson, 26 March 2010.

69 Miya Studio existed as a 'co-operative' studio space for artists from late 1945 until 1949 in Brisbane. The Studio artists were closely linked to the Brisbane-based *Barjai* (1943–1947), a magazine of literature and art aimed at a youth audience. Both 'Miya' and 'Barjai were Aboriginal words, 'miya' meaning 'today' and 'barjai' meaning 'meeting place'. In 1988, the University of Queensland Art Museum presented the exhibition *Young Turks and battlelines: Barjai and Miya Studio*, which first explored this aspect of Brisbane history.

70 Helen Brack, in conversation with Deborah Hart, 6 October 2009.

71 Helen Brack, as above.

72 H de Berg, interview with William Dobell, 10 Feb 1959, Hazel de Berg Collection, Oral History Collection, National Library of Australia.

73 J Gleeson, *William Dobell*, revised edn, World of Art Library series, Thames & Hudson London, 1969, pp 196–7.

74 V Freeman, *Dobell on Dobell*, Ure Smith, Sydney, 1970, pp 66–7.

75 J Gleeson, *William Dobell*, as above, p 189.

76 John Brack, quoted in S Grishin, *The art of John Brack*, Oxford University Press, Melbourne, 1990, vol 1, p 73.

77 Conversation and correspondence with Helen Brack and her daughter Freda, 26 and 30 March 2010. McDonald is grateful to them for sharing this and other insights into Brack's work.

78 J Hetherington, 'Ian Fairweather: gentle nomad who lives a lonely life', *The Age*, 9 June 1962, p 17.

79 See P Ryckmans, 'An amateur artist', in *Fairweather*, Queensland Art Gallery, Brisbane, 1994, pp 15–23.

80 The weighty presence and dense black lines recall the art of Georges Rouault (1871–1958).

81 J Hetherington, *The Age*, 9 June 1962, as above.

82 Ian Fairweather often worked on several paintings simultaneously pinned around the walls of his hut. See also Murray Bail, *Fairweather*, Murdoch Books, Millers Point, revised edn, 2009.

Bibliography

Books and articles on portraiture

Bell, J, *Five hundred self portraits*, Phaidon, London, 2000

Bond, A & Woodall, J, *Self portrait: Renaissance to contemporary*, National Portrait Gallery, London/Art Gallery of NSW, Sydney, 2005.

Brilliant, R, *Portraiture*, Reaktion Books, London, 1991.

Cumming, L, *A face to the world: on self-portraits*, Harper Press, London, 2009.

Engledow, S, *The companion*, National Portrait Gallery, Canberra, 2009.

Friedlander, M, *Landscape, portrait, still life: their origin and development*, Schocken Books, New York, 1963.

Gibson, R, *The face in the corner: animals in portraits from the collections of the National Portrait Gallery*, National Portrait Gallery, London, 1998.

Gibson, R, *20th century portraits*, National Portrait Gallery, London, 1978.

Gibson, R, *Painting the century*, National Portrait Gallery, London, 2000.

Gray, A, *Australian art in the National Gallery of Australia*, National Gallery of Australia, Canberra, 2002.

Gray, A, *The Edwardians: secrets and desires*, National Gallery of Australia, Canberra, 2004.

Heslewood, J, *Mother: Portraits by 40 great artists*, Francis Lincoln Ltd, London, 2009.

Horton, M (ed), *The Archibald Prize an illustrated history 1921–1981*, Fine Arts Press, Art Gallery of NSW, Sydney, 1982.

Kanz, R, *Portraits*, Taschen, Köln, 2008.

McConkey, K, *Edwardian portraits: images of an age of opulence*, Antique Collectors' Club, Woodbridge, 1987.

Miller, J, *On reflection*, National Gallery Publications, London, 1998.

Nairne, S, 'Why do painted portraits still matter?', *Portrait* magazine, no 20, 2006, Canberra.

Radford, R, *Australian colonial art 1800–1900*, Art Gallery of South Australia, Adelaide, 1995.

Radford, R, *Island to Empire: three hundred years of British art, 1550–1850, paintings, watercolours, drawings, sculptures from the collection of the Art Gallery of South Australia*, Art Gallery of South Australia, Adelaide, 2005.

Rideal, L, *Insights: self-portraits*, National Portrait Gallery, London, 2005.

Ross P, *Let's face it: the history of the Archibald Prize*, 2nd rev edn, Art Gallery of NSW, Sydney, 2005.

Sayers, A, *Possibilities of portraiture*, National Portrait Gallery, Canberra 1999.

Sayers, A, *To look within: self portraits in Australia*, University Art Museum, University of Queensland, Brisbane, 2004.

Schneider, N, *The art of the portrait 1420–1670*, Taschen, Köln, 1994.

Simon, R, *The portrait in Britain and America*, Phaidon, Oxford, 1987.

Sturgis, A, *Faces*, National Gallery, London, 1998.

Wilton, A, *The swagger portrait*, Tate Gallery, London, 1992.

Woodall, J (ed), *Portraiture: facing the subject*, Manchester University Press, Manchester, 1997.

'Why call it a portrait? Roi de Mestre at the Students' Club', *Undergrowth*, Sydney, October–November 1927.

Books, articles and papers on artists and subjects

Allen, T, *John Perceval*, Melbourne University Press, Carlton, 1992.

Bail, M, *Ian Fairweather*, Bay Books, Sydney, 1991.

Bail, M et al, *Fairweather*, Queensland Art Gallery, Brisbane, 1994.

Bowen, S, *Drawn from life*, Virago Press, London, 1984.

Bromfield, D, *Elise Blumann: paintings and drawings 1918–1984*, Art Gallery of Western Australia, Perth, 1984.

Bungey, D, *Arthur Boyd: a life*, Allen & Unwin, St Leonards, 2007.

Burke, J, *Australian gothic: a life of Albert Tucker*, Knopf, Milsons Point, 2002

Butler, R, *The prints of Margaret Preston*, National Gallery of Australia, Canberra, 1987.

Clark, J, *Nolan: Sidney Nolan landscapes & legends: a retrospective exhibition: 1937-1987*, National Gallery of Victoria, Melbourne, 1987

Clark, J and Druce F, *Violet Teague 1872–1951*, Beagle Press, Sydney, 1999.

Croll, R H, *Tom Roberts: father of Australian landscape painting*, Robertson & Mullins, Melbourne, 1934.

Dixon, C, *Herbert Badham 1899–1961*, Wollongong City Gallery, Wollongong, 1987.

Donaldson, C, 'Deep and defiant: Dušan Marek, two European émigré artsts in post-war (South) Australia', MA Art History thesis, University of Adelaide, 2007.

Draffin, N, *The art of Napier Waller*, Sun Academy series, Sun Books, South Melbourne, 1978.

Eagle, M, *The art of Rupert Bunny*, National Gallery of Australia, Canberra, 1991.

Eagle, M, *The oil paintings of E Phillips Fox in the National Gallery of Australia*, National Gallery of Australia, Canberra, 1997.

Eagle, M, *The oil paintings of Tom Roberts in the National Gallery of Australia*, National Gallery of Australia, Canberra, 1997.

Edwards, D, *Margaret Preston*, Art Gallery of NSW, Sydney, 2005.

Edwards, D, *Rupert Bunny*, Art Gallery of NSW, Sydney, 2009.

Entwisle, P, *Nerli: an exhibition of paintings & drawings*, Dunedin Public Art Gallery, Dunedin, 1988.

Fry, G, *Albert Tucker*, Beagle Press, Sydney, 2005.

Fullerton, P, *Hugh Ramsay: his life and work*, Hudson Publishing, Hawthorn, 1988.

France, C, *Margaret Olley*, (revised and updated ed) Craftsman House, Sydney, 2002.

Freeman, V, *Dobell on Dobell*, Ure Smith, Sydney, 1970.

Galbally, A, 'Hall, Lindsay Bernard (1859-1935)', *Australian dictionary of biography*, vol 9, Melbourne University Press, Carlton, 1983, pp 164-165.

Gleeson, J, *William Dobell*, Thames & Hudson, London, 1964.

Granek, W, *The art of Laurence Hope*, University of Queensland Art Museum, Brisbane, 2002.

Grant, K et al, *John Brack*, National Gallery of Victoria, Melbourne, 2009.

Gray, A, *George W Lambert retrospective: heroes and icons*, National Gallery of Australia, Canberra, 2007.

Gray, A, *McCubbin: Last impressions 1907–17*, National Gallery of Australia, Canberra, 2009.

Hart, D (ed), *Grace Cossington Smith*, National Gallery of Australia, Canberra, 2005.

Hetherington, J, 'Charles Wheeler: window in the city', *Forty profiles*, FW Cheshire, Melbourne, 1963.

Hoff, U, *The art of Arthur Boyd*, Andre Deutsch, London, 1986.

Hylton, J, *Modern Australian women: paintings & prints 1925–1945*, Art Gallery of South Australia, Adelaide, 2000.

Hylton, J, *Nora Heysen: light and life*, Wakefield Press, Adelaide, 2009.

James, B, *Grace Cossington Smith*, Craftsman House, Sydney 1980.

Johnson, H, *Roy de Maistre: the English years 1930–1968*, Craftsman House Sydney, 1995.

Jones, J, *Robert Dowling: Tasmanian son of Empire*, National Gallery of Australia, Canberra, 2010.

Klepac, L, *Russell Drysdale*, Murdoch Books, Sydney, 2009.

Lee, MA, 'Teague, Violet Helen Evangeline (1872–1951), *Australian dictionary of biography*, vol 12, Melbourne University Press, Carlton, 1990.

Lindsay, D, *The Felton Bequest an historical record*, Oxford University Press, Melbourne, 1963

Lock-Weir, T, *Misty moderns: Australian tonalists 1915–1950*, Art Gallery of South Australia, Adelaide, 2008.

MacDonald, J S, 'Charles Wheeler', *Art in Australia*, no 42, 1932.

Mackenzie, A, *Frederic McCubbin 1855–1917: 'The Proff' and his art*, Mannagum Press, Lilydale, 1990.

McQueen, H, *Tom Roberts*, Macmillan, Sydney, 1996.

Mollison, J & Bonham, N, *Albert Tucker*, Macmillan, Melbourne, 1982.

Murphy, B, *Dušan Marek*, Macquarie Galleries, Sydney, 1979.

Pearce, B & Kolenberg, H, *William Dobell: the painter's progress*, Art Gallery of NSW, Sydney, 1997.

Pearce, B, *Sali Herman*, Art Gallery of NSW, Sydney, 1981.

Pearce, B, *Sidney Nolan*, Art Gallery of NSW, Sydney, 2007.

Perry, P & Perry, J, *Max Meldrum and associates: their art, lives and influences*, Castlemaine Art Gallery and Historical Museum, Castlemaine, 1996.

Polizzotto, C, *Approaching Elise*, Fremantle Arts Centre Press, Fremantle, 1988.

Quinlan, K, *In a picture land over the sea: Agnes Goodsir 1864–1939*, Bendigo Art Gallery, Bendigo, 1998

Radford, R, *Tom Roberts*, Art Gallery of South Australia, Adelaide, 1996.

Rankin, G, Lindsay Bernard Hall Post graduate research project, Deakin University, http://user.ncable.net.au/~chrisran/web/hall.html

Rosenthal, TG, *Sidney Nolan*, Thames & Hudson, London, 2002

Rosenthal, TG, 'Ned Kelly 1948–1992: a magnificent obsession', *Unmasked: Sidney Nolan & Ned Kelly 1950–1990*, Heide Museum of Modern Art, Melbourne, 2006.

Sadie, S (ed), *The new Grove dictionary of music and musicians*, Macmillan, London, 1980.

Sayers, A, *Eric Wilson*, Newcastle Region Art Gallery, Newcastle, 1983.

Sayers, A, *Portraits by John Brack*, National Portrait Gallery, Canberra, 2007.

Smith, G, *Russell Drysdale 1912–81*, National Gallery of Victoria, Melbourne, 1997.

Taylor, E, *Grace Crowley: being modern*, National Gallery of Australia, Canberra, 2006.

Thomas, D, *Sali Herman*, Georgian House, Melbourne, 1962.

Uhl, C, *Albert Tucker*, Landsdowne, Melbourne, 1969.

Underhill, N (ed), *Nolan on Nolan: Sidney Nolan in his own words*, Viking Press, Melbourne, 2007.

Wilkins, L, *Stella Bowen: art, love & war*, Australian War Memorial, Canberra, 2002.

Zubans, R, *E Phillips Fox: his life and art*, The Miegunyah Press, Melbourne, 1995.

Bernard Hall Archive, National Gallery of Australia Research Library, Canberra, 2BH343.

Image credits

Titian, *A man with a quilted sleeve* c 1512
© The National Gallery, London

Peter Lely, *Henrietta Anne, Duchess of Orleans* c 1662
James Macardell after Sir Joshua Reynolds, *Anne (Day), Lady Fenoulhet* 1760
© National Portrait Gallery, London

Gordon Bennett, *Self-portrait (but I always wanted to be one of the good guys)* 1990
Reproduced courtesy of the artist

Elise Blumann, *Self-portrait* 1937
Photograph: Victor France

Arthur Boyd, *Mary Boyd* 1937
Arthur Boyd, *Self-portrait in a blue shirt* 1936
Arthur Boyd, *The brown room* 1943
Reproduced with permission of Bundanon Trust

John Brack, *The baby drinking* 1955
John Brack, *Self-portrait* c 1948
John Brack, *The girls at school* 1959
© Helen Brack

Roy De Maistre, *Self-portrait* c 1945
© Caroline de Mestre-Walker

William Dobell, *Dame Mary Gilmore* c 1956
William Dobell, *Sketch portrait of Dame Mary Gilmore* c 1956
William Dobell, *Self-portrait* 1932
William Dobell, *Sketch portrait of Helena Rubinstein* 1957
© Sir William Dobell Art Foundation

Russell Drysdale, *Margaret Olley* 1948
© Estate of Russell Drysdale

Ian Fairweather, *Portrait of the artist* 1962
© Estate of Ian Fairweather. Licensed by VISCOPY, Australia

Nora Heysen, *London breakfast* 1935
© Lou Kelpac

Laurence Hope, *Self-portrait with mumps* 1953
© Laurence Hope

Dušan Marek, *My wife* c 1952
© Estate of Dušan Marek

Sidney Nolan, *Head of soldier* 1942
Sidney Nolan, *Self-portrait* 1943
Photograph: Jenni Carter
Sidney Nolan, *Ned Kelly* 1946
Sidney Nolan, *S.N.* 1947
Sidney Nolan, *Daisy Bates at Ooldea* 1950
© Trustees of the Sidney Nolan Estate

John Perceval, *Boy with cat 2* 1943
John Perceval, *Self-portrait* 1946
© Estate of John Perceval. Licensed by VISCOPY, Australia

Margaret Preston, *Flapper* 1925
Margaret Preston, *Self-portrait* 1930
© Margaret Preston Estate. Licensed by VISCOPY, Australia

Albert Tucker, *Self-portrait* 1937
Albert Tucker, *Self-portrait* 1939
Albert Tucker, *Self-portrait* 1941
Albert Tucker, *Study for painting 'Self-portrait'* 1941
Albert Tucker, *Sydney Fox* 1946
Albert Tucker, *Man's head* 1946
Albert Tucker, *Self-portrait* 1954
© Barbara Tucker, Courtesy Barbara Tucker

Abbreviations

AGNSW	Art Gallery of New South Wales, Sydney
AGSA	Art Gallery of South Australia, Adelaide
AGWA	Art Gallery of Western Australia, Perth
ML	Mitchell Library, State Library of New South Wales, Sydney
NG, London	National Gallery, London
NGA	National Gallery of Australia, Canberra
NGV	National Gallery of Victoria, Melbourne
NPG	National Portrait Gallery, Canberra
NRAG	Newcastle Region Art Gallery
QAG	Queensland Art Gallery, Brisbane

Contributors

The following entry contributors all work, or have worked, at the National Gallery of Australia unless otherwise noted. Current position titles only have been used, but all have varied backgrounds bringing a wealth of experience to the entries.

Melanie Beggs-Murray freelance researcher; formerly assistant to the Head of Australian Art

Adriane Boag Educator, Youth & Community Programs

Roger Butler Senior Curator, Australian Prints & Drawings

Bronwyn Campbell Assistant Manager, Travelling Exhibitions

Emma Colton Assistant Curator, Australian Prints & Drawings

Georgia Connolly Project Officer, Travelling Exhibitions

Belinda Cotton Head of Development

Julie Donaldson Head of Publishing

Simon Elliott Assistant Director, Curatorial & Educational Services

Deborah Hart Senior Curator, Australian Paintings & Sculpture post-1920

Miriam Kelly Assistant Curator, Australian Paintings & Sculpture

Anne McDonald independent researcher and writer; formerly Curator, Australian Prints & Drawings

Laura Murray Cree freelance writer, formerly editor *Art & Australia*

Dominique Nagy Head of Exhibitions

Sarina Noordhuis-Fairfax Curator, Australian Prints & Drawings

Katherine Russell Manager, Public Programs

Elena Taylor Curator, Australian Art, National Gallery of Victoria

Acknowledgments

I am indebted to many people for their assistance with this exhibition and publication. I owe the largest debt to Ron Radford, the Director of the National Gallery of Australia for his warm enthusiasm and commitment to the project, and for guiding me in the selection of the works and in my thinking about Australian portraiture. He has also provided a thoughtful introductory essay to the catalogue, outlining the importance of colonial portraiture to the story of Australian art. I wish also to thank Laura Murray Cree for the sound writing advice, moral support and generous encouragement she provided to both myself and to all the authors who worked on this catalogue. Her commitment to the project has made a real difference.

I thank Dominique Nagy, who in her role of Manager, Travelling Exhibitions, developed the idea of the exhibition with me, and who then secured the venues and sought the funds to enable it to eventuate. I am grateful to Georgia Connolly, who as Project Officer, Travelling Exhibitions, has shown equal enthusiasm for the project and has now taken on the management of the exhibition and extensive tour around Australia, as has Sara Kelly. My sincere thanks to them all.

In Australian art, I thank Miriam Kelly, Assistant Curator of Australian Paintings and Sculpture, for her great dedication and professionalism in undertaking a wide range of activities connected with the organisation and management of the exhibition and publication, including coordinating the cataloguing, framing and photography of the works. I also thank Deborah Hart, Senior Curator of Paintings and Sculpture post-1920; her enthusiasm and commitment to the exhibition has meant a great deal.

I thank all the authors who have contributed their knowledge to the publication: Melanie Beggs-Murray, Adriane Boag, Roger Butler, Bronwyn Campbell, Emma Colton, Georgia Connolly, Belinda Cotton, Julie Donaldson, Simon Elliott, Deborah Hart, Miriam Kelly, Anne McDonald, Laura Murray Cree, Dominique Nagy, Sarina Noorhuis-Fairfax, Katherine Russell and Elena Taylor. The diversity of voice and discussion has created a richly layered resource and added considerable interest to the publication.

The wonderful ongoing work of the Gallery's conservators is also recognised for their contribution in preparing the works for the exhibition: David Wise, Sheridan Roberts, Sharon Alcock, Jael Muspratt and Greg Howard. They have cleaned and restored a great many paintings for the tour. John Jones provided sound advice and supervised much of the reframing of the works. Jane Marsden was the loans officer from Registration and Ted Nugent supervised the building of the crates for the tour.

I am especially grateful to Julie Donaldson, Paul Cliff and Kristin Thomas for their expertise, dedication and care in preparing this publication. I thank also Nick Nicholson for his work in obtaining the supplementary photographs; and David Pang, Brenton McGeachie, Steve Nebauer, Eleni Kypridis, John Tassie and Wilhelmina Kemperman from Imaging Services for their work in photographing the collection. I would also like to thank my Executive Assistant Juliet Flook who has provided invaluable support.

This publication and exhibition has received generous support from the National Collecting Institutions Touring and Outreach Program, an Australian Government program aiming to improve access to the national collections for all Australians. Since its inception, Visions of Australia has been a strong supporter of the National Gallery's Travelling Exhibitions program, and it is again providing support for this exhibition. It has also been sponsored by the National Gallery of Australia Council Exhibitions Fund. This fund is a bold initiative of the Gallery's Council, and aims to ensure that people across Australia have access to the treasures of the National Gallery's collection.

Anne Gray
Head of Australian Art

Index

Italics indicate illustrated works; numbers in [brackets] refer to the featured portraits.

A

Aborigines 10, 11, 13, 39
Archibald Prize 9, 34, 36, 39–40, 50, 102, 106, 134, 144

B

Badham, Herbert *112*
Self-portrait c 1937 [35] 22, *112–13*
Self-portrait with glove 1939 *112*
Bates, Daisy May 28, *136–7*
Bennett, Gordon, *Self-portrait (but I always wanted to be one of the good guys)* 1990 38, *39*
Blumann, Elise *114*
Charles, morning on the Swan 1939 [36] 24, *114–15*
Self-portrait 1937 *114*
Bowen, Stella 31, 37, *96*
Mary Widney 1927 [27] 33, *35*, *96–7*
Self-portrait c 1929 33, 96
Boyd, Arthur 36, *110*, *124*
The brown room 1943 [41] 24, 26, *124–5*
Mary Boyd 1937 [34] 26, *110–11*
Self-portrait 1945–46 *124*
Self-portrait in a blue shirt 1936 *110*
Boyd, Mary 26, *110–11*
Boyd family 24, 26, 28, 82, 110, 124
Brack, John 18, 23–4, 36, 38, *142*, *148*
The baby drinking 1955 [50] 18, *142–3*
The girls at school 1959 [53] 18, 24, *25*, *148–9*
Self-portrait 1949 *142*
Self-portrait 1955 23–4, *148*
Bunny, Rupert 24, 32, *88*
Madame Sadayakko as Kesa c 1907 30, *31*
Self-portrait c 1920 *88*
Woman in a brown hat c 1917 [23] 18, 24, 32, *33*, *88–9*

C

colonial portraits 9, 10–13, 28–30
commissioned portraits 20–1
Conder, Charles, *An Impressionist (Tom Roberts)* c 1889 *52*
Cossington Smith, Grace *84*
Self-portrait 1948 *84*
Study of a head: self-portrait 1916 [21] *84–5*
Crossland, J M, *Portrait of Nannultera, a young Poonindie cricketer* 1854 *12*
Crowley, Grace *98*
Miss Gwen Ridley 1930 34, *37*
Portrait study 1928 [28] *98–9*

D

De Maistre, Roy 18, 84, *126–7*
Self-portrait c 1945 [42] 18, *126–7*
Dobell, William 20, 34, 36, 134, *144*, *146*
Dame Mary Gilmore c 1956 *20*, *21*
Portrait of an artist 1943 34, 36
Self-portrait 1932 *144*
Sketch portrait of Dame Mary Gilmore c 1956 [51] 20, *20*, *144–5*
Sketch portrait of Helena Rubinstein 1957 [52] 20, *146–7*
Dowling, Robert 13, 28–9, 37, *48*
Miss Robertson of Colac (Dolly) 1885–86 [3] 20, *26*, 28–9, *48–9*
Mrs Adolphus Sceales with Black Jimmie … 1856 *8–9*
Self-portrait c 1852 *48*
Drysdale, Russell 36, 116, *134*
Margaret Olley 1948 [46] *134–5*
Dupain, Max
Russell Drysdale c 1948 *134*
William Dobell 1942 *146*

E

Earle, Augustus, *Portrait of Bungaree, a native of New South Wales* c 1826 *11*
Edwardian and Victorian portraits 28–31

F

faces and facial expressions 15–16, 22
Fairweather, Ian, *Portrait of the artist* 1962 [54] *2–3*, 37, *150–1*
family portraits 20, 24–6, 36
Fox, E Phillips 20, 31, *58*, *68*, *82*
Elsie, daughter of HW Brooks Esquire 1904 [13] 20, 31, *68–9*
The green parasol c 1912 [20] 17, *27*, *82–3*
Mrs James Pirani 1893 [8] 20, *58–9*
Self-portrait from a sketchbook 1905 *82*
Fox, Sydney *130–1*

G

Gilmore, Dame Mary 20, *20*, *21*, *144–5*
Goodsir, Agnes, *The Parisienne* c 1924 [26] 26, 32–3, *94–5*

H

Hall, Bernard *44–7*
J Montgomery, Esquire 1885 [2] *46–7*
Self-portrait as a young man c 1880 [1] *44–5*
Hawkshaw, Geoff, *Fairweather at Bribie Island, Queensland* 1966 *150*
Herman, Sali, *The artist's wife (Paulette)* 1940 [37] 24, *116–17*
Heysen, Nora 27, 33–4, *102*
London breakfast 1935 [30] 27, *102–3*
Self-portrait c 1935 *102*
Hope, Laurence, *Self-portrait with mumps* 1953 [49] *140–1*
Humphrey, Tom, *Tom Roberts in front of 'The Big Picture'* 1902 *60*

I

imaginary portraits 28

K

Kelly, Ned (Edward) 13, 28, *29*, *128–9*
Kemble, Myra *50–1*

L

Lambert, George W 18, 21, 22, 30, 37, *70*, *80*, *90*
Chesham Street 1910 [19] 22, *80–1*
The old dress 1906 [14] 17, *70–1*
Self-portrait c 1906 *70*
Self-portrait with gladioli 1922 *90*
Weighing the fleece 1921 [24] 18, 21, 26–7, *90–1*
The white glove 1921 34, *36*
Law, Benjamin, *Trucaninny, wife of Woureddy* 1836 *10*
Lawrence, Thomas 13
Lely, Peter, *Henrietta Anne, Duchess of Orleans* c 1662 *16*
Lewin, John, *Aged native of Otaheite, New Hollander* 1827 *10*
Liu Xiao Xian, *Reincarnation–Mao, Buddha and I 1998* 38, *40*

M

Macardell, James, *Anne (Day), Lady Fenoulhet* 1760 *32*
McCubbin, Frederick 21, *72–3*
Self-portrait c 1908 [15] 21, *72–3*
Self-portrait 1912 21, *23*
Self-portrait 1916 21, *23*, *72*
McInnes, W B, *Miss Collins* 1924 34, *36*
Marek, Dušan, *My wife* c 1952 [48] 24, 39, *138–9*
Marek, Voitre, *Dušan* 1946 *138*
Meldrum, Max 34, *86*
Poland (Madame de Tarczynska) 1917 [22] 17, 39, *86–7*
Mills, Alice, *Tom Roberts* 1920 *74*
Moore, David, *Sidney Nolan, Western Australia* 1962 *136*

N

Nerli, Girolamo, *Miss Myra Kemble* 1888 [4] *50–1*
Nicholas, Hilda Rix, *The scorned flowers* 1925 *17*
Nicholas, William, *Lady and child* c 1847 *13*
Nolan, Sidney *120*, *128*, *136*
Arthur Boyd 1988 36
Daisy Bates at Ooldea 1950 [47] 28, *136–7*
Head of soldier 1942 [39] *120–1*
Ned Kelly 1946 [43] 13, 28, *29*, *128–9*
Self-portrait 1943 36, *120*
S.N. 1947 *128*

O

Olley, Margaret *134–5*

P

Perceval, John 110, *122*
Boy with cat 2 1943 [40] 28, *122–3*
Self-portrait 1946 *122*
photography 9, 10, 13, 28, 38, 128, 132
portraiture and portraits 9–40
artists' views of 16–19
development of 28–40
subjects of 17, 18, 19
types of 20–8
Preston, Margaret 33, *92*
Flapper 1925 [25] *4–5*, 18, 32, *92–3*
Self-portrait 1930 *92*

R

Ramsay, Hugh 21–2, *62–7*
Miss Nellie Patterson 1903 [12] *14–15*, 20, 30, 66–7, 68
Rosenthal at the piano 1902 [11] *64–5*
Self portrait in a white jacket 1901–02 66
Self-portrait: bust showing hands 1901-02 [10] 22, *62–3*
Reynolds, Joshua 16, 20, 31, 32
Roberts, Tom 16, 20, 29–30, 37, *52–7*, 60, *74*
An Australian native 1888 [5] 29, *52–3*
G Rivers Alpress c 1895 *30*
Madame Hartl c 1909 [16] *74–5*
Mrs Leonard Dodds c 1893 [6] *54–5*
Portrait study of Lena Brasch c 1893 [7] *56–7*
Sketch portrait—Senator JT Walker 1901 [9] 20, *60–1*
Rosenthal, Moriz *64–5*
Rubinstein, Helena *146–7*

S

Sargent, John Singer 30, 66
Scharf, Theo *78–9*
self-portraits 21–4
Shepeard, Jean, *Roi de Mestre (Roy de Maistre)* c 1930 *126*
situation portraits 26–8
Spiden, Percy, *Max Meldrum in his studio* c 1952 *86*

T

Taylor, Howard, *Double self-portrait* 1959 37, *38*
Teague, Violet, *The boy with the palette* 1911 [18] 30, *78–9*
Titian, *A man with a quilted sleeve* c 1512 *19*
Trotter, Eliza H, *Lady Caroline Lamb* c 1811 *26*, *27*
Tucker, Albert 18, 22–3, 36, *108*, *118*, *130*, *132*
Man's head 1946 [45] 18, 28, *42–3*, *132–3*
Self-portrait, 26 Little Collins Street, Melbourne 1940 *130*
Self-portrait 1937 [33] 22, *108–9*
Self-portrait 1939 *108*
Self-portrait 1941 [38] 22, 36, *118–19*
Self-portrait 1954 22–3, *132*
Study for painting 'self-portrait' 1941 *118*
Sydney Fox 1946 [44] *130–1*

V

Victorian and Edwardian portraits 28–31

W

Wainewright, Thomas, *The Cutmear sisters, Jane and Lucy* c 1842 *13*
Walker, Sen. James Thomas 20, *60–1*
Waller, Christian 24, *100–1*
Waller, Napier 24, *100*
Christian Waller with Baldur, Undine and Siren at Fairy Hills 1932 [29] 24, *100–1*
The man in black 1925 *100*
war 116, 118, 120, 122, 130, 132
Wheeler, Charles 76
After the ball 1910 [17] 22, *76–7*
Before the ball 1910 22, *76*
Whistler, James, McNeill 17, 30, 64, 70, 102
Wilson, Eric *104*, *106*
The artist's mother 1937 [32] 24, *106–7*
Domestic interior 1935 [31] 28, *104–5*
Self-portrait 1945 *106*
women artists 7, 11, 13, 29, 33–4, 39, 78, 92

nga.gov.au

The National Gallery of Australia is an Australian Government agency

Produced by the Publishing Department of the National Gallery of Australia
Research and writing assistance: Laura Murray Cree
Copy editing: Paul Cliff* and Julie Donaldson*
Design: Kristin Thomas*
Rights and permissions: Nick Nicholson*
Indexer: Sherrey Quinn
Publishing manager: Julie Donaldson*
Pre-press and printing: Bluestar Print, Melbourne
* National Gallery of Australia

National Library of Australia Cataloguing-in-Publication entry
Author: Gray, Anne, 1947–
Title: Face: Australian portraits 1880–1960 / Anne Gray
Edition: 1st ed
ISBN: 9780642334152 (pbk)
Notes: Includes index.
Subjects: Portrait painting, Australian—History
Portraits—Australia
Portrait painters—Australia
Other Authors/Contributors: National Gallery of Australia.
Dewey Number: 704.942

Distributed in Australia by
Thames and Hudson
11 Central Boulevard Business Park
Port Melbourne, Victoria, 3207

Distributed in the United Kingdom by
Thames and Hudson 181A High Holborn
London WC1V 7QX, UK

Distributed in the United States of America by
University of Washington Press
1326 Fifth Avenue, Ste 555
Seattle, WA 98101-2604

Published in conjunction with the National Gallery of Australia's travelling exhibition *Face: Australian portraits 1880–1960*

The University of Queensland Art Museum,
Brisbane, Queensland
29 January – 27 March 2011

Museums & Art Galleries of the Northern Territory,
Darwin, Northern Territory
9 April – 10 July 2011

Warrnambool Art Gallery,
Warrnambool, Victoria
23 July – 4 September 2011

Queen Victoria Museum & Art Gallery,
Launceston, Tasmania
17 September – 20 November 2011

Hazelhurst Regional Gallery & Arts Centre,
Gymea, New South Wales
3 December 2011 – 29 January 2012

Gladstone Regional Art Gallery & Museum,
Gladstone, Queensland
March–April 2012

Please note itinerary dates are subject to change. Please contact venues before visiting.

Face: Australian portraits 1880–1960
is supported by the
National Gallery of Australia Council
Exhibitions Fund

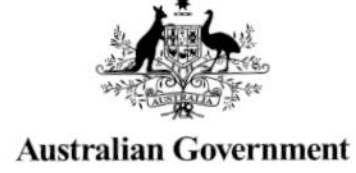

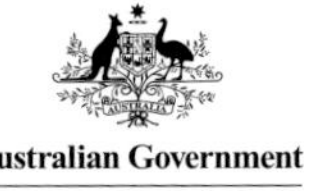

This exhibition is supported by the National Collecting Institutions Touring and Outreach program, an Australian Government program aiming to improve access to the national collections for all Australians; and by Visions of Australia, an Australian Government program supporting touring exhibitions by providing funding assistance for the development and touring of Australian cultural material across Australia.

Media partner

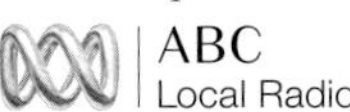